Voices from The Farm

Adventures in Community Living

Edited by Rupert Fike

Book Publishing Company
Summertown, Tennessee

© 2012 Book Publishing Company
Cover design: Jim Scattaregia, Warren Jefferson
Interior design: Warren Jefferson
Photo editors: Barbara Jefferson, Warren Jefferson, Rupert Fike
Photo repair and restoration: Sal Jefferson

Published by
Book Publishing Company
P.O. Box 99
Summertown, TN 38483
1-888-260-8458

Printed in the United States of America

17 16 15 14 13 12   1 2 3 4 5 6 7 8 9

ISBN13   978-1-57067-288-0

"Honoring Our Dead at the Burial Ground," p. 213 reprinted with permission from Communities magazine, (#96 Fall, 1997)

Library of Congress Cataloging-in-Publication Data
Voices from the farm : adventures in community living / edited by Rupert Fike. -- 2nd ed.
    p. cm.
  ISBN 978-1-57067-288-0 (pbk.) -- ISBN 978-1-57067-921-6 (e-book)
  1. Communal living--Tennessee--Lewis County. 2. Collective settlements--Tennessee--Lewis County. I. Fike, Rupert.
HQ971.5.T2V65 2012
307.77'4--dc23
                       2012015941

Printed on recycled paper

Book Publishing Company is a member of Green Press Initiative. We chose to print this title on paper with 30% postconsumer recycled content, processed without chlorine, which saved the following natural resources:
• 16 trees
• 7,464 gallons of water   • 7 million BTU of energy
• 1,655 pounds of greenhouse gases • 473 pounds of solid waste

For more information on Green Press Initiative, visit greenpressinitiative.org. Environmental impact estimates were made using the Environmental Defense Fund Paper Calculator edf.org/papercalculator..

From the photo editors:

The photo editing for this second edition of *Voices from The Farm* has been an intense and nostalgic experience for us, full of emotion, joy, and sadness. As we went through The Farm's vast collection of images, we were transported again and again back to a time of our youth, a time of optimistic purpose and dedication, when we all worked collectively to build this wonderful community called The Farm.

As much as possible, we have included photographs of the actual people, events, and places described in these stories. There are photographs of people who have lived here at one time and moved on, people who lived here then and live here still, and people who lived here, passed away, and rest in our cemetery.

We think you'll find that these photographs help the stories come alive and give one a unique view into what life was like on The Farm during our early years.

Photographer Listing

Albert Bates	Warren Jefferson
Craig Bialik	Nancy Jones
Jenny Bryant	Jeffrey Keating
Clifford Chappell	Edith Lucas
Ramona Christopherson	Daniel Luna
John Coate	Gary Maclaughlin
Michael Cook	Dennis Martin
Edine Davis	Laurie Praskin
Valerie Dyess	Alan Praskin
Don Edkins	Ann Queeney
Clifford Figallo	Linda Rake
Karen Flaherty	Gary Rhine
Mary Flannery	Ivan Rijhoff
Nancy Fleckenstein	Peter Rockwell
David Frohman	Peter Schweitzer
Stephen Gaskin	Edward Sierra
Ina May Gaskin	Douglas Stevenson
Linda Gavin	Melvin Stiriss
Chuck Haren	Lisa Wartinger
Peter Hoyt	Thomas Wartinger
Jerry Hutchens	Gerald Wheeler

Preface

The Farm has been, like all communities, a constantly changing landscape of people and situations. From 1971 to the present, The Farm has been an ongoing experiment in collective living that is still evolving and has always been as diverse as the people that inhabit it.

This book is a collection of stories from members of The Farm both current and past, a series of snapshots of Farm life at various stages. There are stories of everyday life as well as important events in the community's history—memoirs of our families, friends, jobs, and households; our hopes and fears; agreements and disagreements; our successes and failures. Our hope is that these stories convey some of the wonder, great pure effort, bewilderment, frustrations, fun, love, and lasting friendships that are part of the experience of living in community.

This book in no way intends itself as a definitive history of The Farm. Rather it is only as the title implies—a sampling of personal histories from those who devoted their total being to a grand experiment.

Preface to Second Edition

The Farm's individual stories remain as important today as they were fourteen years ago when *Voices from The Farm* was first published. And with this new edition we are pleased to include the family photographs which bring these varied accounts of idealism, determination and yes, disenchantment, into the even sharper focus they deserve.

A sentence like, "The water tower fell straight into the Big Pick Up, bouncing one big time then laying still," is arresting in its own right. But the image of an outsized cylinder's crumpling effect on a sawed-off school bus with "beatniks" standing stunned in the aftermath of a near tragedy, staring at what the laws of physics had just done, completes the story in a way words could never do on their own.

And on the micro level, one can observe the expressions of these young people who were engaged in what was unabashedly called, "Out To Save the World" in a time and place when each person's job, however menial, linked to the whole, to the success of perhaps the most important social experiment in this country's past century. It was a time when hundreds of the best and brightest of a generation decided to try and do something special with their lives by sharing fortunes, holding "all things in common" and living as "voluntary peasants" in a "spiritual school" while creating sustainable village technologies that would work just as well in Haiti or Guatemala as in Tennessee.

A teenage boy pumps a stationary bike hooked up to spin a car alternator in hopes of charging a household's 12-volt battery. Soon–to-be world renowned midwives surround the country doctor who provided their early back-up. A former moonshiner dispenses backwoods wisdom to his new neighbors who sometimes (at their peril) disregarded it. Twenty humans push a truck out of the mud (some pushing on each other's butts to get the job done). A new mother with her baby in a front-sling carries two buckets. Another mother gazes with sudden recognition at her new baby.

These are just a few of the images that enliven this book, a book that has been assigned by college professors because of its balanced perspective, a book that has attracted "new" residents to the community, a community still dedicated to the on-going vision to which this new edition of *Voices from The Farm* hopes to contribute.

Acknowledgements

Without the assistance of Sylvia Anderson, editor of *The Farm Net News* and *The Whirling Rainbow News*, this book would have been, if not impossible, severely limited in scope.

A special thanks to Marilyn Friedlander for her friendly encouragement and expertise in copyediting, as well as to Albert Bates, Dorothy Bates, and the many dozens of Farm residents, former and present, who contributed materially and psychically to make this book possible.

"This is the true joy in life, the being used for a purpose recognized by yourself as a mighty one; the being thoroughly worn out before you are thrown on the scrap heap; the being a force of Nature instead of a feverish, selfish little clod of ailments and grievances complaining that the world will not devote itself to making you happy."

George Bernard Shaw

Introduction

For all of their diversity, there is a common thread running through these *Voices from The Farm*: a deeply understood commitment to creating a spiritual community and taking care of each other.

The roots of the community trace back to California in the late 1960s. Seekers from all over the world converged on San Francisco looking for paths to achieve spiritual growth or fundamentally change society or both. The Bay Area became a cosmic whirlpool of rock 'n' roll, radical politics, experimental communes, and spiritual disciplines from every corner of the planet.

One group that spun out from this intense energy was Monday Night Class, which was organized by Stephen Gaskin, an English teacher at San Francisco State College. These free, open meetings focused on putting the group's shared psychedelic experiences into the perspective of the world's religions. There was a strong emphasis on compassion, developing personal character, self-reliance, and the awareness of the interconnectedness of all life. One key component was the use of meditation to quiet the mind, and nourish the spirit. And by 1969, weekly attendance at Monday Night Class had reached several thousand people. A core group of regulars had begun to consider Stephen as their spiritual teacher.

One night in the winter of 1969, when the American Academy of Religion was meeting in San Francisco, a group of ministers and theologians wandered in and stood at the back of the class, observing the broad-ranging discussion. Believing that Stephen's philosophy might be well received in their own congregations and classrooms and could help heal the rift growing between generations, several of them stepped forward to invite Stephen to come out to the heartland and speak. Stephen agreed and a tour was arranged. Rather than give up their meetings, two hundred or so of his students asked to come along, and any of them who could put together some sort of living quarters on wheels became a part of the tour.

In 1970, a caravan of brightly painted school buses, VW vans, trucks, and campers left San Francisco and followed Stephen on a coast-to-coast speaking tour of college campuses and churches. As they moved from city to city, they attracted other young people who were searching for identity, mission, and tribe.

After being on the road for four months and traveling thousands of miles, the Caravan re-

turned to California. By then there were too many vehicles to park in one place in the city and too many strong ties for everyone to go their separate way. By their shared experiences on the road, the Caravaners had become a community—a church. The decision was made to pool their money, head back out across America, and buy some land. Tennessee had seemed like one of the most inviting places they had visited—land was cheap and the people were friendly. These pioneers became Okies in reverse, trading the spectacular vistas of the Bay Area and a relatively easy way of life for the underdeveloped farmlands and blackjack oak forests of middle Tennessee. South of Nashville, a thousand acres were purchased in the backwoods of Lewis County, and The Farm was born.

For this exotic group of hippies to plop down and thrive in the deep South was a long-odds gamble. These were times of crisis in this country—Vietnam and urban riots controlled the front pages. Willie Nelson had not yet grown pigtails. The Easy Rider boys had met a bad fate in Dixie. There was no such thing as Charlie Daniels's long-haired country boy who just wanted to be left alone. Indeed, if you had long hair in the South at this time, a country boy would likely NOT leave you alone.

From the beginning Stephen likened The Farm to a skin graft that the surrounding area would either accept or reject. During the first years, Stephen's charismatic leadership was clearly pivotal in developing the community's relationship with its neighbors. He understood universal manners and instilled the value of being just plain folks in suburban young people who were anything but plain and who had never thought of themselves as folks. The Farm shared with local Tennesseans the values of honesty and hard work. Long-haired, overalled young men and women were eager to learn from wizened Tennessee farmers who knew how to grow food and survive at a subsistence level.

The Farm was founded as an intentional spiritual community. Monday Night Class and the Caravan had been a testing ground for the principles that would guide it. Recognizing that it was difficult to support a concept of universal oneness while living in a society of haves and have-nots, The Farm organized itself on a communal basis as in the Book of Acts: *And all that believed were together and had all things in common; and sold their possessions and goods, and parted them to all as every man had need.* — Acts 2:44, 45. Each member of the community signed a "vow of poverty" and pooled whatever possessions he or she had. The Farm was considered a family "multistery" (as compared to a monastery) in the East Indian tradition of "householder yogis," where spiritual discovery and family life went hand in hand. Hard work was seen as an act of love and a path to enlightenment.

One of the ways members expedited personal growth was to agree to engage in nonstop interpersonal interventions, sort of a never-ending encounter group. Your inner business was everybody's business. Each person had the responsibility to suggest changes for others while gracefully (in theory) accepting input about themselves, in order to elevate their consciousness.

Anyone who became a member of the community took Stephen as a spiritual teacher. This gave The Farm, in its early formative years, one person who everyone agreed was the ultimate arbitrator, "the head man," as the local Tennesseans sometimes called him. However, this role of spiritual leadership meant different things to different people. For some, the relationship between spiritual teacher and student was a formal one, like the relationship between abbot and novitiate, where the teacher was looked to for guidance in all aspects of life. For others,

a spiritual teacher was a good friend with common sense and good judgement, someone you could go to when you were in a bind and needed advice, like a trusted aunt or uncle.

The "teachings," as they came to be called, were a mix of common-sense virtues filtered through Christian, Buddhist, Hindu, Sufi, Jewish, and Native American traditions. Through a process of trial and error, the community continuously refined its agreements to be compassionate, nonviolent, and vegan (a vegetarian who does not use dairy products, eggs, honey, and leather); to avoid tobacco, alcohol, and hard drugs; to shun consumerism; and to be a good planetary citizen, a "voluntary peasant."

Early in 1972, the Farm's homegrown rock 'n' roll band began a series of coast-to-coast tours with Stephen, playing in parks and student centers for free while promoting the community

in Tennessee. The community also established its in-house press, the Book Publishing Company. Its first publication was an upbeat magazine called Hey, Beatnik!, which used a layout reminiscent of Fillmore rock posters to portray life on the land as visionary teamwork. That same year, an adjacent seven hundred and fifty acres were purchased.

In 1974, Stephen and three other men spent most of the year in prison for growing marijuana. Stephen had not been caught in the field, but as a full partner in the community, he accepted equal responsibility for anything that happened to it.

While home on a weekend pass in the spring of that year, Stephen suggested The Farm form a charitable organization as a way to extend assistance to neighbors and communities beyond its borders. The name Plenty was conceived from the idea that if the world's resources were shared equitably, there would be plenty for everyone. Plenty started cautiously by giving away canned goods and crop surpluses. In 1975, Plenty joined with the Mennonite Central Committee to ship several tons of emergency relief food to alleviate chronic famine in Haiti and to help out after a massive hurricane in Honduras. Volunteers were sent to assist in cleanup and reconstruction after natural disasters closer to home. Two Farm couples jetted off to Dacca, Bangladesh, to set up a clinic near a railway station where smallpox was making its last stand.

When a devastating earthquake struck Guatemala in 1976, killing 23,000 and leaving a million homeless, The Farm decided to send several volunteers to determine if Plenty could be of assistance. It became apparent that the technology the community had developed for a nutritious vegan diet, home birth, primary and emergency medical care, and village utility systems, such as water, sewage, and communications, were exactly what was needed in the reconstruction effort in Guatemala. As the scope of Plenty's projects expanded, these village technologies were brought to other countries in Africa, the Caribbean, and Central America. Plenty also sent volunteers to assist the ship Rainbow Warrior during many of its campaigns to save the whales and block the dumping of nuclear waste.

Closer to home there were various inner city projects begun in the South Bronx, Miami, St. Louis, Chicago, and Washington, D.C. These projects covered a range of community needs that included emergency medical care, clinics, care for the elderly, and youth programs. Plenty's free ambulance service in the South Bronx, which responded to emergency calls in an area virtually ignored by city services, was covered by the CBS Evening News and The Wall Street Journal. Plenty's legal crew sued the Nuclear Regulatory Commission in an attempt to shut down the nation's nuclear power plants. Native American men and women from the Haudenosaunee (Iroquois) Confederation came to The Farm to learn midwifery, ambulance skills, and how to operate a community radio station. These were only some of the projects taken on by Farm members from the mid-1970s to the mid-1980s. With no apologies, "Out to Save the World" was rolled into the

destination slot of the community's old Greyhound Scenicruiser that was used for tours and to deliver crew and supplies to various projects.

As the scope of the outreach began to expand, a steady flow of visitors continued to increase and so did The Farm's population. By 1975, there were more than 750 people living on The Farm, including 160 married couples and 250 children. Farm midwives had delivered over 250 babies, and in subsequent years compiled statistics for home birth that challenged high-intervention birth practices in this country. Besides delivering children for community residents, the midwives placed an invitation in *Hey, Beatnik!* to any woman considering an abortion to have her baby delivered on The Farm for free. This included prenatal and postnatal care at The Farm's clinic. A woman with an unwanted pregnancy could leave her baby with a Farm family and have the option of returning for the child whenever she wanted. This offer found many takers; however, after giving birth, most of the new mothers bonded strongly with their babies and opted to keep them.

The Farm was not the first group to forsake eggs and dairy products in a totally vegetarian diet, but it certainly was the largest. Its success with raising healthy children on a vegan, soybean-based diet helped raise the status of vegetarianism from a cult fad to a respected dietary option.

The Farm was a magnet for visitors of all types—locals, relatives, school tours, and media of every sort. There were film crews and reporters from CBS, NBC, ABC, Germany, France, and Japan. The Farm also became one of the stops on the "psychedelic seekers tour." The overflow of new spiritual students led to the creation of satellite Farms in Wisconsin, Missouri, Colorado, Michigan, Louisiana, West Virginia, Texas, California, Virginia, Kentucky, New York, Florida, Alabama, Canada, Ireland, England, and Spain. *The Wall Street Journal* referred to The Farm in a front-page article as "the General Motors of American communes."

By 1977, there were 1,100 Farm members, and out of 14,000 visitors that year, 6,000 came through the front Gate (The Farm's combination visitor welcoming center and security checkpoint) and stayed overnight. Sanctuary was granted to anyone who had been physically

or emotionally abused or was mentally ill. Judges remanded troubled teens to The Farm who otherwise would have done time. Convicts were sent to The Farm on work release. Elderly relatives were "sprung" from nursing homes. Many families were healed emotionally in The Farm's protective environment, and children from broken homes who would have fallen into society's cracks found foster parents. Bonds of friendship were kindled from circumstances of adversity that turned strangers into family.

From the start, the community's main source of income had been construction crews who went out every morning as far as Nashville on jobs. But over the years, income for the basic operating needs of the community chronically fell short. There were "on-The-Farm businesses" that the community hoped would eventually be the main, if not the sole, sources of income: The Book Publishing Company, producing books on philosophy, vegetarian cooking, midwifery, natural birth control, CB radio, and satellite TV; Solar Electronics, installing photovoltaic panels and windmills, designing and manufacturing radiation detection equipment, and installing satellite receiving systems; Solar Energy Works, designing and building solar homes and water heaters; Farm Foods, creating and selling vegetarian foods for the health food market. These and many other endeavors were undertaken.

It was not enough. In 1976, the Farming Crew made an attempt to go from growing food just for the community to being a commercial agri-business and incurred heavy financial losses. Medical bills were piling up and other creditors were becoming impatient. A third source of income, windfalls from members' inheritances and wills, brought in sporadic chunks of cash, but over time the community gradually became overextended financially, physically, and psychically. By the late 1970s, the debt service began to get out of hand, and by 1980 morale was definitely beginning to suffer. In the midst of its growth and outreach, The Farm found it difficult to improve the quality of housing, the variety of food, and the availability of basic necessities for community members.

The community was starting to collapse under its own weight. At the peak of its population in 1982, it had grown to about 1,500 people, half of whom were children. It received more than 20,000 visitors that year alone, as many as 200 on any given night. There were many large households with up to thirty adults and twenty children, most of them under the age of

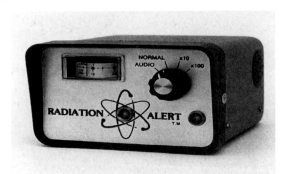

seven. Ailments related to sanitation were a fact of life. In some cases, parasites and tropical diseases were imported from the countries The Farm was trying to help.

Hopes that any of the community's business enterprises would suddenly become a great success and save the day were growing faint. In spite of many meetings and much brainstorming, The Farm continued to slide deeper into debt. People began to leave, slowly at first, and then in a more steady stream.

In the same blink of an historical eye that saw Communist China allow some free enterprise and many Israeli kibbutzim allow private property, The Farm decided that no longer would all things be held in common, except for the land. In 1983, dues were levied on all adult members who remained. Many more people left, power struggles over Farm businesses surfaced, and like a messy divorce, bad feelings attended much of the reorganization. However, shifting to individual responsibility for personal finances eventually resulted in a debt of hundreds of thousands of dollars being retired. The land was saved for the next generation. But the grand experiment of holding all things in common and using that collective strength to serve the needs of the poor and dispossessed of the larger world was over.

Today The Farm looks much the same, only with several hundred people quietly taking care of business instead of several thousand going in that many different directions. Houses that formerly held dozens of people are now home to individual families. Plenty's international projects continue as before, funded by outside donations. A land trust has been developed and supported by present and past members to preserve large tracts of adjacent Tennessee forest. The Ecovillage Training Center hosts visitors from around the world who can take short courses in alternative energy, buildings, health care, and permaculture. But most visitors these days are virtual, not literal. Hundreds log onto The Farm's websites (www.thefarm.org) and (www.thefarmcommunity.com) every day, downloading files on everything from tips on community plumbing to recipes for tofu.

To walk on the land or down the roads now is to experience more silence and peacefulness than in the 1970s. The core group who stayed and secured the land are being joined by newcomers and former members trickling back. Even though there are differences, there remains an undercurrent, an echo of the community's past. The Farm's vision and voice are not finished—there are still chips on the table, and in many ways there are thousands of legacies and voices, not just one. Here are some of those voices.

Rupert Fike, Cynthia Holzapfel, Albert Bates, Michael Cook

It's a Farmie Thing

One afternoon about a year ago while David and I were walking into an athletic club near our home in Nashville, we ran into an acquaintance of ours, someone we had known only a short time. We explained that we were stopping in to say hello to a good friend of ours, another former Farm resident, who now managed the cafe in the club and whose daughter (along with the daughter of yet another former Farm resident and friend) worked there. David and I started to get into a very involved explanation of all our connections to this cafe and the people who worked there, but she politely interrupted us and said, "Oh, I get it. It's a Farmie thing."

And of course it was, it was a Farmie thing. This person was astute enough to know that there was such a thing, but how to explain this phenomenon, this connection that exists among all Farm folks, whether still there, just left, or long gone, whether long-time or short-time resident?

Well, above and beyond everything else, there is the religion. We were so earnest. We gathered together every Sunday morning to meditate with complete eagerness. There were no doubters (well, maybe a few visitors) in our meditation group. So many of us had taken psychedelics and had our cultural conditioning blown away enough to experience a world of higher consciousness, to know with a certainty that could not be shaken that Spirit exists and that we are all One. This was the incredible binder, a shared psychedelic vision. We were students of religion together, and we were practitioners of religion together. Our lives were dedicated to our path.

The path we choose was to build a village, from scratch. So those experiences we shared creating our little town bind us together. Because you can't be talking to just anyone and in the middle of the conversation say, "Oh, you know how it is rolling tortillas for fifty people." Or, "Wasn't that crazy and fun going on laundry runs to town in the windowless back of the Cracker Truck, totally dark, sitting on seventy-five loads of dirty laundry?" Or, "Remember when we finally declared a ladies' day at the communal shower house?" These are not common American practices. All these memories of our incredibly rich, sometimes sad, very often hysterically funny experiences are ours alone. They cannot be compared to anything else—not to living in another city or another country, or even in another commune. They are absolutely unique, and they absolutely bind us together.

We created a language with words and phrases entirely our own. No one else but those who lived on The Farm would have any idea what "hogany" meant (a state of complaining or whining, usually by a kid). Or what was meant by someone being "into the juice," (juice was our word for energy, so "into the juice" referred to using more than one's share of it). No one else would get an immediate chuckle out of merely mentioning the word "yark" or understand its place in our history. (The Yark was the collective call, the howl of the pack. It was our way of saying, "I'm here, I'm here" and turning each individual voice into one—an affirmation that we were all in the same boat.) Only we would understand who the Bank Lady or the Petty Cash Lady was, or the Housing Lady. Only we knew the significance of Farm Hands, the Pumper Truck, and our annual holiday, Ragweed Day.

We named our vehicles and spoke of them familiarly, affectionately—the Diamond T, the Lark, the Bank car, the Big Pickup. We named our houses, sometimes for the material from which they were constructed, sometimes for their site, sometimes for more esoteric reasons: the Adobe, Kissing Tree (two trees in the front yard, their trunks delicately touching), Honey Base (Anthony kept bee hives there), Philharmonic Hall (Philip, a musician, was an original resident). Over time, the houses developed reputations and personalities of their own: some households were known for how well the core couples got along, others were known for how poorly they got along, some houses always found space for pregnant women, some made room for teenagers, some were "well-manifested," others were not. Their stories and the stories of The Farm's community buildings—the Community Kitchen, Canning and Freezing, the Soy Dairy, the Sorghum Mill, to name a few, became part of our folklore, part of our shared history. We had institutions that belonged only to us: we "did" the Gate, we "did" the Visitors' Tent, got sent to the Rock Tumbler (living quarters for hard-edged men who needed

their corners smoothed a bit), we got sent out for "relativity," occasionally got "put on a thirty-dayer" (a month-long sentence away from the land to thereby better appreciate it).

We all, at some point or another, ran out of wood for the fire on freezing cold nights. We all got ourselves on the laundromat list and then were called by the household ahead of us on the list when it was our turn—3 a.m., twenty degrees, twenty loads of laundry, five or six diaper pails. We all got up and stumbled through the pitch dark to the outhouse. We also all sat in meditation together, then talked about what was in our hearts and minds together. We argued and gossiped together, tried to fix each other, tried to keep our sense of humor when someone else was trying to fix us. We tried very hard and sincerely to take care of those among us who were very young and very old, and to provide a refuge for people who had need of sanctuary.

We were in perfect agreement about doing those things, bound by our ideals. Our collective character was courageous and spunky but also sweet, gentle, and compassionate. And this was our common knowledge.

The land was ours. The open fields fed us and our horses. The meadows gave us our meditation site and a place for all-night boogies. We stomped paths in the floor of the woods from one household to another, from building to building, from hill to hill and hollow to hollow, and along every creek. These were our paths. They became as familiar to us as our hometown streets had been. The creeks showed us their beauty and gave us cool refuge from the heat. We named them and the meadows and, of course, the old logging roads which we reclaimed from the woods with our bulldozer. In the Native American sense we felt a mystical relationship to this land we had bought, and our love for it bound us together.

Our diet was something else that was our own creation. Though some households were more creative with what was available from the store run during a given week, we were pretty much a town that ate the same food every night. Sometimes those foods and the events surrounding their appearance were rather weird—the mere mention of them causes simultaneous laughs and moans: Joshua steaks (early mass-produced vege-gristle that chewed nicely but caused horrific gas); day-old Bunny Bread (originally bought for "sickies," everyone soon got a taste for this nickel-a-loaf white bread that we sometimes had to pull away from pig farmers); survival crackers (just that—from fallout shelter provisions); and then there was wheatberry winter, where every night, there they were on your plate, beside the blighted potatoes: boiled wheat berries.

But mostly our diet was creative, innovative, and delicious. It nourished us in more ways than just physically. We loved our tofu and soymilk—we built our own dairy to make them and exported the soy dairy concept to protein-poor peoples in other countries. Soybeans and soft tortillas—simple, nutritious, wonderfully satisfying—became our national dish.

We are like the Jews of the Bible, those of us who lived on The Farm and left. We created our own diaspora. When our paths cross, we recognize each other with a kind of recognition that goes beyond mere sight. We may not have hung out or even liked each other all that much. We may not have too much to say to each other beyond the initial how are yous. But we have a shared past which creates a connection, the tie our friend referred to as "a Farmie thing." We are bound by religion, by language, by institutions, by land, by diet, by this unique experience called The Farm.

Marilyn Friedlander

Landing in Homer's Back Yard

When we came to Lewis County, Tennessee, it was because Philip had met one of the Martin girls in the music store where Philip had gone to trade one guitar for another. After hearing about the Caravan from Philip, Rose Martin's daughter, said, "No one has lived on my mother's old home down in Lewis County for thirty-five years. I bet my folks would let you stay there while you look for a place." Peter, Phil's brother, talked to the Martins, and they loaned us the Martin Farm to park on until we found land.

The caretaker of the land was Homer Sanders, who lived across the road. The county judge of Lewis County was Doug Humphries, who was a friend of Mr. Martin. Well, Lewis County is a dry county, so Mr. Martin sent a fifth of whisky to Judge Humphries and one to Homer Sanders (which was kind of funny since Homer was a moonshiner), and asked them to be good to us and take care of us. Homer organized the Democrats in our end of the county and became one of our connections to the local power structure.

Homer was one of those small vigorous men who was so strong and vital that his size made no difference whatsoever. He wore one of those little tweed, stingy brim hats, and when he took it off, his wiry hair was the shape of the inside of the hat. He had had a cancer operation, and part of the root of his tongue had been removed. Because of this, it was kind of hard to understand him sometimes, but I realized that the load of different accents that we had brought to Tennessee was probably just as hard for him to understand. Homer made the effort. His speech cleared up for us. He treated us as individuals and when he was your friend, his loyalty was steadfast. After he got to know us, he would stick up for us if he heard anyone disparage us. It didn't matter if it was in the bank or grocery store; he would tell them that he knew us and that he liked us.

We found out later that Homer was pretty technically astute. He had helped build Redstone Arsenal and had been called out of retirement to help decommission it. He had a sawmill which he rigged to work from a remote control number pad. He had other talents as well.

He was a naturally kind man. He was not used to black people, but when he met Elizabeth, an elderly black woman who was a Farm resident, you could see them both resolve to do the right thing in front of the children (us), and they embraced warmly. Homer and I became close friends. When we had a cold winter, Homer told us how many of us he could sleep warm in his house. When we had hard times on The Farm, Homer always referred to it as "our" troubles.

He took us on walks in the woods and showed us the good herbs and wildflowers and taught us the trees. Although he was armed to the teeth and had many fully automatic weapons, he respected our ways and never carried guns on The Farm, although he had great familiarity with our land. One time he told me that he had built a whisky still on every spring on our land and

that he had made a quarter of a million dollars' worth of whisky on that land.

Sometimes our clinic would purchase a quart of Homer's White Lightning as a base for making cough syrup. You could shake a quart fruit jar of Homer's whisky until it was all bubbles and when you stopped, the bubbles were gone in half a second. It had a very low viscosity. The stuff must have been 190 proof. Homer sometimes spoke of buying "store bought" whisky to sober up on!

Homer had migraine headaches and a Farm person gave him some pot which he took in tea. It worked well for him and when he heard about magic mushrooms, he said, "Give me some of those mushrooms. I'm going to go home and tie my leg to a tree and try some."

Stephen Gaskin

A Backwoods Vo-Tech School

I first met Homer Sanders in the fall of 1971 while we were still on the Martin Farm. When we arrived as guest tenants he must have felt a proprietary duty to help us out. He did this, according to him, by personally holding off a version of the white citizen's council on Drake Lane who wanted to literally "run us off."

I was very dark from working in the fields all summer, and I recall our first interaction was his asking me if I was an Indian (phonetically it came out, "Youunsan Injun?") I said no, I was Russian, and he literally got a knee-slapping kick out of that. I left out the part about being Jewish.

My father had died in May of that year, and in a strange conjunction, Homer Sanders took on that role somewhat of mentor, teacher, and friend. Homer had an ancient, very rigged-up sawmill and access to tracts of timber, both of which we needed. What he needed was labor, which we were long on, so we made a deal whereby we'd split all the lumber and expenses. In addition, we could buy his share and cut all the firewood

we wanted. All this barely a mile from The Farm.

Somehow I was elected strawboss of this crew of ten or so long-haired, bearded men. Plus we had Robin, Homer's teenage son, and Barnabus, a yearling mule who we had given to the Sanders rather than accept the karma of "shaving" (gelding) him. A close neighbor, Scott Shrader, also helped out, mostly with an incredible ability to get his mules to snake logs out of the deep woods with only the occasional "gee" or the barely audible "haw."

That first summer or two Sanders Lumber Co. became a backwoods vo-tech school for all us middle-

class white boys with ponytails and beards. I learned how to drive a logging truck with a dual rear-axle, how to cut trees and snake logs out with a tractor, how to build with oak 2 x 4s (hint—two pound sledge and a grease gun), and basically how to survive in the woods. College was no preparation for felling giant tulip poplars that yielded eight 8-foot logs.

This whole operation was what was called a peckerwood mill. Mostly we cut red oak, white oak, post oak, and poplar with the occasional cherry or walnut and beech.

Homer knew plumbing, electrical, construction, mechanics, hydraulics, everything. We learned about a cut-and-paste universe from him. Our operation wasn't as "zen" or neatly organized as some of the nearby Amish mills we visited, but it could definitely put out some lumber. Many of our early buildings were constructed with this wood.

Homer had a goat named Miriam who lived on top of his trash pile eating whatever she wanted. She was chained up so she couldn't roam and do serious damage. There were many dogs, of course, and a few catfish ponds scattered around. Junk and machinery were scattered

everywhere in his sheds, but Homer knew where everything was. One rainy day we decided to organize his sheds, "spiff things out." After that he couldn't find anything and complained bitterly. Years later, long after I'd quit working with him, he'd drive over to ask where a certain power-take-off was. "Youins with yer cleening, usins can't find a damn thing."

Logging is a dangerous business, and we had our share of close encounters with disaster. Once a felled tree didn't go the way it was supposed to and would have landed on two guys, but it hung up in the branches of another tree. Another time we managed to get the loaded log truck stuck on the main railroad line between Nashville and Birmingham. And on cue, here came the train. Homer grabbed a t-shirt to use as a flag, ran down the tracks around the bend, and got the train to slow, then stop—just in time.

The fact that we landed almost right on top of Homer is full of poetic implications—was it an incredible convergence or is the world full of such men, resourceful, smart, entertaining, and generous as long as you're on their good side? Either way, Homer was having an incredibly rich existence whether The Farm ever came his way or not. He and his wife Irene, who was also incredibly accepting of us, certainly contributed to our making it those first few years.

Homer and his family barely scraped through the Depression in North Alabama by selling logs. Later he got into illegal whisky and gave the slip to the revenuers many times before getting caught with a whole carload of sugar. He tried to cut through the woods and actually pulled the rear end off his car on a stump. Went to jail. Got out and worked maintenance at the Redstone Arsenal in Huntsville. One winter there was trouble with a large boiler, and he refused to go in and fix it. Said it was too dangerous. The guy on the next shift went in and got killed when the thing blew. Homer was stubborn like that.

Mostly we took his advice on matters like how to slowcook sorghum, or water-main logistics, or where the best chert pit was for our roads. Occasionally we ignored him, like during the construction of Kissing Tree, one of The Farm's first large houses. Homer took a look at the hearth and went crazy; we'd made the throat so big it wouldn't draw properly. Too much work to redo it, we forged ahead. Years later when I lived in that house, I came to understand what he had meant. Your butt could be hot as the sun, but your front would be cold as Pluto.

Homer died in July, 1985, by which time I had moved to Nashville and The Farm had gone through enormous changes. I felt bad that I had not kept up the friendship more over the years. Wilbur, the head of our trucking company, was driving his semi the day of the funeral, and even though the police escort tried to keep him out of the procession, Wilbur forced his Kenworth in. It seemed fitting.

David Friedlander

Ed.: This a copy of the vow of poverty that was signed by everyone who became a member of the community.

Vow of Poverty

We are organized on a communal basis according to the book of Acts of the New Testament, Acts 2:44, 45:

And all that believed were together and had all things in common; and sold their possessions and goods, and parted them to all as every man had need.

We have a common treasury. All money from whatever source is given to our bank which distributes the money according to need—to further our religious and educational purposes, and to provide everyone in our community with food, clothing, housing, and ordinary medical and dental supplies and services. No individual member of our Church owns property.

No part of the earnings of The Foundation, the corporation that handles the material affairs of our community, inures to the benefit of any particular shareholder or individuals and if an individual or member has given money or property to the community or corporation, he is not entitled to get that money and property back. This vow does not apply to property or money acquired by someone after leaving our Church and our community.

"It Was Hot, and We Were Tired, Ready to Get Home ..."

We had just got off work from Consolidated Aluminum in Columbia. It was hot and we were tired, ready to get home, but when we got up to the stop-light at the hospital three cop cars had stopped all traffic because the chief of police was leading this long line of different colored school buses through town. They had stove pipes coming out the window and everything. We had never seen anything like it.

They were heading down [Highway] 43 towards Mount Pleasant, and once the police let us go we fell in behind them. We were so hot and tired. We were ready to get home, but those school buses were barely going thirty-five. There was four of us in our car, and we were talking back and forth towards each other, "Boy, I wished they'd just hurry up and get on out of our way. Maybe they'll turn off at Hamilton Court."

Well they never turned off. Then once we got to Mount Pleasant we said, "Man, maybe they'll turn down towards Hampshire and get on out of our way." Nope, they kept on going down 43 and started up Rockdale Hill which had a passing lane, but even then we couldn't pass them because they was passing each other. "Well maybe they're going on down towards Lawrenceburg," we said.

But when we got to the top of Rockdale hill where we could see, well they started throwing them right-hand blinkers, turning onto Highway 20, right where we was wanting to go. "What's going on? They're going through our town!" We saw they were different people from what we was accustomed to. Long hair and beards and all that. Kind of like how I am now. But I was clean-cut then.

Anyway, they came on through Summertown, and when they got down to the Henryville Pike we said, "Man, maybe they're going to turn down towards Henryville and get out of our way." But no, they kept going on out 20. All we knew about hippies was a few things we had seen on TV from San Francisco, the hippie movement and all that. If you only had a radio you wouldn't know about them at all.

Finally when they got to Drake Lane which was our road, well they started throwing them right hand blinkers up. "Whoa, what's going on here? Is somebody going to invade us?" Nobody had said nothing about this was going to happen. Not a thing. This was the road I was born on. It was a trip for us to see something like this happening. We hadn't seen that many school buses even when we were going to school. And every one of them with a stove pipe.

Well they pulled off there at the Martin land, and we finally got around them and went on home. The next few days though some neighbors got together and were saying, "Now there ain't no sense in all them coming in here to live." But I always said, "Now this world is a great big world. And if I am allowed to be here then anybody else can be here too." I said, "Man they got as much right as anybody to be there. If they don't bother me, I'm not going to go up there and jump on them." And after a few weeks everything settled down except for all the State Patrol cars we started seeing on Drake Lane. We used to never see State Patrol cars here, but after they pulled in, boy you saw them all the time.

Bud Runyon

Martin Farm Summer

Here is the image—a rainbowed formation of sixty or so school buses, vans, and trucks proceeding deep, deep into the back regions of Tennessee, quite unannounced yet coming to stay. It is Saturday afternoon, May, 1971.

Several highway patrol units began trailing us around Columbia when we exited off I-65, and by the time we got to Drake Lane there were more. We parked the buses on the dirt road and sent search parties into the dense woods of the Martin's old home place where we had been given permission to live. The scouts came back with news of a secluded meadow up against some railroad tracks about a half mile in.

There was an existing road down to the meadow, but the first hundred yards or so were in dispute. Mr. Smith said it was on his land. Homer Sanders, caretaker of the Martin Farm, said no, it was on the Martin's land. "Shootin' scrapes," Homer said, had come up less on Drake Lane.

It was decided to bypass that section of the road and any possibility of a "shooting scrape." We nosed one bus into the woods and started hacking a path in front of it. There was some urgency to the task as it was getting late, and no one wanted the Caravan to spend the night out on this strange county road. Cars and trucks full of curious locals were already slowly cruising, pointing. The highway patrol had their radios turned up. It was becoming a scene. The buses stretched the whole frontage of the Martin Farm all the way up to Mr. Smith's house, easily a quarter mile.

The "road" we cut that afternoon was just two tire tracks through felled blackjack oak and hickory, the stumps left high because the ancient buses had huge ground clearances. But there was one short stretch, a quick down-then-up crease in the woods where the dirt became mud, chewed up and slick after the first few buses went through.

John Coate—From the days of the Caravan on, we never had a shortage of manpower—monkey power we called it. And quite often that was how any large job got accomplished. With thirty or so men and women at your disposal just from yelling, "Monkeys" at the top of your lungs, you could, lift, pull, push, or yank just about anything to anyplace you wanted it.

Rupert Fike—No problem now, we had monkeys, hundreds of them to push each bus or truck up the little rise. It was well into dusk before we'd driven, pulled, and monkey-powered the buses down into the meadow, and blessed seclusion.

The smaller, lower-to-the-ground vehicles, like our VW bus, only made it a few yards into the woods. It was determined they needed to stay out near the road for town-running duties.

Kathy and I had spent the last six months we were in San Francisco fixing up our van. I'd relied on *The Complete Idiot's Guide to VW Repair*, and Kathy had transformed the interior into a homey little vessel, everything in its place.

We kind of saw it coming, how our van was going to be nationalized, but still it was a shock those first weeks, somebody with "priority" business in town knocking on our window early, us vacating, waiting all day for our bedroom to return. Some days we got dispatched ourselves—since we were from the South, we knew the manners, how to let it slip we were from Georgia. Plus we were among the few who could understand (barely) the advice Homer Sanders kept giving.

Kathy and I were the first to go visit Homer—well it wasn't so much a visit as an emergency that cropped up the day after we landed, Sunday. We needed hay real quick. We had bought a team of Belgian mares from some nearby Amish, and now the horses were hungry. They had been sledding supplies down to the meadow over the rain-slickened ruts we'd made through the woods. We had no wagon so Jon, one of our few country boys (he'd grown up on a Nebraska farm), had hitched up Belle and Mabel to a pallet-type deal which he stood on like Ben Hur and "hyaed" them in what I thought was a very uncompassionate voice. But

the team responded. Belle and Mabel, God bless them, dug in, bowed their necks, and sledded in load after load of propane tanks and groceries. Likely they were thinking—did we have to get sold to someplace where the wheel hasn't even been invented?

So Belle and Mabel were hungry. We had some sweet feed, but they needed hay. Kathy and I drove over to Homer's trailer. He was watching *Gunsmoke* with the volume way up. There was a shotgun and shells next to the door. Everything smelled of gun oil. We expressed our desire for some hay and waved a few dollars around, but all Homer wanted to talk about was parties. Except he said "artees!" since he was missing part of his tongue.

I had many relatives with heavy Southern accents, but he was a challenge to understand, especially with Marshall Dillon shooting at the same time. Finally Kathy got it, elbowed me, and said, he's asking about parties, wild parties. I said, oh no, we don't have wild parties. We're spiritual, blah, blah, blah. And Homer said, "Shucks! Guess I ain't got no hay then!" Then he slapped his knee and had a big laugh which, after a moment, we nervously shared. He took us out to a shed and helped us throw a few bales on our purple bedspread of Krishna and the cow maidens.

The next few weeks was the transition into "all things in common." And where it might have been cleaner for me to completely "cut loose" of our van, I had such an attachment to it, I

began working in the Motor Pool (mostly on the VWs) as a way of keeping tabs on my baby. Soon the van was getting used so much we had to move out and put together an A-frame in the woods made from stapled plastic and skinned saplings.

From the fertilizer factory we were tearing down in Mt. Pleasant, I scammed some 1 x 6s and hammered together a rude floor to get our bed and junk up off the ground. It was a very wet summer, mushrooms growing everywhere (orange chanterelles pan fried with brown rice—yum).

Soon there was a succession of people coming to inspect our place. We'd hear a "knock, knock," voices actually saying that since there was nothing substantial enough to knock on. "We heard Rupert and Kathy had a floor. Can we see it? Wow. Stoned," they said in wonderment. "A floor." Some of the more conservative were openly critical, wondering if a floor might be breaking some rule that we were all hazy about but determined to have. Perhaps having a floor meant we were abandoning the Mahayana (great boat) concept of taking care of everyone for the Hinayana (small boat) concept of just covering ourselves. That would be bad. The astral conservatives (people who would hold you to higher standards than they held for themselves) were out in force that first summer. It was still getting figured out, how exactly to be "spiritual." We were watching each other very closely, all of us insecure about being spiritual students.

Word got back to Stephen about our floor, and he came by, took a look, and commanded no more plastic tents or temporary structures, since it was becoming evident that we'd soon buy the Black Swan ranch and move over there. But since we had voluntarily thrown our bedroom/vehicle into the communal pot, we got an exemption.

Meanwhile at the small clearing we called the Motor Pool, Jose was the straw boss because he was the only real mechanic. Jose was from Puerto Rico via New York City, and he did not think highly of an auto manual that called itself a guide for the "complete idiot." This did not seem like "positive manifesting," one of the few "rules" we were sure about. But since more VWs kept coming in as stragglers from the Caravan caught up, and since I was one of the only so-called mechanics, I was allowed to keep using the Idiot's Guide. Which was good because I would have been lost without it.

This was a time for acid-head English majors to find a niche on the material plane where they could actually do something productive—a bit more difficult than it sounds. For the past year or so, our only occupation had been rearranging each other's heads, and that was continuing, but now we all had to become householder yogis.

From early on, your gig, your day-to-day job, sprung more from the direction you needed to grow spiritually than from what you were good at or had previously done. In fact, being proficient at something might make it detrimental for you to keep doing that every day. If you were too much into your head, you needed to get into your bod, go out in the fields and hoe the sorghum. If you used to manage a health food store in Berkeley, you probably shouldn't do the food buying even though you might know ten times more about it than anybody else. Why? Because you'd get into old ego places—bossy or full of social position and self-importance.

The Martin Farm summer was a psychic, if not an agricultural, hothouse. It was just us and the woods, very little contact with the outside world (the word in neighboring Mt. Pleasant was that we were "mating") but much contact with each other's heads. I walked up late one night to one of the few town-runner cars that had a radio. I slowly turned the AM dial, amazed at the realization that the world was going on, that this was not a summer of isolation and sorting out subconscious for the rest of the world. Nothing made much sense on the radio. There was a discussion through the static about some papers at the Pentagon. I imagined there had been a big demonstration there that had left the grounds littered.

We did many dumb things that summer like planting the sorghum way too close together so it grew like grass, its biological family. We literally hand-cultivated a small field breaking each dirt clod with our fingers, thinking such was zen practice, the plot barely large enough to feed a family of eight, much less nearly three hundred. After a midsummer thunderstorm, a panicked message appeared on the community chalkboard—"Corn on its Side!" Which was really no big thing. Corn occasionally gets whacked down by summer storms, then over the course of a few days, it straightens back up. But oh, no. Monkey power had to intervene, rush into the fields, and try to personally hand-straighten each stalk, the result being we broke or wounded most of the field.

We spent ridiculous amounts of money (from inheritances) on groceries including corn flakes, Soyagen milk (Stephen had once said he liked it), health food brown rice, and adzuki beans. It had not sunk in yet that the days of co-op buying and organic veggies were over. Twice a week, we made ice runs to Columbia, returning with huge blocks of ice, the kids running up and down the road, screaming, "Ice at the store." We were classic grasshoppers who needed to be ants. The coming winter would not be kind. Money would dry up. Food, if not scarce, would become bland and the same old same old—wheat berries, soybeans, sweet potatoes, the occasional canned goods.

Near midsummer there was a serious outbreak of hepatitis from some contaminated watercress that someone had picked in a local creek. Whole buses became sick bays. Jaundiced faces stared out windows with barely the strength to wave. Mt. Pleasant officials became justifiably concerned because the little house down in the meadow where we'd first parked was the pumping station for their water supply, and here we had hep right on top of it.

Several babies were born that summer. Ellen gave birth to Naomi who was premature and did not even weigh a kilogram. The nurses at Maury County Hospital called her "the littlest hippie." Naomi had to stay in Columbia for some time, so Ellen used a breast pump to bring her milk in, the idea being that Naomi would drink it for its antigens when she got home. There was zero electricity on the Martin Farm so Ellen's milk was stored in the only refrigerator we had, a propane powered unit on Anthony and Janine's bus. Thing was, the milk kept piling up, so instead of just throwing out the older stuff, Anthony and Janine made ice cream out of it. This became an epic scandal.

Finally as autumn approached, the deal got signed, money changed hands, the Black Swan ranch became ours—one thousand acres, almost exactly what we'd spent months looking for, and here we'd been given permission to squat on the Martin's land not a quarter mile from what would become The Farm. Buses got cranked up, many for the last time. Others had to be towed, but by mid-September we were on the land, our land. The paperwork was executed deeding it to the Zen Center in California should anything befall us.

The sorghum mill was under construction so we would soon be in the syrup business.

We hosted a series of "debates" with local Jesus-only ministers that got front page coverage in the Nashville Tennessean. The reporter on the scene was the young Al Gore. We were on our way. The Martin Farm summer had been precisely what we needed—a few months of isolation and getting out of the buses, transitioning from head to body, discovering what exactly we were about—because the world would soon be calling.

Rupert Fike

Bow Saw Yoga

We often assigned someone to do a "yoga"—doing something on the material plane to help with their spiritual development. For example, on the way to The Farm my bus was traveling alone, a couple of days behind everyone else. We were driving through Kansas when we were pulled over by the cops for going too slow. Barbara, who was driving, was doing the self-imposed yoga of a word fast, no talking at all. She did break the fast to talk to the cops.

The first winter on The Farm, I was living in a single people's tent. There were maybe a dozen of us. We were a quirky bunch, the dregs of the single folks. That's why our material plane manifestation was so bad, about the worst on The Farm—it reflected our level of agreement. We were in a 16 x 32-foot army tent with a straw and canvas floor, a major fire hazard. One guy wanted skylights. Without anyone else's agreement, he cut holes in the ceiling and glued plastic over them. We could never figure out a way to make them stop leaking. It was maybe the coldest winter we ever had—the temperature got to seventeen degrees below zero one morning. We bathed in a two-foot diameter washtub, standing in water we'd heated up on the woodstove, behind a curtain at one end of the tent.

One day Robert and I had been hassling with each other. We couldn't seem to get along at all. So the other people in the tent sent us outside with a two-person handsaw. It was our yoga to saw firewood until we could get along. It was freezing outside, with icicles hanging from the trees and cloudy. Now, we were so mad at each other that when one of us wanted to push, the other one, just out of spite, would push too instead of pulling. It took us awhile just to get in enough agreement to make the saw move. Then we started getting into it. We sawed away, got it going pretty fast. We sawed a good pile of firewood, got nice and warm from the exercise, and just let the anger fade away. Bow saw yoga worked!

Rachel Sythe

The Hippies Come Clean

Arriving in Tennessee after what for many of us had been more than a year of living on the road, we found ourselves finally able to focus on something other than locating rest stops and dump stations and generally keeping our buses in good working order. We could spread out into the woods around us and explore the possibilities of living in a nonmobile environment. We had only the faintest hint of what was in store for us, but we had been living on the edge for quite awhile by then so there was little apprehension about our most uncertain future. Somehow the fact that we had successfully circled the country as a kind of gypsy community made us confident that together we could solve those unknown challenges now that we had landed.

First on my list of priorities was to take a shower. Sponge baths just weren't going to cut it anymore, and if there was one unpleasant fact of bus life, it was the difficulty in finding a good shower along the highway. Of course, there was the small detail of finding a spigot somewhere in those Tennessee woods. Not that there wasn't plenty of water, in fact that was one of the critical factors in our decision to locate ourselves in Tennessee. Turned out there was about as much rain there as in the Pacific Northwest, and springs were plentiful. Unfortunately, most of us liberal arts majors had neglected to take Plumbing 101 at any point along the way. We did have some basic "how-to" skills, I guess, at least enough to know what questions to ask. And we found no shortage of friendly locals ready to tell us how to do things.

We located one of the many springs at the bottom of a ravine, bought ourselves a submersible pump which we ran on a VW engine (suddenly our vast supply of bus and van parts became a most valuable resource) and we were on our way to running water. We ran a length of plastic pipe up the hill and built ourselves an outdoor shower building, complete with a hand-dug drain field that we learned how to make with a government manual and a few hints from the neighbors. I was sure they had at least some vested interest in keeping the hippies clean.

It was summer by then, and the creek served the purpose while we built our shower house, but the water didn't exactly come preheated. For the new shower we went out and bought the biggest propane hot water heater we could find, right from a factory outside of Nashville. Of course, the biggest hot water heater around isn't going to keep the water hot for two hundred people, cycling through the system at least every couple of days. We ended up only using half the shower heads we had installed, since that was all the little pump and the water heater could support. It became a real challenge to pick the right time to come for a shower, since the line could be an hour or more long.

But that was only the first lesson we learned. The second one was when the first real freeze came along in the fall of that year, and the entire system of plastic pipe burst into splinters. I remember being amazed at the destructive power of ice and wondered out loud why we hadn't taken some precautions (like turn off the water?). By then we had moved onto our new property next door and were working on a "state-of-the-art" building, fully enclosed and insulated. We had, however, planned to use the parts from the outdoor system for our new shower house, but now there was little left that could even be recognized as once-functional plumbing fixtures. We would have to start from scratch.

Philip Schweitzer

How We Dropped Our Water Tower But It Landed In the Right Place

David—After a few weeks on the Martin Farm it became apparent we needed running water, showers, all that. Using a crew of men all day every day to collect, then distribute, spring water was an obvious energy loss. Somehow we found out that Vanderbilt University had an old summer retreat in Sparta, Tennessee, out on the edge of the Cumberland Plateau, and there was this water tower there we could have for the taking.

It was quite an expeditionary force we sent for the tower—two school buses, about twenty-five people, a station wagon, and the Big Pickup, a school bus that had been converted into a very strangely proportioned yet heavy-duty truck. A large wooden cradle made from 2 x 10s and oak logs was built to the dimensions of the actual tank and placed in the bed of the Big Pickup. We planned to be gone probably a week.

Steven—I got involved because I had an engineering degree from MIT and had always wanted to do something big and mechanical. Seemed like a great fit. My first step was to prepare

a derrick tall enough and strong enough to lower the tower off its three-legged perch and into the cradle on the truck. A derrick is nothing but a frame that allows you to mount a pulley high enough in the air so that you can do some business. Through that pulley a cable was then to be attached to the water tank so it could be lowered to the ground.

We could have rented a crane to lower the water tower, but the thinking was why do it that way when we can do it ourselves and impress everybody with our know-how. (Mistake Number One) So I spent the next week or so talking to one of the heavy-equipment experts in Columbia and built a stiff-legged derrick in the Motor Pool. It was roughly the shape of the letter A with a pole in the middle that extended up past the point of the A. It was made of old telephone poles and held together with steel I-beams and monstrous U bolts. My friend in Columbia said this would work. He also lent us enough steel cable and blocks to get the job done.

The "job," in hindsight, was actually quite mammoth for the level of "tools" we had. Here was a five-thousand-gallon water tank on top of a three-legged fifty-foot high tower, and here we were with a funny looking truck, a slapped-together cradle and derrick, and some cable. The tower was located maybe one hundred yards from the edge of this cliff that was, in essence, the end of the Cumberland Plateau. Below us was a one-hundred-mile vista of the Nashville Basin, absolutely breathtaking in the early summer mornings.

At the tower site we assembled the derrick, almost like a huge tinker-toy set. For support we cabled the derrick's legs to the concrete blocks that the tower was resting on. From there we winched the derrick to vertical using a cable attached to the water tank, the pulley on top of the derrick, and for pulling power, a pickup truck. This was also how we were going to lower the tower. The middle of the derrick was tied to some trees via cables to make sure it wouldn't fall the other way, toward the tower.

Kenneth, at that point, wanted to also tie a cable from the trees to the top of the derrick, but I said, no. We would have had to lower the derrick again to do that, and besides, I got my degree from MIT and the derrick was okay as it was. (Mistake Number Two) Then we positioned the Big Pickup so that the oak cradle on its bed was right where the tank would be when it was lowered. (Mistake Number Three) We were ready!

David—The plan was—when the tower was unhinged at ground level, I'd slowly back the bus up which, via a cable through the derrick's pulley, would lower the tank down gently into the cradle that was waiting in the bed of the Big Pickup. It took us several days to get all of this together. At the last minute we hired a local welder to strengthen the framework with an arc welder. He said it would never work.

Steven—Two of the tower's legs were pivoted on its base so all we had to do was disconnect the third leg, lift it enough for clearance, then let the tower pivot on the two hinged legs and slowly lower it to the ground. So with all in place, we unbolted, then jacked up the third leg of the tower, and for a brief moment there we were, this huge water tower balanced on two legs. I was a little nervous about now, but it's sort of like jumping off a high dive; you just have to do it. The signal was given to the bus holding onto the derrick to start backing up, and here it came, over center, putting weight on the derrick.

It looked okay for a while (seconds turning into minutes). The top of the derrick was deflecting a little more than I thought it should have, but we didn't stop and reassess (too exciting!). So we lowered the tower a little more, and then a little more. At this point the whole contraption—tank, tower, derrick—was a good fifteen degrees off plumb, and the top of the derrick, the single middle pole, was beginning to bend like a fishing pole. It wasn't a graphite fishing pole though. It was just an old, recycled, dried-out telephone pole that didn't stay bent too long. I don't recall hearing the crack, but things were happening pretty fast by then.

David—As I backed the bus up, the rope attached to the derrick broke, the metal and wood framework bent, and the tank fell.

Steven—Nobody said anything, whoa, stop, look out, any of that. All of our impulses were overcome by what our eyes were seeing—the water tower coming down in free fall, yet still accurate as per our preparations.

David—I can close my eyes and still see it perfectly, my view from the bus, the water tower falling straight into the back of the Big Pickup, bouncing one big time, then laying still.

Steven—When the tank hit the truck, the old school bus door flew open, the hood popped up,

the tank bounced back into the air, and the truck amazingly went with it, all six wheels off the ground. They both came down, the hood slammed shut, the door closed itself. They went up one more time, the hood and door again opening before everything settled, except for a last bounce from the tower—and then all was very quiet. (And still, if you don't count this huge cloud of dust around the truck and a long plume of rusty air curling up from the main outflow pipe on the bottom of the tank.)

David—Luckily we had been smart enough not to let anyone sit in the cab of the Big Pickup just in case our calculations were off. What happened was the tank fell exactly into the cradle in the bed of the truck. Steven may have been wrong about certain stress tolerances, but he had the trajectory down perfectly.

Steven—We all stood there, holding our positions, quiet for a good ten seconds before we started laughing. And then we were roaring.

David—We swarmed all over the poor Big Pickup, expecting the worst. It was fine except for the sides of the bed that were crumpled and later had to be rebuilt with wood without our signature red and blue stripes. The leaf springs were completely bowed, almost going the wrong way, the frame a tad bent. We chained the tank down, tightened the boomers, disassembled the tower, cleaned up the area, and left the next morning. The tank had a good-sized crease in it that remains to this day. It got cleaned up inside and out and was raised on our new land, by a crane, and served the community for twenty-seven years before it was replaced.

David Friedlander and Steven Levin

VW Spring Pump

With the water tower in place and a cistern full of spring water in the hollow approximately two hundred feet below it, we bought a water pump and built a shed for it next to the cistern. The only problem then was how to power the pump—it needed a ten horsepower electric motor, and here we were miles from the nearest 220 electricity.

Meriwether Lewis Electrical Co-op said no way could they run that much wire, that many poles, all that manpower for one water pump. It was out of the question. We were stumped, but something needed to be done. Much energy was expended each day in the pick up and delivery of five gallon (40 lb.) water jugs for home use. It took a truck and a full crew of men to make the rounds, and even so they couldn't keep up. There was always a mother and kids pulling a red wagon filled with jugs. It seemed we might stay in that rut forever because we were electricity poor. But looking around we saw what we were rich in—new spiritual students who had driven 40 hp Volkswagen Bugs to The Farm.

Mary was from Michigan and did not care what we did with her rusted-out '62 Bug. Which was good because that was how the agreement went—when you joined The Farm you threw in everything you had, which in Mary's case was the rest of her travelling money, maybe two hundred bucks, and a good-engine, bad-body green VW Bug.

The guy at the Columbia machine shop gave me an extremely long stare when I explained what we wanted. He took off his safety glasses, looked at the dirty old brake drum. Then he looked at the clean new pulley. Drum, pulley, pulley, drum. "You want to what, now?"

I tried to explain it again. We want you to weld this double pulley to this Volkswagen brake drum because we've got a Bug we're gonna jack up down next to the spring house and . . . he held up his hand. He tried to get out of it, but we begged. He finally shrugged, okay, okay . . . hippies.

The big day came. The pulley was ready, the shower house was finished, hot water heaters in place, water lines run, all we needed was to get the water up into the tower and then a town of over four hundred would have running water. Well, showers and spigots. We backed Mary's VW as far as we could down Spring Road which was really not much of a road at all. From where the old moonshine tracks gave out, we got some machetes and hacked a path for the Bug. The blackjack oak at the top gave way to poplar and hickory as we neared the spring.

Once we'd backed the car up to the pump house, it took some doing to jack up the car, put the new drum/pulley where the left rear wheel used to be, get the thing aligned with the pump's pulley, and put the belts on. Then we had to tighten the belts by monkeying the three-wheeled VW forward. Somebody installed a water pressure gauge from the pump on the car's dash, and that was it. We fired her up, got ready to whoop and wave our hats, gave the engine some gas, put it through the gears—but wait. The pulley was barely turning even in fourth gear. We revved it some more, but still nothing. This couldn't be.

Somebody finally noticed the right wheel was turning, doing sixty it looked like. Oh yeah, in all rear ends that aren't posi-traction, power goes to the axle with the least resistance, in our case, the axle that wasn't trying to turn the pump. This is why cars get stuck with one tire in the mud.

For another bad moment we were defeated. If we put the right rear tire on the ground, the new pulley would be too low in relation to the pump pulley. All seemed lost. No showers tonight after all. And then someone, I can't remember who, reached in between the front seats and yanked up on Mary's emergency brake. The right rear wheel stopped. Power surged to the pulley. The belts started flying and then came a new noise, the whump-whump-whump of our pump—blessed sound. We touched the three-inch PVC pipe snaking up the hill. Water was pulsing through. We put the Bug in fourth gear and found the perfect creek rock to lay on the gas pedal, one that kept the pressure at 120 psi. And that night we all had hot showers.

Later came problems. Not so much with the VW and the pulley as with the human element. A crew was needed to fill the tower twice a day, and where we'd been ecstatic at the clatter and

whump-whump that first afternoon, "pumping" soon became known as a boring, ear-splitting chore—start the car, position the rock on the gas pedal, then sit there an hour or so.

Pumpers quit too early or put the rock on the gas pedal, went home, and forgot to come back to turn it off. This resulted in either no water or the sound of "slop, slop," water overflowing the tower and dropping thirty feet making a huge mud hole. And of course, inevitably, someone kicked over a gas can, gas leached into the cistern, then got pumped into the tower—contamination of the whole system. The tower had to be emptied, scrubbed down.

I was on call for the thing, day or night, and it always seemed I got the news that the VW wouldn't start after the tower had run dry. Plus it would be a two- or three-birthing night. One weekend night I had to go to the Visitors' Tent and take a distributor out of a "soaker's" (a prospective member) VW because the one at the spring had burned points, two ladies were having babies, and there were no auto parts stores open. The owner of the car was going to join and throw in everything he had in the next couple of days at the next "soaker's meeting," so it wasn't like I was stealing part of his car—in fact I had him hold the flashlight for me—but still, he looked a little shaken about the whole deal. I told him to think about his distributor giving everybody showers on Sunday.

Then I ran back down to the spring, and while I was changing it out, somebody yelled down from Second Road, "Hurry up, Marlene is dilated six centimeters! They need water." I remember thinking, God, what a place. The poor woman's getting her cervix measurements shouted out through the woods.

I finally got the thing in, wires on in the correct order. I stood up, arched my back, and listened to the woods. A hoot owl was calling. Tree frogs and crickets were buzzing, lightning bugs and stars twinkling. So much for all that. I started up the VW, destroyed the peace, and set the rock on the pedal.

Rupert Fike

Lozier Was One of Our First Teachers

David—After the water tower project, Marilyn and I and some other folks went up to Lozier Lawson's place near Old Hickory to help him get in his hay. Lozier had come to know the Caravan while we were parked at Percy Priest campground looking for land. He became impressed with us after seeing us working long hours outdoors on a very cold day. Lozier was one of our first teachers in the way of down-home, strong, and centered local farmers. He was always ready with a crack or a laugh, but he could get mad too. Like when I drove his tractor and on the way to the hay field I hung the blade on a tree limb. I drove it back and said something was wrong, it wouldn't cut. Boy, was he pissed, but he got over it, fixed the thing, and sent me back out to mow this twenty-acre field. All day it took, around and around. Later in the week we were "bucking bales" from another field, and somehow I lost a twenty-dollar bill which represented our expense account for the entire week. I was devastated, but Lozier smiled, put me on the back of the hay baler, then drove it slowly up and down the field until I spotted it in the stubble. That's the kind of man he was.

Another time, he had me stand at the bottom of his lane and wave my arms so when this herd of a hundred or so cows came at me, they would turn into an adjacent fenced field rather than run me over and escape into the surrounding countryside. So I stood my ground, arm-waving and shouting, go that way, pointing to the sharp left turn as the herd headed toward me. They were picking up a little steam as they came down the lane. It looked like a scene from Rawhide. Head 'em up. Move 'em out—right at me. Either I wasn't doing it right or they always waited until the last second to turn. I didn't wait to find out. I made like Curly of the Three Stooges, pivoted on one foot around in a circle and nyah, nyah, nyah, woowoowoowoowoo, exited stage left. I did not want to be an item in the Tennessean the next day, "Vegetarian Trampled By Runaway Cows." Needless to say, the herd did not stop at the bottom of the lane.

Lozier was pissed again. It took us several days to recover the herd and get them back in the right pasture. There were cows jumping hedges on adjacent land, cows wandering down county roads and stopping traffic, cows grazing on pampered lawns in nearby subdivisions.

Lozier died a few years later in a farming accident, hitting an underground electrical cable with his chain saw. He was a good friend of ours in the early days who taught us the value of hard work while maintaining a wonderful sense of humor that really made you feel glad to be around him.

Ellen—When I was nineteen and had lived on The Farm for about a year, my fiancee was working construction in Nashville to earn money for the community. The house that was rented in Nashville for Farm construction crew families and for families of patients in Vanderbilt Hospital was full. So we joined ten or fifteen other Farm folks who were camping at the Old Hickory Lake Park in a school bus and army tent.

It was fun living in the park. There wasn't much work besides preparing food for the meals, so I spent much of the day in the water or on the rocky shore. As soon as I woke in the morning, I could swim far out into the wide expanse of Old Hickory Lake. I have always found the experience of being in the middle of a large body of water to be of a strengthening and liberating spiritual nature.

I was sitting on the rocks looking out at the lake when I first met Lozier. I was told by friends that he had a farm nearby. Lozier had a nice, respectful way about him. He seemed to genuinely like the idea of The Farm and was pleased that a Tennessee girl had joined up. I had dropped my Southern accent around my Northern and Western friends, but it drawled right out as soon as Lozier and I started shooting the bull. He had a sense of humor that was light and quick on its feet.

Every time he came by the camp, he'd come looking for me, and we would share some of that good ol' Southern-fried humor.

I was walking up to the camp from the lake several weeks later when a park official drove by the bus and army tent. His face was a picture of astounded outrage. By the following day, we were firmly told that our camping privileges had expired and would not be renewed.

The night before we left for The Farm, Lozier came over to say goodbye. The bus was lit by kerosene lamps which threw soft shadows on the Indian tapestries. I immediately launched into telling Lozier the story about the park official. I told him that my fiancee had decided to join the construction crews that worked in the area surrounding The Farm and that we would not return to live in Nashville. Then, I asked Lozier point-blank would he come to The Farm in about three weeks to visit us. The stage was set for one of the most astounding experiences of my life.

Lozier looked at me in the dim light, and his eyes were pools of darkness. Lovers may have the sensation of falling into each other's eyes, and my initial experience was similar to this. However, I did not drift into some romantic feeling for Lozier, who was old enough to be my father, but rather into a waking dream which overlaid the quiet conversations around us in the bus. Quite unbelievably, I found myself experiencing the distinct visual and kinesthetic sensations of floating in space. I was keenly aware of having been transported to the edge of the solar system, facing out into the galaxy. From the distant but brilliant stars came wafting the sweetest, wildest song. It was the kind of song that can pull the heart free, just by listening to the longing and the love that it holds. To hear that music was to experience such a poignant summons, that if possible, I would have traveled the unknown distance stretching out before me in galactic space to find the singer of that song.

Then someone spoke to Lozier, and suddenly, the experience was gone. Lozier didn't immediately turn away. He looked at me for another long moment. This jovial, gregarious man had nothing to say to my light-hearted invitation to visit in three-weeks time. There was a deep sorrow in his eyes that I didn't understand. It was not in any way proportional to our return to The Farm. But after what had just occurred, I understood very little. It seemed as if centuries had passed since I was laughing over being kicked out of the park.

The entire experience was too strange for me to discuss with anyone at the time, and I thought very little about it in the excitement of my return to The Farm and upcoming marriage. Actually, for most of my life, I never told anyone what happened that night. The experience was so vivid that it never faded in my memory. Yet, I had never heard of waking dreams and found the experience difficult to reconcile with my concepts of reality.

It was three weeks later when Stephen told us at Sunday service that Lozier had been killed working on his farm. As the tears poured down my face, I understood the depth of sorrow in

Lozier's eyes. I remembered how Lozier had looked at me, and I strongly believed that he must have known. Then I knew that sweet, loving song was Lozier's call home.

David Friedlander, Ellen Piburn

Like a Frozen Asimov Robot

Howard Warf was one of the Lewis County old-timers who didn't welcome our moving to Lewis County at all. Mr. Warf was an old time political boss. When we first came to Lewis County, we told the sheriff that we were not going to upset the political balance until we knew what was going on. Politics was not our first priority.

We heard tales of Mr. Warf controlling the whole county. It was said that if you crossed Mr. Warf and someone in your family had a job serving food in the school cafeteria that they would lose it. We took the stories with a grain of salt until I actually found a national magazine article that mentioned Mr. Warf along with some other famous political bosses. One was Mayor Daley Sr. of Chicago. One was Huey Long of Louisiana. One was the guy who controlled Duvalier County, Texas, and one was Howard Warf of Lewis County, Tennessee. He was the real thing.

We had a good relationship with Finley Brown, the county road man and, at one point, the county helped us with some of the roads on The Farm, which had stirred up some controversy, at least among the Republicans. The Democrats' position was that everybody in the county got driveway connections to the county roads and our road situation was just more of that, if you considered how many people were on that "driveway."

I was visited early on by the sheriff, T. C. Carroll, Finley Brown, and Judge Humphries. As seemed to be Southern custom, they took me for a little ride around the county while we talked. It wasn't like they were giving me my orders, it was like we were some of the Democrats, dealing with an issue that had become a mutual problem. They felt that it would be easier if we, The Farm, just made The Farm roads be county roads to get them out of trouble for helping us with roads. I said, "No, I'm sorry to be a hassle, but we like it so it takes a search warrant for anyone to come onto the property. That lets us keep control over our own land." They took me back to The Farm, and we parted friends, but I knew that it might not be the end of it all.

Sure enough, not long after that a sheriff's deputy came to pick me up and take me to Mr. Warf's office at the county seat for an interview. He said, "You ought to go along with Mr. Warf, he just likes to make it nice. You just go on in there and ask for a road and that will make it all nice and legal."

The interview with Mr. Warf was surreal. It was obvious that I was to accept a favor from Mr. Warf which would signify my support for him in return for this favor. I just chatted and didn't try to start anything. Mr. Warf kept starting sentences which had blanks for me to fill in, but I just acted as if I didn't understand the verbal cues. The deputy was on the side trying to get me to do the right thing by making encouraging faces at me.

By the time we got to the end of the interview, Mr. Warf seemed a little confused. I guess he thought someone forgot to brief me on my lines.

When we had first come to Lewis County, some people planted some pot. This got us busted. We weren't on The Farm yet and some people thought they were in the trackless wilderness and that no one would notice. Unfortunately, they did notice. I and three more men from The Farm were arrested.

At our trial, while the jury was out, I went to Mr. Warf and stuck out my hand and asked how we could register to vote. (One of Mr. Warf's jobs was registrar of voters.)

Mr. Warf's reaction reminded me of Isaac Asimov's first three laws of robotics and how a robot can be frozen by conflicts with these three laws. Howard Warf was frozen by some of the first three laws of politics.

Number One was never be seen being friendly with some low-class hippie, especially while the jury is actually still out. This was in conflict with law Number Two, which had to do with the existence of about five hundred voters living on The Farm. His hand went back and forth, to and from that handshake, like a frozen Asimov robot.

We did register to vote, and eventually we came to a point where we had two representatives on the county commission. There were three positions open in our district. We could have had them all, but we left the "At Large" position open for the neighbors so they wouldn't have to be represented by a hippie if they didn't want to. We figured that two representatives was about our share according to the size of our population.

Mr. Warf continued to become more controversial, and on one meeting night of the county commission he walked in and started talking about something he wanted done. Well, the commission was already in a conversation about something and one of the members said, "Does Mr. Warf have to wait his turn to speak here like everyone else or does he just get to walk in and take over?"

This began a discussion that culminated in a vote about whether Mr. Warf would wait his turn or not. The vote went against Mr. Warf, who apparently knew his time was past. He left after turning in twenty-two unelected county jobs that he had been holding on to for dispensing to the faithful.

Many years later my oldest son Sam was at the local community college in his political science class when the teacher told the class about Mr. Warf and about him being the political boss of Lewis County. The lecture finished with the story about how The Farm's influence ended Mr. Warf's reign in Lewis County.

Stephen Gaskin

The Music Is the Message

There was a bit of exploring that we began to do once we were sitting still after the Caravan for the first time in over a year. Many of us had played music, having been a few of the wandering hippie minstrels of Golden Gate Park and the like, but had been forced to abandon our playing, at least temporarily, while we navigated the U.S. interstate highway system on our great mission of peace and love. I say that without sarcasm, since despite whatever naiveté we may have labored under, we most certainly had only the most lofty goals that drove us from state to state in those days of Vietnam, cultural upheaval, and mystical revelation. But it was this very idealism that caused us to both in-

terrupt our music-making while on the Caravan, and then to begin it again in Tennessee. Why not use music to make some noise of a different kind?

Perhaps it began somewhat less pretentiously, when a few of us were sitting around outside our parked buses in the woods, picking guitars and singing and generally enjoying the fact that now we were home. We started writing songs, but from the first there was a simple though unwritten rule of the composing process: the lyrics had to meet the rigid standard of

not bringing you down, even with the subtlest subliminal reference. It was assumed that if you wrote while you were in a truly spiritual state of mind, only the highest level of consciousness would pervade your music. The reality was that you endured a critical process of sanitizing so that you revealed nothing that could be construed to be at all demeaning, depressing, or heaven forbid, demonic. No blues, no whining about your problems, no metaphors that could be misconstrued, no heart on your sleeve, tears on your pillow, or of course, coke up your nose. We were determined to be the clean alternative to what was quite accurately perceived as the self-indulgent pop culture that had long since sold out to big money and fleeting fame.

We were acoustic musicians out of necessity, but we felt our roots were in rock 'n' roll. Once we had moved to our new property, there was at least electricity at the one house and a barn that was located there. We began to piece together electric instruments, and got serious about creating something that was, if not mass-marketable, at least a statement about who we were and what we were thinking about. Then something happened that could only be described as a strange twist of fate.

One of our people had been hitchhiking through Nashville and was picked up by a country musician named Claude Gray. He had had one hit some years before, something about "One Last Cup of Coffee," and was currently associated with a new label called "Million Records." He was in the process of promoting a new single that he had done with the label, and in the

course of the conversation with the woman from The Farm, he became interested in this new music from the hippies on the commune. When could he come down and check it out?

We were happy to oblige and scheduled a concert in the barn for a convenient weekend. Of course, we weren't loaded with material at this point but that didn't mean we couldn't crank up a set of jams and feedback-laden psychedelia that was certain to energize the otherwise musically deprived among us. We knew how to have a good time.

Claude arrived with a few unidentified friends while we were engaged in our routine of exploring rhythms and simple modal structures that allowed us to go completely experimental, unrestrained by convention. Somewhere during the evening everyone in the barn was waving their hands above their heads, swaying and dancing, caught up in the mesmerizing atmosphere of the loudest rock we could generate with the gear we had assembled.

Claude Gray was, well, tickled pink. He was certain that he had somehow miraculously stumbled on the very next wave in pop culture. Nashville was still reeling from the knock-down punch rock 'n' roll had put on country music, and this was an experience that he believed could be exported from right out of the heart of Music City itself. Wait until the honchos at Million Records get a load of this!

Not long after Claude's Barn Rock adventure, we were booked at a sixteen-track studio outside of Nashville. Never mind that we were hardly ready for prime time, we had enthusiasm, ample chops (individually if not collectively), and a few pretty good tunes to jam on top of. We left our kerosene-lit, woodstove-heated buses parked in the Tennessee outback and headed for the high-tech recording studio to turn on the world. Nothing could stop us now.

The session itself is a bit of a blur to me now. Maybe that's at least partly the result of the fact that we filled the coffee pots with peyote tea and stayed pretty well on another plane the entire time. We recorded an entire album, only to scrap it all and start again with a revamped lineup of players. We played live, no baffles, no overdubbing (much to my chagrin at the time), and no fancy techno-tricks. Honest, raw, and natural was the only way to go. Listening to it today I am impressed by some of the jams and embarrassed by the vocals. But the point wasn't to make elevator music anyway. We were idealistic kids who really did believe that we could make a difference by being who we were and not compromising. At some level, I think we succeeded in contributing to a continuity of faith in a new way of thinking and living, at a time when the greater culture around us was succumbing to a surreal artificiality.

But we were also soon to be victimized by another little twist. Shortly after the pressing of the record, a double album complete with a full-color poster and a front-page ad in Billboard magazine, Million Records was busted for bootlegging. It seems they had made their money selling eight-track recordings of the likes of the Rolling Stones and Simon and Garfunkel. Million Records, and our new album, went unceremoniously down the tubes.

Our musical adventure, however, was far from over. We went back to the barn and practiced, honing our skills and getting ready to tour the country with a series of free concerts designed to get our message out, and maybe even pick up some more people who could help us turn The Farm into one of the biggest statements on reinventing culture that this country had ever seen. The only problem with this plan was that The Farm was running out of money while we were spending it out on the road. While we did bring in many new people who contributed mightily to our community in the years that followed, it sowed more than a few seeds of resentment among those who stayed behind, laboring to keep The Farm alive while we toured around the country telling everyone how really great it was.

But despite the controversy, the music never stopped. More bands sprouted up, and more of us found ways to express ourselves with artistic talents in many artistic fields. This was a critical element in our first decade of survival and would help us to remain closer to the cutting edge of the technology in publishing and recording.

Our next album, however, was the very antithesis of "cutting edge." Recorded in an Army tent set on a wooden platform, the control room was housed in a step van parked with its nose inserted into the side of the tent, the windshield providing the view between the musicians and the engineers. We worked with a two-track mastering deck that was perhaps the only piece of professional gear we possessed, but it couldn't overcome the limitations of the rest of our makeshift assembly. We still managed to actually press a record, but it quickly became a collector's item among aficionados of the truly obscure. The point was made, however. We would let nothing stand in the way of making our statement, certainly not our lack of the technical facilities available to the pop musicians of the day. We were nothing if not inventive.

As we continued to make our music, slowly, even haltingly, we had begun to assemble the building blocks of a real studio. Our small tape company had grown to be pretty self-sustaining by recording, editing, and distributing tapes of Stephen's lectures. Out of this base we created a practice studio and a small control room for the tape decks we had acquired. By 1978, eight-track recording equipment began to appear that was accessible to the consumer. This was roughly equivalent to gear that had been state of the art only ten years previously, and to us it meant independence from the grip of the record industry—which we had no chance of penetrating anyway. Our stubborn insistence on doing whatever it took to get out beyond the confines of our isolated Tennessee refuge led finally to the creation of what came to be known on The Farm as "Bandland," The Farm's recording studio. Known locally as Village Media Services (a "cousin" of that company using that name is in existence today), we formed a small business that supported itself by working with local musicians making demos and even a couple of albums. "Bandland" became the headquarters for a wave of musical creation that added enormously to the quality of life within the community in those years.

The band that had evolved out of the original Farm Band, was known as the "NRC" (after the infamous Nuclear Regulatory Commission; we were deeply involved in a protest of the nuclear industry), produced an album that, while now showing signs of age much like other music of the period, still has remarkable style and energy. And while the music we made could not break out of The Farm box and into the mainstream, we continued to make every effort, on several different fronts, to impact an increasingly self-obsessed culture as it veered down what to us was an obviously destructive path.

Philip Schweitzer

Prison Softball

Early in 1974 after years of appealing on religious grounds, Stephen and three other men went to jail for growing marijuana. Stephen had not been actually apprehended in the patch, but in a gesture that certainly solidified his moral leadership and holds up even today as courageous, he stepped forward and took equal responsibility for the actions of some of the members.

The morning they were to turn themselves over to Sheriff Carroll was a stressful, doubt-ridden one for the community, which gathered in force at the Gate to see them off. The sentence was a vague one to three years, but even one month without Stephen's hands-on guidance seemed fraught with insecurities. His vision had turned this ragtag invasion of hippies into The Farm, a respected religious community. Plus his unassailable policy setting (which we would quote as "Stephen says . . .") had provided the hidden benefit of stopping personality clashes or power struggles before they ever got going. Once "Stephen said . . ." whatever—that was it, end of story, united front, no arguments. But now with his going to jail, we would be, in a way, on our own, and even though the party line was, "Well, with the Teachings we can get by without the Teacher," there was definitely a vibe of worry about the coming months.

This was underscored by a car traveling at a high speed sending up clouds of dust before stopping at the gathering by the Gate. Out popped a brightly dressed couple just back from Hohenwald, the county seat, where they'd gotten their blood tests and marriage license early that morning. Stephen took their hands, married them right there, got in the Lewis County police cruiser, and by that afternoon he and the others were behind "The Walls," Nashville's gothic state prison that dated only to the previous century even though it looked medieval.

Word quickly spread the next few days that the community, in a gesture of solidarity, would embark on a "grass fast" for the duration of the prisoners' jail time. However laughable this may seem now as a response to our spiritual teacher getting tossed in the slammer, the "fast" was undertaken in complete seriousness and strict adherence.

Of greater significance was the fact that The Farm now began an ongoing outreach program to all those in jail. We came up with many ways to show "solidarity"—penpals, band gigs at various "joints," taking in any parolee who showed up at the Gate, doing personal business for the friends our men had made "inside," all of this became a new and vital priority.

Which is how we, the community's closet jocks, got committed a year later to playing a softball game against the prison team at the Turney Center, which was located near Only, Tennessee. By this time Stephen and the three other men had been paroled back to The Farm, but during their year in "the system," they spent several months at the Turney Center, and it was there that Stephen

had been locked down in "the hole" for refusing to wear leather boots to go out on work detail. Stephen had offered to supply his own nonleather boots for the job, but his offer was rejected. No leather boots—no work; no work—"the hole." It was that simple.

Stephen's time in solitary was only a few days, but with that history at the Turney Center, it put our thrown-together softball "team" in an impossible situation. I mean, it was good we'd scheduled the game because the prisoners couldn't get many teams to come play them, but there was one very important aspect we'd overlooked—gloves. What were we going to do about using leather softball gloves?

For us to go up there with leather gloves was clearly not an option. It caused guilt pangs to even think about it—wear leather to play a game in the very same facility where our spiritual teacher had refused to do so and been thrown into solitary confinement? Absolutely no way.

We'd been practicing without gloves down in First Road meadow, but that didn't seem like the one either—to show up barehanded for a serious, competitive softball game. The inmates would surely be offended. It would turn the game into a joke, creating ill will instead of good-will. Thought was given to cancelling the game. Those who had come up with the bright idea of this outreach now saw it as a no-win hot potato.

Salvation, however, came from the local general store, the Lawrenceburg Big K. I was on a quickie parts run, but the Gateman held me up and quietly told me I'd have to take a pregnant visitor to town. She'd come to have her baby here and needed a few diaper-type items to put her mind at ease that all was in readiness for her birth. The midwives had sanctioned it—get her into town and let her buy her things so she'll relax.

I really didn't want to have her along because she'd see me stop and guzzle a Dr. Pepper the first chance I got. Plus she'd see me drink one on the way back.

John Coate—This little situation went straight to a common problem of communal life: Simple corruption, sandbagging small amounts of money. When you got five bucks from Petty Cash to buy some new sneakers, you looked to spend about four dollars and twenty-five cents and blow the rest on snack food like a Dr. Pepper and a candy bar. You were supposed to bring back the change, but almost nobody ever did, and after a while it became an accepted practice. So on the way home everybody's medicating themselves with carbonated water and caffeine elixirs (which actually helped with the digestion of soybeans). And all the bottles and wrappers went on the floor.

Rupert—But okay, okay, I'll take her, and after I got my auto parts, I found myself following her through the back aisles of the Big K, trying to hurry her up as she slowly filled her buggy with baby supplies.

But there, on a shelf near the toy department, there they were—gloves, mitts. Obviously too shiny to be leather, they were horrible and wonderful at the same time, naugahyde and poor workmanship, perfect. My hand barely fit into the "Little Slugger" glove. I punched the pocket. It was hard, unyielding, not much bigger than a softball itself, but this was IT! I checked the shelves; there were ten or so of them. We were saved.

The Turney Center is set deep in the backwoods of Hickman County, not far from Grinder's Stand, by the Duck River. As we drove up, the first thing we saw were the guard towers along the prison walls. Beyond the walls were open fields that led to a dense wilderness on the other side of the Duck.

There were many other weekend visitors in the long entrance hall, but still it seemed the guards stiffened at the sight of us, long-haired, bearded men in patchwork jeans, sneakers with exploded toes, braids, pigtails. And immediately as we passed through the metal detector, "Brrnnggg . . . Brrnggg" the thing went crazy. We were searched. Ahhh, here we go, one of the guards held it up—a half-inch wrench forgotten in the back pocket of our shortstop's jeans. They inspected it carefully, looking for a possible hidden hacksaw blade while we explained that he had been combining last night, and that the combine had a loose sprocket because . . . they held up their hands—enough, shut up and move on. They kept the wrench, but now we were eyed with a certain suspicion, or maybe it was respect, for having set off their alarms.

The Turney Center team was already on the field, completely uniformed down to socks and cleats. The ball was pop-popping its way around the infield as the bleachers filled with inmates waiting for us, the afternoon's entertainment—the good vibes, vegetarian whipping boys from the commune. We put on our Little Sluggers and tried to loosen up, but there was a huge intimidation factor. For one thing our jeans suddenly seemed too tight. Perhaps, we joked quietly, we should squat for ground balls instead of bending over. It got a nervous laugh.

For the first few innings, though, we held a two-run lead. They were smacking the ball all right, but it was going right at us, who in absolute self-defense, were catching it. And with each line drive caught off the bat of those hairy-armed, tattooed men, our plastic play-mitts made a pitiful "splat" sound as if they were saying, "Hey, I'm just a toy."

Meanwhile the onlookers were yelling from the bleachers, "Hey, come on three-hundred-year infield! You're getting beat by a bunch of hippies." We asked the umpire, also an inmate, what that meant. "Well," he said, "the first baseman is doing two sixty-year terms for murder/robbery, the second baseman has a fifty-five-year sentence for robbery/kidnapping . . . " We held up our hands. We got it. All we had were two guys who'd done "thirty-dayers" (been sent off The Farm for thirty days to get some "relativity").

In the third inning things started coming apart—literally. A vicious line drive actually took the Little Slugger off our second baseman's hand. Ball and glove rolled into right field as one.

The batter was speedy, he rounded first and headed for second. Our right fielder had a problem getting the ball out of the exploded glove. The runner rounded second. The hard throw went to third base where that Little Slugger came apart, the ball rolling over to the dugout. The batter rounded third and scored for a two-exploded-glove home run. The crowd went crazy, pointing, replaying the whole thing, their hopes of entertainment having come true.

We gathered in a huddle around the destroyed gloves and attempted triage, life-saving surgery involving hair-ties and shoelaces. It was hopeless. The game continued, but another glove came apart the next inning, and then two more exploded in the fifth. The prisoners now seemed to be aiming their shots directly at us just to see our gloves go to pieces. The crowd loved it too. The rout was on, but we hung in there and finished the game, wearing the gloves just for show the last few innings. The final score was something like twelve to five.

On the way home in the van we were a tired, defeated, yet somehow a happy bunch. We had actually done some prison outreach, we'd made a showing, scored a few runs, and actually led for a while, answered a thousand questions about why we wouldn't use leather. And on the van's hard floor, several of us lay back and found the perfect use for our split-open Little Sluggers — as pillows.

Rupert Fike

The Night The Farm Came to Prison

The word was out on the compound: a band was coming to play tonight! What made it especially appealing to everyone was the fact that it was not going to be gospel or country music. At least that was the rumor.

It did not really matter though. We prisoners were starved for some kind of diversion from the normal routines of our lives. Anything which could take our minds off of death, robbery, rape, fear, and intimidation was a welcome relief.

It is strange the way men turn violently on each other when crammed into a small space. Both the prisoners and those who guard them become capable of mean and vicious acts. I often wonder why. Anyway, the word about the coming band was out, and I was looking forward to the distraction.

I had never heard of The Farm. Other prisoners had, though. They related the story about how some of them had stood up to Uncle Sam (the government) over an issue of some importance to history and The Farm community. They had done some time, got out, and, according to the word, had not forgotten from where they came (which is pretty unusual).

I personally had no love for hippies. I could take them or leave them. I had no opinion on them either way. On the night of their show, I was an observer. I watched from my seat way up high on the gym pullout seats as the hippies from The Farm went about getting everything together as more and more prisoners filed in from their respective units.

I noticed right away that the hippie girls looked very doe-eyed and that the guys all had far-away looks in their eyes. It was if their internal dialog was "stay busy, don't look up, stay busy, don't look up . . ."

I also noticed how aggravated the prison guards looked. They really did not like it when outsiders came in. It interfered with their routine. Tonight, they looked even more hostile than usual. I enjoyed that. My smile was an expression of my delight at the nervousness of the guards.

When the music began, I felt something stir within me that I had not felt in a long time. It was a connection to something nonviolent, a connection to some peace. To this day I cannot remember a single song that they sang, but I will never forget the energy of love that they released into the gym that night. It spread throughout the entire prison and gave calm to a negative place.

After the show was over (way too soon), the prisoners wanted more. The guards would allow no encores, however, so the show was done.

Then the most amazing and unprecedented occurrence happened. The hippies from The Farm were hugging prisoners and shaking their hands. Guests visiting the prison just did not do that! The guards would usher everyone out quickly, and the guests would usually leave without ever having come close to a prisoner. But these hippies were having none of that!

I was mesmerized. I sat glued to my seat at the top of the gym watching all this hugging. I felt that if I smiled any wider my face might break. I was one of the last ones out of the gym. As I walked out, I heard one guard telling another that they had lost control tonight, those people were not supposed to come in contact with any prisoners. The other guard replied that he sure wasn't going to tell anybody. I laughed all the way back to my unit.

That night I laid in my prison rack and thought about the show. I replayed the night's events in my mind. I kept thinking about Jesus being amidst the unclean lepers in the Bible and how that must have been much similar to the scene in our gym.

You know, I never did get a hug that night. I was too high up on the gym seats to make it down to the floor. Besides, I was an observer and what I observed was LOVE!

Yeah, I never got a hug that night but I got something much better—a piece of my soul was returned to me.

Andrew Dixon

Grass Fast Sunrise

During the incarceration of Stephen and three other Farm members for growing grass, The Farm went on a "grass fast." Since grass was considered only a tool for raising your consciousness, this did not preclude us from seeking the state of mind that we sometimes referred to as "stoned." We simply had to work out other means of attaining it. There was always meditation, sorting out the group head (discussing the subconscious problems of your crew, your household, etc.), walking in the woods, and for me, like many others, there was farming. After all, just following your path, doing your work, and staying focused are all you need to do.

I was on the Farming Crew during its most ambitious years from 1972 to 1976. For the first four years, we were constantly expanding the number of acres we farmed. At one point we had 80 to 110 people working full or part time on the crew. We were long on people power but short on farming equipment. One of our solutions to this dilemma was to institute the twenty-four-hours-a-day, six-days-a-week tractor schedule. We rotated the night shifts so periodically it would be your turn to show up late in the evening, well after dark, and do whatever the next task was. We plowed, disked, planted, and cultivated at night by the headlights of the tractors.

One time it was me and Willy on the evening shift. We were supposed to cultivate a field up near the Gatehouse. Willy got a call just before our all-night shift. The previous driver said the tractor was in the Tractor Barn and needed engine work, and the cultivators needed to be fixed before we could clean up the field. So we met at the tractor barn and went to work.

The barn itself was a massive building with a high ceiling and doors large enough to accommodate combines and large tractors with implements attached. It was your basic post and beam structure built with telephone poles and sided with rough-cut, grey oak that was milled by our own crew at Homer's saw mill. At one end there was a raised platform that held the humble Farming Crew offices. At the other end was a long bench that ran the full length of the wall and held the tools and spare parts. One of the unique features of the "parts stash" was a huge pile of bolts and nuts that were the floor sweepings from a large manufacturing plant. This was a great resource. It could also be a great source of frustration.

You see, the bolts and nuts were of many different sizes and had different types of threads. Finding a matching nut for the perfect bolt you had just located was not always quick and easy. Still, it was a lot easier than trying to get some money and a car to go to town. Besides, on a night shift like ours, that wasn't an option anyway.

We were working on an old International Farmall. It was well used when we bought it, but it was a reliable machine that we worked hard for many years. Willy and I began with the engine problems and slowly worked our way through them. Then we turned our attention to the cultivators. This project required some serious sorting through the massive nut and bolt bins. With a lot of banging and tightening the task was finally completed. What had originally been designed as a night in the fields had turned into an all-night mechanic session.

When the tractor was ready to roll, we fired it up and drove out to the field. Willy drove and I rode on the fender. Just as we arrived at the field, feeling triumphant, the sun began to rise. We parked the tractor at the beginning of the first row facing the coming morning. We shut it off and stood there quietly as the sky filled with wonderful shades of gold, orange, and pink. We watched as the dark, then grey, of night gave way to the bright blue of a clear spring day. Just as the sun was cresting the hill, we could both feel the rising energy. Willy turned to me with a huge grin on his face and said, "Who needs grass?" It was a perfect natural high.

Michael Cook

The Community Kitchen

When we first moved onto the land that was to become The Farm, there were but three buildings on the entire thousand acres—a small, ranch-style house with its own well, a large, tin barn, and then about a mile down the main road that bordered the fields was an ancient, grey shack made from rough-cut oak. It was approximately twenty by thirty feet with an unfinished plank floor, a solid oak plank door, and minimal frame windows.

Homer Sanders called it the "line shack" because that was what it was—a leftover from the nineteenth century when the road that ran through our property was the old carriage trail that led east from the Natchez Trace to Columbia, Tennessee. It was a "shack" situated about a day's travel from the Trace which provided shelter for travelers who were following the "line" towards Columbia.

It was a classic "if these walls could talk" kind of place. The poor, the well-to-do, statesmen, highwaymen, anyone getting off the Trace at Grinder's Stand (where Meriwether Lewis died) and heading to Columbia in the last century would have passed and perhaps taken comfort in the Line Shack. Later, as the population of the area increased, moonshiners used the building for sugar storage and the like.

But the action that building would see was far from over. Before it was torn-down in the mid-1980s, it served as The Farm's Community Kitchen, a meeting and eating place, bustling with energy all day. A large "dining" tent was set up next to it where thousands of meals were served. Then for many years after that it housed our flour mill. And if indeed there were still ghosts from robberies or deaths or ambushes in the Line Shack, they had to scramble to keep from getting run over by sweating women yelling, "Hot stuff!" as they carried large pots of hot beans from the stove to the counter.

Rupert Fike

The Front Door

The Front Door, that's what we named the Gatehouse and its ongoing scene. There, at the end of a turn off dusty, unremarkable Drake Lane, we greeted the world. And in some cases we sent the world back on its way. But always the Gate crew of the day tried to make sure it was understood exactly what we were doing there, and sometimes during the explaining, we educated ourselves.

We were living out a huge-scale vision of all things in common. We were an intensive spiritual school, all teachers, all students. We were developing Third World village technology. Meanwhile, right across the chert road in something of an eloquent counterpoint, sat eighty-year-old Grady's cinder block house and sheds, trucks up on blocks, chickens in the yard, cows mooing, the screen door slam and hollering of tow-headed boys going on the same as it ever had.

In the 1970s there was a sizeable diaspora on the road—refugees from a homeland that was no more and may never have been—Woodstock Nation. The Farm soon became a stop on their search. We had been fairly loud about landing in Tennessee and had put out a full-color magazine, *Hey Beatnik!*, that soft-focused and air-brushed the rigors of Farm life. So it was really no big surprise when they came; it was just the unendingness of them.

They showed up happy and together, testy and on medications, able-bodied, frail, all stages of pregnant, some down-to-earth, some delusional, many with only the slightest idea of what we were about, many perceiving The Farm as "open land" where there were no rules. The Gate crew's job was to figure out each individual case. Were they nice enough for an overnight stay? Two nights? Did they just need a tour? Were they candidates for sanctuary? Sometimes they had to be driven back out to the interstate to spare our neighbors the rantings of some barefoot anarchist.

There on the front porch of the Gatehouse, sincere seekers, professional charlatans, and hippie nomads mingled with just-plain-curious Mom and Pop Tennesseans stopping by for a look-see after church. Then came college professors with classes, various police, FBI, Immigration Service, film crews, reporters, new additions from Central State Mental Hospital, and hey, here's the propane delivery man wanting a check. There was always the daily in-and-out Farm traffic, plus the function of the Gate as a nerve center and clearing house. For a while it was also the base of the community's ambulance and EMTs and holder of the oxygen tanks for fifteen or so birthings a month. Add to all that rattlesnake cages in the back of the gatehouse filled with captured snakes, and basically you had an intense twenty-four hour scene.

There was an official Gate crew whose job it was to set various policies, deal with local authorities, track down visitors, decide who fit our "sanctuary" requirements. But in addition, Farm couples rotated through for twenty-four-hour shifts of separating wheat from chaff, the possible from the undoable. No one was allowed "down on The Farm," even to the Visitors' Tent, until it was certain they understood we were a spiritual community commanding a certain reverence and respect.

Inevitably mistakes got made. Nice people were sometimes lectured sanctimoniously. People with mental problems occasionally made it to the Visitors' Tent. The traffic hardly ever slowed. Often there was a new group pulling in before you had finished sorting out the last bunch. This frequently wore down the regulars on the Gate crew.

One of the main continuing problems for the Gate crew was its function as a vibe-filter for the community. That meant that all the potential problems with visitors got sorted out there. Innocent, good-vibes visitors or curious locals would sit on the porch with some bipolar hippie who was convinced that, like baths, he didn't need his lithium anymore. On any shift there was from one to four such "trippers" living at the Gate. Sometimes ambiguities over who actually was the crew resulted. In many ways it was a mental emergency room, often feeling like a full-moon Saturday night. And at the end of each shift, the Gate crew would try to sit a moment and find time to write a few words for continuity with the next shift, to pass the exhausted, sore-throated dharma. These are excerpts from those logs.

6/3/78 — Had an old hobo, Human Humorous, come in, signs all over his back and on his hat, dollar bill hanging in front of his nose, pulling a sort of golf cart with more signs and stuff. Nice guy who took off most of his stuff when I asked and put it on the back porch. He was opposed to work on principles and decided this was not his trip. He gets checks from the government — total disability — ulcers.

H. at Gatehouse, laying about. Got him to sweep and mop upstairs and down. He has a hard tropism towards spacing out in a corner if you don't keep after him.

We need more snake sticks up here, plus containers with tight fitting lids. A woman came in who had a prior agreement to leave her baby here. D. (a neighbor) walked over from next door with an apparent broken arm. Ambulance took him into Maury County Hospital. Later a lady from Australia with three kids came in. She saw Stephen there. Also a nice guy from Germany.

We need fly swatters and scrubbers.

6/5 — Quite a few visitors today. More from Australia. A group from Findhorn, and reporter-from the Washington Post. In the midst of all this, a visitor who'd been kind of quiet, jumped up and blurted out, "You guys aren't spiritual," ran out, and caught a ride to somewhere with a crew. Then a car ran the Gate going out, an irate husband it turns out.

6/14 — Help! No Gate wheels. Visitors' Center has about fifty folks. Farming Crew is picking lettuce across from the Gatehouse so we have been plugging visitors in while we worked on getting them a place and a way to get there.

Lady flying in from Norway to Nashville. Need a Music City Welcome Wagon. Stephen, crew, teenagers, EMTs, ambulance, and Scenicruiser all off to the Longest Walk, Seabrook nuclear plant protest, and the Bronx Plenty Center. Book Company crew right behind in the Clark mobile home — off to Minneapolis for Birth Control Convention.

6/26 — Amazing day, was covered though. Sonny Jones (FBI) spent several hours here talk-

ing with Joel and Leslie. Finley Brown (Road Commissioner) came later and saw Leslie. Joe Churchwell, running for county clerk, visited for awhile, then Sheriff Bennett came—Mercy Sakes!!!

6/27/78—Never thought I'd see the day when the gate would be closed, but due to hepatitis, that's now the situation. Taking day visitors and visitors from other countries only.

8/13/78—Still getting visitors from Germany. If we don't get any more cases of hep for the next two weeks, the quarantine may be over. One of our visitors was tripping (acting out uncontrollably) last night. She went to Leslie's house and proclaimed him the incarnation of Jesus and said she was his soul mate. She was pretty rambunctious so Leslie had her shipped to the Gate. About 5 a.m. she got away and made it all the way to Leslie's bedroom. Back to the Gatehouse. Got away again, twice more actually—a lot of Bible talk. It seems that giving her a good back rub helps the most. No tours past the Head of the Roads due to hep!!

8/14—Not much traffic today which was fortunate.

8/22—A lady named E. made it from San Francisco hitching all the way. Said she'd been in and out of mental institutions and jails, needed some sanctuary to try and figure it out. Stephen said flat out we couldn't take on any more sanctuary cases that needed a crew to maintain them. That is just the way it is. We're maxed, unable to keep up with who we've got cooking. Plus all those tripping buddies that are spending almost all of their time with the sanctuary cases are productive, trucking folks who could be holding down some part of our thing that's flapping in the breeze. We were out front with her about all that, and she agreed to be cool so she's got a temporary three-day sanctuary. She seems like a real sweet lady. Hope we can help out. Just discovered she quit taking her lithium two weeks ago.

10/24—Ten Army helicopters (the real big ones) with machine guns and other weapons buzzed The Farm for some time at very low altitude, less than one hundred feet. Scared some kids and horses.

10/25—Helicopter trip made it into the New York Times. Hueys and Cobras doing a village intimidation trip à la Nam was what it was. Army folks, officers, flew in today in a single helicopter to "check out" what happened yesterday. Landed at the school, reporters were there along with all the kids and Stephen and Leslie. Lawrence County news came and got a good interview with Stephen. Then a guy came in wanting to tell us that the helicopters were UFO illusions. He almost got into the juice with the WSM-TV guys who were here doing the story. Channel Five came to get our reaction to the General's statement.

11/22/75—We talked to a tour of twenty-four folks in morning from U. of Alabama. Just as they were leaving a class of twelve from U. of Kentucky showed up for the night although we had no knowledge they were coming. In the midst of all that, we got an ambulance call that there was a baby that was a slow starter, blue. We made the run in good time—three minutes. Thought we were headed out to the hospital at first, but the midwives kept slapping the baby's feet until he got going. Nice big boy that started turning pink and squawking real nice. Made us rush and rush to watch him come on.

Got back to the Gate in time for another group from Carbondale, Ill. A guy came in a little soused and wearing about an eight-inch buffalo skinning blade. He seemed nice enough after talking to him and putting his blade away.

11/30—There were five weddings today, so a big chunk of the traffic was the families coming in.

12/1—Monday, your regular busy day, crews out early, store fixed us up for bread. A woman up on Hickory Hill went to pour what she thought was water on her pot belly stove, and whoosh it was kerosene. It caught fire. She got her kids out before the place burned to the ground. We coordinated the fire-fighting efforts through the CB—absolutely priceless.

12/4—R. (one of the neighbors) and a pal rode in last night drunk. One of them was on Barnabus the mule and hyaed him up on the porch. Quite a scene, a mule on the front porch. I needed to be a bit stronger about establishing our turf. Leslie went over today to tell him where that was at.

Kissing Tree Lodge

Lynette—Going into our infamous second winter, most of us were shivering in surplus Army tents or crammed into buses and vans in many strange configurations. This was called "Wheatberry Winter" because that was one of the main staples that was served over and over that winter. Stephen and The Farm Band were out on their debut tour of free gigs in an old Greyhound Scenicruiser we had bought just for that purpose. All the band members and support crew wanted to take their families along, so over fifty men, women, and children were living on the road in that bus for a couple of months.

Meanwhile back on The Farm, we California types were having a pretty rough time adjusting to life in the woods. The Tennessee winter had a strong tendency to mold or rot anything we didn't keep close, but not too close, to a woodstove.

Plus we were seriously broke. We'd used up all the trust funds and inheritances of the few rich kids among us, and everyone had already pitched in their savings. Then the expense of fielding The Farm Band's tour pretty much wiped us out. We had no idea how we were going to support this many people.

Stephen had appointed a steering committee to guide The Farm while he was away, and I can't recall the details now, but somehow building a nice house for Stephen and his family became a top priority, even though they had definitely not asked for one and were living in pretty much the same conditions as everyone else at the time—a 16 x 32-foot army surplus tent pitched on the ground with a wood burning stove for heat and a propane stove for cooking. But somehow The Farm wanted to surprise them with a finished house when they returned from the tour in November.

So a large crew of our best carpenters went racing all fall trying to finish this grand (by our standards) house. One of its most important features was a large, native stone fireplace that was supposed to heat the entire house. And what a house it was, a stone foundation with massive oak beams as floor joists. They were joined by large oak pegs which went through both beams at every intersection. It felt very strong.

As the structure was going up, the leaves were starting to fall. Soon you could see the new house from the main road and across the hollows. This sight was in a bit of counterpoint to the rest of The Farm as we were quite out of money. The shelves in the community store were practically bare. We were scraping! Mark, the store man, got disgusted around this time and left with his family, saying he didn't see how we could afford to send out The Farm Band and build a nice house when we couldn't even afford beans. (He and his family came back later.)

Somehow we held body and soul together until the middle of November when the Scenicruiser got back. What a homecoming! It was as if they'd been orbiting Jupiter or something. The bus had been in communication with The Farm by ham radio, so we knew pretty much when they were coming in. Almost everyone in the community was waiting up at the barn, right next to the front Gate. So there we were, a few hundred of us, kids too (couldn't leave them at home alone) on an absolutely frigid night, all of us huddled around a small wood burning stove in the barn, with Belle and Mabel, our draft horses, over in their stalls.

It was about 2 a.m. when the Cruiser finally made it to Drake Lane, The Farm's "driveway." We were so excited! Then it seemed like a really long time before we finally saw the bus's headlights coming up that last short but steep hill toward the Gate. The road was layered with mud from the storms we'd been having, and the bus was quite loaded. With only a few hundred yards to go, the bus stopped. It could not make it up that last slick grade. Somebody from the Farming Crew cranked up the old Oliver tractor and went out to rescue the bus. After what seemed like forever, here came the Oliver, churning through the gate, hauling the bus. Home at last! Everyone piled out, and a big reunion was in full swing for several hours before folks started the long walks home in the cold dark carrying their sleeping kids. Stephen and his family went home to their old army tent because the house had not been quite finished.

It wasn't very long before we heard what Stephen thought about his new house. He laid into us for building such a thing when we hardly had enough to eat, and didn't blame Mark for splitting. He also ranted and raved about a lot of other shortcomings that had surfaced while he was gone. After he and his family moved in, it became immediately obvious that the huge stone fireplace was not going to heat the house. Instead, it actually sucked cold air through

every crack in the uninsulated walls while all the heat collected up in the high ceiling of the great room. It was impossible to heat. Plus Stephen became uncomfortable living in a better place than anyone else. He called it a drafty old mausoleum, and pretty soon his whole family moved back into another army tent. This one was built with a wood floor and was located over on the next ridge, fronting a pasture that eventually became an apple orchard.

Michael—I recall the carpenters trying very hard to get Stephen's house finished before he got back from the band tour. Our financial resources were slim that fall, so the Bank Lady was under pressure from every direction to allot the small amounts of money The Farm had. All the people pressuring her were, of course, friends, and all their individual projects seemed necessary. But the building crew must have "leaned" hardest because she spent money on Stephen's house that was needed for some of our basic necessities.

When Stephen returned from the tour, he noticed that the Bank Lady was avoiding him and that there was no cooking oil at the store. After looking into it further, Stephen decided not to live in that house after all. His family moved out and gave it to some people who had taken on the care of an elderly relative of one of the members. That house on Schoolhouse Ridge was one of the few "real" houses on the land at that time, and I thought that this was one of Stephen's best moves. It showed he really stood behind his principles. And he did this rather consistently, being one of the last to still live in a tent, get running water, and such.

People may wonder why young, smart Americans raised in a very individualistic culture and valuing independence perhaps above all, would put their faith to such an extent into another individual, would grant anyone the power to be his or her spiritual teacher. For me it certainly had to do with the way he exemplified the teachings under pressure.

By moving out of his new house, in one healing gesture, Stephen had reset the tone of The Farm, reinstilled the proper attitude going into winter. Give to those who need rather than worrying excessively about yourself, and don't get so anxious about your project that you pressure the Bank Lady or anyone else to give you what you want. Most of all, forgive. It was moves like giving up the best house that reinforced my respect for Stephen enough so I'd come to him with my problems and at least be open to his answers.

Stephen, of course, was only human, and had personality, quirks, ego, just like the rest of us. And yet without his and Ina May's sparkplug leadership, we would not have had The Farm at all, or the midwives, or Plenty, some of the things that make me the proudest to be associated with the community. As far as I know, most of us are all still trying to live by the teachings, each in his or her own way.

Lynette—The house eventually became known as Kissing Tree Lodge because the trunks of two trees near it were touching in a distinctive way. It was a bit remote from where everyone else was living at first, so to get to the area where the Store, Soy Dairy, and Canning and Freezing were located, you might opt to take the path that followed the wooded crest of the ridge down into a deep hollow, across a shallow creek, and up a very steep hill on the other side that connected with the bottom of the next road. This was a beautiful walk at anytime of year. Just a little bit downstream from where the path crossed the creek, there was a meeting with another creek underneath a limestone cliff that was always wet with springlets. In the winter they became icicles, a spectacular winterscape. At night it was dark, so deep below the ridges, and without a flashlight on a moonless night, you had to take baby steps to stay on the path.

Lynette Long, Michael Traugot

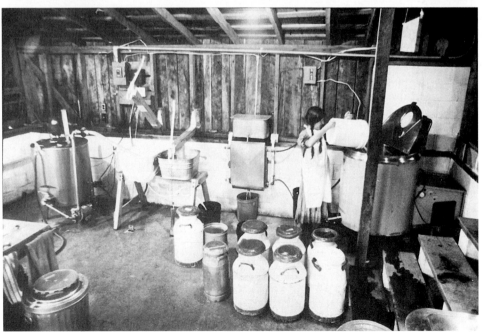

The Farm Was a Sea of Mud

In November, 1973, Heather and I left Tennessee and lived for a few years on two of The Farm's "satellite" communities—in Seattle and Northern California. We returned in 1978. After living in a large, action-packed commune in downtown San Rafael, moving back to muddy roads and dimly lit tent houses was a big change. It was also winter, even though we had arrived in the midst of a warm spell. That meant The Farm was a sea of mud. In many places there was no way you could get around it—you had to walk right through it—bogs of thick, sucking mud that stuck to your boots with every step.

By this time all houses had a "mud room" for an entry way, but you couldn't really get your boots off without mudding up your socks, then tracking it in. I had forgotten just how muddy it got there. Not long after we got back, I was going around saying hello to all my old friends when the rain turned to snow. A couple of hours later the temperature plunged, and the wet mud covered with snow froze solid and stayed that way the entire month of January. The roads were like glass, walking was a balancing act, and driving was crazy.

Lynette Long

Winter Gate Logs

January, 1978

1/6—If water ever freezes, don't wait three days before telling the utilities crew! The longer it's frozen, the longer it will stay frozen (sigh). It's now frozen underground so we won't have any water until it thaws or we get a deeper line dug.

1/7—We tried last night to get the water going. First we heated the pump with the wood-shop's kerosene heater. Then we thawed under the tank with the heat lamp and under the porch with an electric heater. Then Fred started fires under the tank and under the house. That seemed it would get everything really thawed out. But still no wah-wah. Oh, well.

1/12—Water still frozen, doing jug runs from the house.

1/14—Ice Station Zebraville. Snow through the night to cover the ice sheet now three to four inches thick. Any car stopping at front door tends to slide towards Gate steps. Have to go out and monkey power them along.

WATER STILL FROZEN. Our Gate car done broke on first run of the day (for water). Wheels situation is scarce. Visitor car brought us food and water from down on The Farm.

The neighbor's kids came over to catch a ride to the Summertown store. Got the print shop run to take them in. We fixed them up with a box of food from our store as well.

Entropy rules. Roads slicker 'n spit. Never stopped snowing and blowing all day. Most of the phone traffic is calls for wood and water. All of three visitors came in. At dusk, five full trucks of firewood and twenty men came in from the county road forest. What a scene. Entropy is also defined as the liberation of energy.

Dominion Over Snakes

One particular Bible verse Tennesseans were especially fond of throwing at us went something to the effect that God had granted man dominion over Earth and all its creatures. This, to the locals, meant that we were silly being vegetarians, and as for refusing to wear leather boots, they just shook their heads.

After taking possession of our one thousand acres though, that verse came back to haunt us because we were now the "owners" of many rattlesnakes. Like it or not, we had dominion over them. The prevailing wisdom in middle Tennessee was to shoot rattlesnakes on sight, or, lacking a gun, put a sharp hoe through their head. We certainly could do neither of those things. On the other hand we had to do something. We were settling many acres of woodsy terrain that had not seen any class of human residence for many years. We were walking narrow, just-made paths through underbrush and woods. We had children, toddlers, and crawling babies.

A slow day at the ambulance shed was the norm for Bill and me. We were a team, both state-certified EMTs staffing The Farm's state licensed ambulance, lights and siren, the works. Mostly we provided emergency backup to the fifteen or so births a month that started happening once the midwives in the community put out their call to all women to come have their babies for free on The Farm.

This particular morning, Bill and I were nodding off at 10 a. m. because we'd been up all night shuttling birthing supplies, but when Suzanne, our teenage dispatcher answered the phone and started snapping her fingers at us while she scribbled on a pad, we woke right up. She turned to us, "Rattlesnake. Schoolhouse Ridge kid herd (baby-sitting group). Go!"

I grabbed the snake stick and off we went, sending up huge clouds on the roads where every vehicle was supposed to go very slowly for just that reason. I remember the look of concern of the faces of folks moving back from the road as we sped by. Anytime the ambulance moved that fast, something serious was up. I wanted to roll down the window and yell, hey, it's okay, it's only a snake, but then I thought, no, it's not okay, I'm the one who's going to have to deal with it.

When we got to Schoolhouse Ridge there was a knot of people showing us where to stop. We ran down the hill into this little grove of sumac. The snake was coiled on a broad rock, enjoying the sun not far off the path. One of the kids had spotted it. It was pretty big, maybe three feet long with a bunch of rattles. Two of the kid herd ladies had sent the children inside and were now keeping watch.

Our snake sticks were nothing but broom handles with an eyelet on the end, like for a screen door hook to latch into. Through that eye looped a length of quarter-inch nylon rope which was nailed to the end of the stick so that a noose could be formed by the rope that stuck past the eyelet. You were supposed to ease the noose over Mr. Snake's head and pull back hard on the rope. Then you had its head trapped up against the end of the stick a good four feet away from you. Other EMTs had already captured rattlesnakes, but Bill and I had only practiced on long sweet potatoes behind the clinic.

There was a single mother who was in charge of this snake. She had come to have her baby a few months earlier, then stayed on. Young women like her kept piling up faster than you could keep track of their names, but I knew her face, and she knew mine. She said she had the wind angle figured and for me to be careful not to throw a shadow across the snake. She motioned me around to where I should be. I went.

Leaning towards the snake from its back, I played out a circle of cord from the stick, dangled it just over the snake's nose, and then gracefully it lifted its head. I noosed it and pulled back on the cord, wham, castanets like they were hooked up to 220, mucho life force suddenly at the end of my stick, pissed-off life force, whipping around pissed life-force. I had it. Or did it have me? I did not want it anymore. "The bucket," I yelled to Bill. "Get the bucket!"

Bill gave me a blank look. The snake whipped itself almost around the stick. "Where's the bucket," I yelled.

"I think we forgot it," Bill said. I knew he was right. I'd grabbed the stick but forgot to pick up the snake bucket.

"I can run get a diaper pail," the Single Mom said.

"Yeah, great, go." The thing was heavy at the end of that stick. While she was going I tried to ease the snake down because my stomach muscles couldn't take it much longer. But as soon as it touched the ground, the snake went nuts, sensing it was about to escape. I put my elbows into my stomach and held on with both hands. Bill and I discussed having him take a turn, but it looked too tricky, keeping tension on the cord.

She came back down the path with one of those green bottom, white snap-top diaper pails from the Big K in Lawrenceburg. It had her baby's name all over it with a very large S on the top. I remember thinking couldn't she have at least brought a pee pail instead of a shit one, but mostly I just wanted to get rid of the thing.

Bill now had the more dangerous task of holding the pail steady while I lowered the snake and then loosened the rope. It was quite different from sweet potatoes, the rattles curling up, not wanting to start their way in, but after a couple of tries we got the critter in there, its diamonds of earth colors now not looking so good inside a green plastic S diaper pail.

We started back up the path with it. "Hurry," I said. "There's a screwdriver in the ambulance tool kit. We can poke some air holes in the lid." The Single Mom frowned. "No," she said. "You can't do that. What good is a diaper pail with holes in it?" She had us there. Flies to shit to our mouths was the etiology of many diseases in the community. A diaper container with holes in it was sure to bring a "Where's that at," in the Laundry.

Still, the poor snake had to be suffering in there. "It's gotta have air," I said. "We can get you a new diaper pail." Getting a new diaper pail was doable, it just might take a few days, or, okay, a week. It, as did many things, depended on the Petty Cash Lady's mood and pockets.

You might get your money right then or you might, worse case, get put on some "list" awaiting the next "run."

"No holes," she said. "I offered you my pail, now don't ruin it."

Bill and I eyed each other. Some arguments you were better off losing. On a level, two on-duty EMTs outranked a Single Mom. But she'd just done some heavy bonding with the midwives, the heaviest of the heavy hitters in our community. We weighed our allegiance to the land's wild life force versus a possible run-in with one of the midwives over "leaning" on one of their Single Moms.

We put the screwdriver back in the tool kit and set the pail in the front seat of the ambulance so as not to contaminate the back which got scrubbed spotless every day. We told her thanks, we'd be right back with the pail, and headed up to the Gatehouse where the snakes were kept until somebody from the state wildlife commission came for them.

The snake, of course, would have been fine there in the pail for those five minutes or so, but I decided it really needed a whiff of fresh air on the way up to the Gate. I popped the clamps down. Bill said, "What are you doing?" I said, "It's okay, just keep driving." I eased the top off, just a few inches, for some air, but here came that head and tongue—jailbreak from the S pail, its stink coming out just as fast as the snake. The thing was strong, pure muscle. It almost tipped the pail over, but I crammed the lid back on which trapped the head on the outside. Bill tried to jump away while still driving, and all that made the ambulance swerve from one ditch to the other out near Apple Orchard curve.

I jumped up on the seat and got the snake all the way back in. Bill was mad and told me not to do that anymore. That's when a beat-up farming crew truck coming the other way stopped. The driver said, "You know, that's really not cool, hot-rodding the ambulance around." Two other men in the front seat nodded sternly. They drove away in, as always, a huge cloud of dust.

Behind the Gatehouse were proper, mesh-covered snake boxes provided by the state. They used them for school shows, venom milking, etc. Again the rattler was uncooperative; now he didn't want to leave the pail. Perhaps he was methane-dazed. We ended up using a stick to poke him down into one of the mesh boxes where he hit with a thump. Several visitors came around to watch the transfer and seemed to find it highly entertaining.

The snake was now so still I bent down to make sure it was alive. It moved a bit, and for a moment I questioned whether shooting or hoeing the thing might have shown a more compassionate dominion. Later that night when we got relieved, Ben and Gregory complained that they smelled shit in the ambulance. Bill and I sniffed and said we didn't smell anything.

Rupert Fike

The Letting Go and the Taking Hold

Don and I and Benjamin, age two, arrived at the Gate on a lovely October day. After we explained our hope that we could stay, we were served a lunch of pinto beans, collard greens, and popcorn sprinkled with nutritional yeast, a perfect meal still memorable in my mouth.

After lunch Benjamin took a spill on the porch, so I picked him up as was our custom, and I began to coo to him that it was okay, go ahead and cry. The Gate man came up and said, "We don't encourage our kids to cry. If you don't think it's heavy, he won't think it's heavy." I practically stumbled backwards. No one had ever questioned my parenting before. I was shocked and more than a little hurt. I ended up holding Benjamin more for my own comfort than for his. My mind was reeling.

We first stayed with Lawrence and Janie on Huckleberry. Imagine me, a somewhat tight-lipped New England Yankee, daughter of a Maine chicken farmer, learning The Farm ropes from a very Southern woman whose accent was as thick as her hair. I didn't know a thing about pressure cooking beans or rolling tortillas, but Janie, even with two kids of her own, was very patient and began to teach me everything.

One night early on as it got time for bedtime stories, I asked Janie, "Have you seen Ben's book, Where The Wild Things Are? I can't find it anywhere."

Janie gave me a stern look and drawled, "Why, Ah threw that book in the fahr." I fell back, horrified, assuming she had burned our copy, but what she meant was she had burned a copy her parents had given her because of its "vibes." I took this very seriously even after we found our book because I believed she spoke for The Farm. How could Maurice Sendak not be okay on The Farm? Later I found out there was much pressure to keep the vibes clean at every level, and sometimes the dogma of good intentions overrode common sense. I think it was the very next day I met Mary at the Dry Goods Store, and she, as a lifelong New Hampshire resident, connected with me on a deep level. Mary explained and laughed away the book incident. It took me a while to understand that not every opinion I heard stated was "party line."

In a way it was like Don and I were always playing catch up. We had come to The Farm when it was really too late to get to know Stephen personally. It was like The Farm had two phases—the Letting Go, which was Monday Night Class, the Caravan, and the Martin Farm, and then there was the Taking Hold, everything after that—which was when we showed up, when the men were working fourteen-hour days and the women too, and there just wasn't time to get bonded to everyone in the community anymore.

We next stayed with Don and Cory Ford at the little Round House. Again I considered everything Cory said, since she was a Farm veteran, as gospel. Once she criticized me for being lenient and sentimental with Benjamin so the next time he acted up I instructed Don to spank him, which Don was not into, being the designated spanker, but I insisted. Afterwards Cory said the vibes were terrible around all that. I hadn't pleased her at all.

When Benjamin came down with an earache, Mary Louise checked him out and mixed up a bottle of amoxicillin with dosage instructions. Cory came home from the clinic lab where she worked and said, no way would she give antibiotics to her child, Kopi, for just an ear infection. She probably just said it in passing, but I took it as instruction. A few days later when Mary Louise came back by to check on Ben, his ear was no better, and she spotted the full bottle of medicine on the counter. From there the story came out.

The next day Cory was very upset that, as she put it, I had gotten her in trouble with the clinic ladies and jeopardized her lab job. These were transition times from hippie reliance on homeopathic remedies to a judicial use of Western medicines. Cory and I were simply caught in the change, but I clearly remember feeling "blamed."

After a few more months of bouncing around Farm households (tent-holds actually), Don and I landed at a large (16 x 32-foot) army surplus tent on Dogwood Lane, squeezed in among two other couples and some single folks. We were thrilled. Our bedroom was a curtain drawn across a corner of the tent which was typical accommodations. In another tent, one woman became known as "the voice from behind the curtain" because of the household conversations she joined from that position.

There were always comings and goings among the single men and women who lived there, as they'd first decide they needed a break from the larger single tents, and then after a month or so with us decide we were Dullsville.

Our Dogwood Lane time was hard work but exhilarating. One strong teaching I got on parenting may seem trivial, but since it's stuck so hard in my memory it must not be. Myra and

I were on a blanket in the school for a winter boogie, and Vivian, who was maybe three, was having a bad kid day. "Stop crying," Myra said to her. Vivian toned it down from "Waaah" to "Hur . . . hur . . . hur." Myra said, "Stop, hur." Vivian immediately got a look of hurt and changed to a much quieter, "Um . . . um . . . um." "Stop, um," Myra said. She continued pursuing her in that manner until Vivian was quiet and then pretty soon was playing nicely on the blanket.

There were also struggles and sorrows. Two nearby homes were lost to fire that winter, the first from some clothes being hung too near the stove. A heroic sidelight to that fire was that Betsy Sharlet was doing the phone switchboard when she found out that her house was burning down but she stayed at her post to keep communications flowing, patching in directions to the water truck from CB calls. Her cat died in the fire. Everything was lost, actually.

At least no one was hurt in that fire. Little Andrew, near the end of that bad day, asked his mother Jeannie about his shoes, where were they? He had run out in his socks. "They burned up, honey," she said.

"Well, what about my coat?"

"Burned up. Practically everything you can think of is burned up, Andrew." She knelt to tell him this.

"Oh." He seemed to take such news philosophically.

The second fire a few weeks later was far more tragic, involving deaths of two babies and serious burns. It was in the early evening. Sparks and floating bits of flame were carried by thermals from the intense heat of the large house going up like a torch. We looked up at our Dogwood tent and saw fire settling all over our roof.

Don had just that day built a ladder to help around the tent (later this was considered quite telepathic), so he pulled it out and up went Rob onto the roof of the bread truck bedroom where he could get up on the one beam of the tent's roof. Three of the men formed a chain up to Rob and handed him pitchers of water the women began filling at the kitchen sink. Just that summer running water had come to Dogwood. We kept that up over an hour, relaying water to Rob who doused the sparks as they hit our dry canvas roof.

After the thermal died down, I went further down on Dogwood where there were folks from the burnt-out house. I was going to tell them of space for one family at the Rainbow House, but what I walked into was a scene where shock and trauma were on every face. Gayle was holding a tiny baby boy, who did not make it. He was not crying. The EMTs were wrapping Thomas' arms in bandages. I felt I had intruded on a situation so full of unspeakable pain, I simply backed on out after mentioning my housing message. Reuben and Margaret moved into Rainbow that night and when their daughter was born later that year, they named her for the other baby girl lost in the fire.

The next morning we woke to a clear, blue sky easily seen through the hundred or so holes, dime- to quarter-size, in our tent roof. After breakfast Don went up with canvas and tar to patch each hole.

Through all the hardships and tragedy there were daily reminders of how great the whole experience of living in community was. I recall sitting in the living room at Mango Manor nursing Samuel and listening to a conversation. Our young Guatemalan single man, Frank, was talking with a visitor from the Netherlands. Frank, whose first language was Cakchiquel, also knew Spanish, and he understood Dutch enough to kind of get by, which corresponded with the visitor's understanding of Spanish. So they had immediately worked out a way to converse using three or four languages. I knew a bit of French and German and Spanish, enough I could get the drift of what they were saying, but what a wonderful experience—where else could I have sat in my own home and been party to it?

Since leaving The Farm I have had to be careful not to say, "When we were in Guatemala . . ." because I, personally, have never been there. But I tend to forget that. Those of us who stayed on the land or the satellite farms helped front out the ones who were there, and I felt I was an integral contributor to everything The Farm did. I still believe in the worth of those missions, in the intentional community we created, in the idea of several families sharing living space and basic services. Even more, I believe in the goodness that comes from living close enough to others so that nothing can go terribly wrong for one family without others nearby to lend wisdom or muscle. I truly believe in learning how to relate and raise children from watching and imitating others. All these things worked for me.

Patricia Lapidus

There Was Great Incentive to Get Married

There were two major problems about being a single person on The Farm. First, there was more social position if you were married. I think it was commonly assumed that if you were single for any period of time, that there was something the matter with you. No one wanted you. You were "too trippy" to try and "work it out with." Also, since you were single, there was no one working full-time on getting rid of your subconscious like a Farm spouse does. So naturally it was perceived that single people had more unmined subconscious than did married people. Thus, there was great incentive to get married.

Then there was The Farm's edict that, "If you're having sex, you're engaged, and if you're pregnant, you're married." You have to understand that The Farm was essentially a very small town so there weren't that many single people on the land, and since it was taboo to even consider looking for a mate in the nearby towns, the search was confined to this closed society where out of, say, one thousand people, half were kids, more than half of the adults were already married, and of the balance only half were women. I had worries: "From among the single women on The Farm, will I be able to find my lifelong mate? Or for that matter, will I ever get to have any sex?" Well, if I planned on staying there, as per another Farm edict—"Two days or the rest of your life"—then I would have to find my mate within that small sampling of humanity. So there were a lot of marriages that were a result of those weird pressures.

Being such a small town there was also a lot of scrutiny put on the single people's courting activities. If a single guy was seen walking down the road with a single woman, that would

start major gossip. Just walking down the road, let alone actually having some interest. So if two people wanted to really hang out together, make out even, the surrounding attention was so heavy, and the implications of marriage were so strong, that I never felt like I had a chance to go slow or, God forbid, shop around—like having sex with a few women to be able to compare and find the right sexual chemistry. Sex on The Farm meant marriage and that meant forever, so single life there was far from the image of a free-sex hippie commune.

I recall a point where I was "courting" the woman I would eventually marry and I was having serious doubts about getting married – "Wow, the rest of my life." It turns out, being new to the Farm, she was having doubts about me too, and about Stephen, and had decided to leave. Before she left, she went up to "the house" which served as a meeting place for the community. While there, she ran into, well, I'll call her Grace, who was often a spiritual advisor to women on the Farm. Grace noticed her and commented that she had heard we were "courting," adding a cryptic, "Well, you know, he don't know shit about ladies!" My wife-to-be left The Farm as planned.

So what am I supposed to do now? Was there ever going to be another beautiful intelligent woman on the Farm that would be interested in me? Especially when the word got out that Grace thought I was ignorant about women? So I signed up! I got out my magic markers and mailed a colorful plea letter for her to return. It worked – she came back, we got married, had 11 good years together, and brought three beautiful kids into the world who are now my pride and joy.

Gary Rhine

Falling in Love

My dear wife is sleeping. I slipped out from under our covers moments ago and looked back in wonder. This morning her breath was soft on my cheek. My prayers are in gratitude. It wasn't always this way.

I was hitchhiking home to The Farm. I'd been gone three months. Darkness fell and I was still forty miles from The Farm. A pickup truck sped by with a couple of boys, one of whom whooped on the way by and sailed an empty beer bottle my way. There was a pop of shattering glass that threw shards against my jeans. I slipped back into the enfolding evening. There was a wide pasture near the corner. Away from the road was a broad rise sweet with fresh mowed hay. I rolled out the sleeping bag and gazed up into the deep sweep of the Milky Way. Behind me was a tumultuous, emotionally exhausting summer in New York. The time ahead was as uncharted and empty as the space between the burning stars. My mind turned to prayer.

The prayer that is most commonly answered is the one that goes, "Thy will be done." So what else is there? But sometimes . . . Tonight I prayed, like I'd prayed for several years, "Dearest source of all creation, if it is thy will, I would like to find a life partner. I don't mean to be picky, but she must be perfect. I want a family. I want to care for children and watch them grow. If this is not your will, I can, of course, live with that, but if there is even the slightest possibility, please know I swear to do my part to be a good husband and father. Amen." My sleep was restless that night. Each time I woke I prayed again, this on-going, years-long conversation between the ultimate ground of reality and the vibrating collection of atoms and Spirit that is me, personally.

Morning came dry and sunny. By late afternoon I was back on The Farm. I'd visited my friend Allen's parents in New York, and they'd sent their love to him. I headed to the Tractor Barn to see if I could find him. "Beetle" Bailey was carrying a battery to one of the Farmall C tractors. "Hey, Hutch," he called, his blond beard parting into a broad grin. "Welcome back. The cucumbers are getting away from us out in front of the Motor Pool."

"Let's sort it out in the morning. You seen Allen?"

"Yeah. He's cleaning up the Farming Crew kitchen."

The kitchen was a maple-sided building across from the potato barn. Just before I got to the kitchen steps I heard a woman laughing. Laughter tumbled out the kitchen door and touched my chest like a tender cloud. In seconds I was up the steps and staring, for the first time, into Kathryn's eyes. Her memory of that time is of the afternoon sun igniting a golden halo around my head. It was years before we had babies, but I believe they were born in that moment.

We started spending time together inside the bustling swirl of the Farming Crew. She was smart and funny and hardworking too. She sang while we worked. A pure sound came through

her that made sorting onions seem like church. Kathryn and I spoke about the most important things in our earliest talks. We were in agreement about Spirit, truth, lifetime commitment, and babies. Laughter always kept our conversations well oiled. I knew we were courting when Kathryn asked me, "Will you still laugh like this when you're really old?"

In contrast to the world outside, on-The-Farm-marriage was working for our generation. It is inspiring to have happily married friends. A couple of sweet married ladies told Kathryn I was a nice guy. I'm still grateful for their support.

It was harvest time for the Farming Crew. One morning we picked tomatoes from a rich field we leased on a horseshoe-shaped bluff overlooking the Buffalo River. A sudden rain drove the crew out of the rows before we got the bushel baskets of tomatoes loaded. In the afternoon Kathryn and I took a beat-up white pickup back to the site.

The mist lifted and clouds opened. Sunlight poured down, hitting the crystalline water drops hanging from the leaves and exploding into millions of emeralds and rubies. Although our shoes were held together with duct tape, we were swimming in abundance. All the dreams we held dear were aching to bloom. I hadn't touched money in weeks, and there was nothing more I wanted. Only to reach out and take the next basket from Kathryn and set it in the rusted bed of the truck. We were wet with honest sweat. I started to ask God if Kathryn was the special one I'd been praying for. Across the field she was coming with a heaping bushel of swollen red tomatoes. Beads of dew hung like jewels from her hair. Her eyelids dropped slightly. She smiled and her lips parted. God couldn't answer any clearer than that.

I put off asking her to marry me. I was afraid she might say "No." Or more likely, since she was so nice, she'd let me down easy, saying something like, "Let's think about it a while." And I had to be sure myself. There was no doubt in my mind and weeks passed and there was still no doubt in my mind. We might have hung like that forever but the Farming Crew would not stand still. At the end of the season in Tennessee a big chunk of the farmers would head down to south Florida and grow food all winter. I was scheduled to go and Kathryn seemed hesitant. I didn't think she would come unless it was really heavy. One day, after loading the pickup with supplies for Florida, we sat in the front seat in the driveway at Fourth North, the household where Kathryn lived.

I said, "Will you marry me?" She stared at me for a couple of seconds and said, "Yes."

That was it. Years roll by. Kids come and grow. The Farm changes. The Earth spins. Our hair turns silver. I wish all the world could be this happy.

Jerry Hutchens

Nothing to Say

In the early days of The Farm, we had meditation in the Second Road meadow every Sunday for an hour just before dawn. The meadow is a beautiful place, a gently rolling hill with trees that open into a clearing leading down to Cox's Branch Creek. Sitting there in the dark, still meadow waiting for the first glimmer of light to fill the sky was always a renewing experience.

Most of us sat in the traditional cross-legged zazen position. Just as the sun began to crest over the hills and forest, we would Om together until the sun was fully up. After the Om was over, Stephen would stand and talk. This was usually followed by questions and discussions.

One of these Sunday meditations still stands out clearly in my mind. It was Easter Sunday, and, although we always meditated at sunrise on Sunday, there was something different about this one.

Easter Sunday has its own special feeling. The first Sunday after the first full moon after the vernal equinox—the renewing of life in the northern hemisphere.

As we sat in the beautiful crisp air that drifted through the trees and open meadow, I thought of all of the people who were celebrating this moment. I thought of the Christians who held all-night vigils in prayer and contemplation. I felt connected to all of the ancient rituals of celebrating life renewing itself.

As the meditation continued, my thoughts become slower and fewer until I, we, consciousness was all that existed. There were moments when I had just enough awareness of myself to realize that everyone else was drifting through those moments of seamless existence. I could also feel that there were people of good heart and different faiths all over the world celebrating life. The feeling of peace and harmony with all of creation was deep and real. Just before the sun rose, I thought, what could anyone possibly say after this.

The sun rose and the Om was strong and pure. The resonance with universal consciousness was deep and clear. As the Om slowly faded, a deep, still peace flowed through the meadow, through us, through the universe. Stephen stood up, took one long slow breath, looked at us all, and said "I have nothing to say."

Michael Cook

Up-Close Relationships

As with many things, The Farm took communal living to its own, personalized extreme. During the years of peak population, the mid to late 1970s, most houses, some of which were customized tents, had four or more families, i. e., couples with two to four children, a few single men and women, a single mother or two, some with several kids, maybe an "adopted" teenager, and then there was always the Gate crew calling trying to fit in one more new "sanctuary" resident.

Living with that many people was, to put it mildly, intense; but then add in no electricity, a sporadic running water situation, no flush toilets, meals for forty having to appear from absolute "scratch" three times a day, and whew, it could tend to the stressful and no-fun side of the meter. But when it was working, it was like an adrenaline rush, manic gleams in our eyes sharing a secret—This is a blast!

The whole thing began gradually, so we were able to grow into our "large household" situations. At first there were just the Caravan buses that really couldn't hold more than one family. The only exceptions were several "four-marriages" that had formed in San Francisco when two couples united as one after going through a shared psychedelic experience. These were the forerunners of our communal life. Even though gradually they all dissolved, for a time these intimate extended families demonstrated how by living and working together, we could grow spiritually through sacrifice and sharing. Soon couples were living together without having a sexual relationship. It seemed only natural that we would share living quarters.

In late summer, 1973, my wife Deborah and I had only been on The Farm a few months and needed a place to call home. We were living out of our VW van, but soon we became friends with another couple who had just "inherited" a school bus with an old bread van attached to the bus's back door. This became our first "permanent" home.

We hit it off quite well as a little group, and, I admit, in my young and naive mind there some fantasies bubbling—Will this bond last forever? The end result, however, was much more predictable. Before long everything they did started to drive us up the wall, and I'm sure it was the same for them. We quickly developed the dreaded "subconscious"—which was Farm lingo for a build-up of interpersonal stuff that bugged you, but which either you didn't talk about (and not talking about it was completely against "the agreement"), or you were unable to resolve through "working it out."

To "work it out" meant you had a "sort session," wherein the underlying details and motivations of someone's learned behavior got sorted out or talked about. An obvious example would be to try to tell someone what it was they did that got on your nerves. Or perhaps somebody had said something which caused hurt feelings or showed a self-indulgence on their part.

The major goal of all this was to "stay current" and not let things build up, and in doing so, "working it out" covered the complete territory of human relationships—from subtle anger, intimidation, and crafty conditioning of others to the infinite levels of greed, selfishness, and desire that lurk in us all. We bravely attempted to talk about unmentionables, "calling" each other on petty issues. Through the whole process we aspired to lifelong relationships based on truth. Since we had a lifelong commitment to each other, we might as well start dealing with what bugged us about each other in a sane manner.

We soon learned that the better friends you were, the easier it was to say what you really felt, and that a friend would be more likely to listen and actually consider the information. (This was vital to the whole process, that one consider the input of others before firing back with a "Well, here's what you do.") Ideally, when several friends told you the same thing, it was time to drop your defenses and do some serious introspection.

Of course it wasn't always friends that "got into your thing" (confronted your ego). Supposedly altruistic sort sessions sometimes turned into a battle of verbal karate depending on who had the strongest word skills. But more importantly, if you tried to work it out with someone you weren't that close with, they often turned it around, got defensive, and in effect said, "No, you're the one with the problem." Then the whole interaction became a stalemate.

This is what happened between us and the other couple in the bus, so we moved out and started "bus hopping," living from place to place while the regular residents were off visiting their folks or perhaps on the road selling books for a week or two.

Soon we became friends with a couple who lived in a tepee. We both needed better housing, and after getting to know each other better, we decided to work together to build a small cabin. All of The Farm's building materials at this time came from salvaging old houses and barns. The deal was you worked on the crew during the week, but on Saturday you could go out and get materials for your own use.

Our cabin was built onto the end of a Railway Express truck, a big box about eight feet by twelve feet. It had a small woodstove and a sink. The area where the driver and passenger seats had been was outfitted with a bed. With the windshield and the two door windows, you had a panoramic view of the deep Tennessee woods. There was even a bubble skylight, so it was truly a magical little space. The cabin itself was ten feet by sixteen feet with ten-foot walls which allowed us to make a loft, more like a really high bed. It was all very cozy, and although we had our periods of emotion and "working it out," we remained good friends throughout the winter and into the spring.

Deborah and I had our first child (Jody, a son) in that Railway Express van. Not long after that, it just felt like each couple needed their own space for awhile, and our friends moved elsewhere on The Farm, leaving us by ourselves in the cabin/van.

We were going through our own changes around this time as we were one of the youngest couples in the community and didn't carry much responsibility. So for the next few years we lived on "satellite" Farms in Kentucky and New York that followed the same basic agreements as in Tennessee. It was during our time on the Green River Farm in Kentucky that, in order to stay closely connected to Tennessee, I and another couple, Stephen and Susan, began studying to get our ham radio licenses. The Farm used ham radio as a free communications tool, meeting with the other Farms daily at a designated frequency. Stephen Skinner was the first to get his license, and on our initial contact with the Tennessee Farm from Green River, we knew it was time to go back to where the action was.

When Deborah and I had returned to The Farm a year earlier to have our second child, Leah, we had been well taken care of in our role as a pregnant couple. But arriving from Kentucky

we were on our own, not sure at all where we would be landing, and that's when we got a real taste of just how bad living with other people could be.

We started at one couple's place which was "theirs," because they were the couple who stayed put while other people moved in and out. It was a small tent with two adjoining bedrooms and a kitchen. Each couple shared their bedroom with their kids, plus there was a third couple in a nearby bus who had come to have their baby.

We soon learned that it was the man of this couple who ran the show with his dominant Southern male flavor. His wife took the brunt of his intimidation tactics in that he ripped her off on a daily basis. As far as energy trips go, this one was fairly obvious to diagnose, as well as uncomfortable to be around. But as soon as we got in the middle of it (as per the agreement), the wife would suddenly become her husband's staunchest defender, and then you'd have both of them united coming down your throat. Every night seemed to evolve into some type of sort-out, and the atmosphere stayed pretty much uptight to say the least. I was working in town at The Farm's electronic shop, and going home at night became something I dreaded. My stomach would be in knots, I couldn't eat dinner; even our baby daughter became sick, then dehydrated, leaving us to somehow feel it was all related.

According to the teachings, when someone stubbornly refused to "cop," you didn't sit there and argue with them, you brought in others, an appellate court of peers, so to speak, a wider range of viewpoint to see, in a more dispassionate way, what was really going on. The theory was that eventually, faced with a circle of friends, it would become an untenable position to say they were all nutty and that you were the only sane one.

Which in a way was what happened. A couple we'd gotten close with at the New York Farm came down to have their baby, so we got them to move in. The New York Farm had a high standard for good vibes, and together we knew we could stand up to the emotional flack we were dealing with. This helped the situation, but it was actually the pregnant lady's relationship with the midwives that turned up the heat on the crusty husband.

One thing you did not do on The Farm was to intimidate (or even dance around attempting to intimidate) a pregnant woman. They shared a special relationship with the midwives, one of absolute trust, and the midwives were the community's ultimate power figures. They dealt with life and death issues and could get whole projects begun or cancelled with a phone call. They commanded respect and set the tone for how a "lady" should be treated. So as the midwives got closer to our new pregnant resident, this focused the energy spotlight closer on our "tripper."

The husband continued to indulge his ego in a number of ways as he came under the microscope. At his job on the Farming Crew, he always seemed to be the one driving the truck on a soda run. He would "liberate" (help himself) to frozen vegetables from the community freezer. Plus, he continued being a pain on the home front.

When the midwives turned up the heat on him, he and his family very quickly left town. However, after all that working it out, Deborah and I were ready for a change. We moved out in search of a group head, some people that already had a telepathic connection, where we could settle down with for a while. It took six moves in the next six months before we found what we were looking for.

The scene was an old (even by Farm standards) army tent that housed two other couples. It was exhilarating to be having fun again—just simply hanging out together at dinner and afterwards was a joy. Unfortunately, this tent was doomed from the start. It was perched on the side of a hill, and when the spring rains hit, our floor became a wash. The uphill side was at ground level, and on top of that the canvas roof was worn and leaked badly. Each couple had to huddle on their bed to stay even somewhat dry. We soon had to face the fact that the best thing we could do for the community was to tear that place down.

It was 1975 when an evolutionary event hit Farm households—television. None of the house/ tents were wired for electricity, but in an effort to move away from kerosene lamps which had

been the cause of several fires, twelve-volt car battery lighting became our new technology. It was amazing the amount of light that a taillight bulb reflected by molded aluminum foil could bring to a dim tent. Soon DC trickle charging lines were strung from a source of AC power through the trees to almost every house.

This new source of power opened the door for DC-powered TVs which were being made for campers and boats, etc. Those nine-inch screens were, to us, a window on the world. We could watch the nightly news, Sesame Street became a baby sitter for the dinner preparation crew, Saturday Night Live was the buzz of every weekend. Since I had a connection with my folks for work, I hitched home to Kentucky one weekend to earn enough money to buy an incredibly huge thirteen-inch black and white TV.

Meanwhile, with our flooded tent scene condemned, Deborah and I once again found ourselves without a place to live. Thomas and Sylvia, one of the couples from the washed-out tent, arranged for us to come have dinner at Mango Manor, which was a close-knit group of families who had bonded in Florida while staffing and running a green bean packing plant for The Farm. It goes without saying that the household was already crowded, but Thomas and Sylvia pled our case, telling everyone what good folks we were—and, oh yeah, we had a TV!

Mango Manor felt strong. Deborah and I stayed in a bus that we shared with a woman who had come to The Farm to have her baby. Right away we all started working on an eight-room addition. Our old friends from Green River, Stephen and Susan, were there along with four other couples, three single men, a couple of single women, and always at least one single parent. Initially it was a single father with two boys who, without a mom, were a bit wild. The dad tried to make up for that feminine need, but unfortunately his efforts became sentimental coddling that his sons innately learned to exploit. As pseudo aunts and uncles, we tried to help him reel them in, and even though we didn't work miracles by any means, the Mango Manor family was able to help him out.

These up-close relationships gave everyone in the community a dynamic look at how families work and the difficulties of being a single parent. We saw how children absorb what is going on around them. We learned that how people treat each other really does make a difference.

Next we worked it out with a woman who had a Farmwide reputation as being difficult. Her husband had been one of the first people to build a "real" house (no canvas) even though we would think of it as a shack today. The early Farm, however, considered it a palace, and they were promptly kicked out of it by the powers that be. The teaching on that one was that if you put that much attention and energy into fixing up yourself, then you must be on an ego trip and not giving enough of your energy back to the community. So this couple and their three energized sons became a hot potato. Looking back, there are likely many people who wished, after having lived with this couple, that they could have remained in their isolated little cabin.

Then came Eddie, an idiot savant who could play the piano beautifully, but he had the personality and vocabulary of a cartoon character, switching voices and personae constantly, adding in old movie dialogues. He was the younger brother of a woman who lived with us. She and her husband were trying to do the honorable thing and care for Eddie, thereby keeping him out of an institution. Eddie Spaghetti was a master at getting your gourd, and it was hard to understand how he could be so nonstop wacky. It was like a game he was playing, and you wanted to yell, "Game Over!" (which we frequently did) but to no avail. The Farm tried to help Eddie by letting him be something of a front man for one of our bands, and he actually did pull off a few pretty good performances. Of course you could never be sure what he would play or where he might drift to between songs.

As with most large households, Mango Manor worked by scheduling. Men had mop nights. Women had dinner nights. Couples shared kitchen cleanup duties. There was a baby-sitting/ kid herd schedule so that the women could go out and do things in the community. It was a pretty tight ship. In the evenings another guy and I would entertain with guitars and song. At knee level there was a whole other scene—ten or so kids from newborn to eight—and they were as much a family as we were.

Doug Stevenson

Beatnik Bell

Two hallmarks of a successful modern society are good transportation and good communication. It was obviously going to take a while to develop good roads through the mud and hills of The Farm, so we placed our bets on a phone system.

By the time I arrived in the spring of 1973, there was a burgeoning system of interlocking phone lines powered by batteries to which about a dozen phones were connected. Affectionally thought of as one step up from two tin cans and a string, it was a hippie party line—anyone could pick up a phone connected to this system and join in on whatever conversation was ensuing. This necessitated the creation of a certain code of conduct regarding "When To Listen and When Not To Listen." If you got on and there was obviously a personal conversation going, you were obligated to hang up quickly. If there was a conversation of public interest, you might feel free to listen and put in your two cents. Some days there were conversations that flowed freely from which work crew was going to use what vehicle, to could that crew take someone's laundry to the mat, and what number was next in line in the Laundry Mat, to where was it at to have a numbered turn at the mat, to we need to fix more washers, to let's see if that work crew can stop on the way out of Columbia for washer parts. It was a free-form, but efficient, way to take care of all the business at hand. No matter that the more people on the line at one time, the harder it became to hear one another. For as difficult as it was to get around (especially during mud season), and considering the vast distances between the outlying areas of the community (as measured by being on foot leaning into a strong headwind), the phones were magically instantaneous.

Ringers on a phone are a luxury. It takes a much more elaborate electronic setup to generate the distinctive signal that makes your phone, and only your phone, ring. More than the basic system we first had. So we

settled for beepers on the phones and assigned each phone (be it in a household or public building) a signal that corresponded to a letter of the Morse code. Every time you worked the beeper on your phone, it simultaneously beeped every other phone in the system. As the number of phones grew from a dozen to stretch the limits of the Morse alphabet, the cacophony of beeps became a constant background noise on The Farm. You could get a pretty good measure of what was happening on the phones by the type of beeping that was taking place. There was the "Oh, no, I know that everyone's going to hear this at 3 a.m." tentative little bleets and the "When the heck is the Gateman going to hear this and pick it up?" insistent and annoyed blaring. Also, your house's particular signal became a subconscious call to attention. Carol, one of the midwives, said it always amazed her that she could wake up from a deep sleep to the sound of her beep. Hey, honey, was that dit-dit-dah-dit-dit or dit-dit-dah-dah-dit? The ultimate

beep was the all-points, a constant beeping that wouldn't stop until the person beeping was sure that the whole Farm had picked up the phone. At that point they would deliver a message of consequence that everyone needed to know. Services will be an hour later. There are peaches at the store.

Initially, the Farm's only phone line to the outside world was a party line with several neighbors. Five hundred hippies—four Tennessee families. We instituted a policy of waiting five minutes between our phone calls so our neighbors would have at least a fighting chance to use the phone every once in a while. It was obvious that this was not a long-range working arrangement, so we managed to trade the party line in for two outside lines of our own. Just one catch. Neither of these lines could be patched into our internal phones without reducing the quality of the transmission to about zero. And would you really want to talk to your mom while having twenty people jumping in to try and get a number in the laundromat line?

While you could always trudge up to the main house where the phones were located to make your connections to the outside world, it would be a whole lot easier to have a Farm receptionist—someone who could make your calls for you and take care of your incoming messages. Enter the Phone Lady. These women (and, eventually, several guys) became the conduit through which much of The Farm's business was conducted. They made doctor's and dentist's appointments, called in car parts orders, told you your mom called, and told your mom you'd call her Friday. As a result of performing this community-wide message service, the phone ladies became adept at knowing where anyone could be reached at any given moment. This skill was enhanced through years of experience, and we also used to think that sitting around all that electrical equipment gave us a psychic edge.

This became my first permanent job on The Farm. I was one of about three ladies who rotated shifts day and night to provide nonstop coverage of the community phone needs. It was a tremendous responsibility. I walked to work for the first year in sheer terror, summoning up the courage to match the rapid pace, and even more rapid karma, involved in being a phone lady. Barbara came up after my first shift and looked over my neatly arranged rows of hanging messages. "Did you try and get this person for this?" she asked over and over again as she inspected each message. Well, no. I guess I figured that sooner or later I'd come across that person on the line and deliver the message. Within about ten minutes Barbara had dispatched all my messages with an efficiency that took my breath away. One of those little lessons that molded my entire career. If only she had known.

If you can imagine all the daily goings-on of a community of five hundred, then seven hundred, then one thousand people, you'll have a picture of the vast range of events that crossed a phone lady's path. From the most mundane activities to life-and-death situations, whoever was on that phone was responsible for smooth sailing at a moment's notice. The heaviest situations were birthings—getting all the midwife crew there quickly—and ambulance runs. They were inevitable in a community that large and with that many children. Even though no

two emergency situations were ever the same, you had to build up a bank of experience that would guide you through the next one. It was somebody's baby quit breathing—quick, get all the on-call medical people to the scene, call the Gate, clear the way out, call the police in Mt. Pleasant and have them ready to clear the intersection in the middle of town, get to the emergency room at Maury County Hospital and let them know what's coming. It was Eric calling and saying that Thomas's scalp had just been pulled off by the farming crew's combine. It was Richard saying, "Everybody's OK, but the crew in the blue van just had an accident north of Columbia."

It was also this is CBS News. We want to come down and shoot a story next week. It was hi, I'm Swami So-and-So and I have the secret teachings to bring The Farm. My girlfriend and I were on our way to visit, and now our car is broken down in Summertown. There was never a dull moment.

Soon after I began as a phone lady, The Farm acquired a hand-me-down public phone system big enough to service a small town. It was being put out to pasture by a local phone company nearby—one of the few remaining independent local phone companies in existence in the whole country. To us, it was the ultimate in telephonic experiences. Ringers, private lines. Ah, banks and banks of lovely relays. Beatnik Bell, we called it. Sure it was an old system, and prone to being finicky, but what a leap into the twentieth century. It involved so much equipment we had to construct a climate-controlled cinder block building the size of a large garage to hold it all. It was the highlight of the year for Farm techies, amp meters quivering in anticipation.

Once more the psyche of the community and the state of the phone system were indelibly intertwined. No more beeps. We discovered that man is not destined to listen to a dial tone when picking up a phone—we replaced the droning sound with a lively message of the day's news, a revolving all-points bulletin. And to the delight of the phone ladies, we got an ancient switchboard, complete with plug-in cords and Ernestine-like headsets. We actually acquired this set up to handle an alternative phone system that we developed, called "hot lines." These were private connections wired directly into the switchboard that would always get through if the other system was being ornery. After our new equipment was installed, the switchboard could handle dialed calls down onto The Farm that could then be connected to the outside world. Another leap into the twentieth century.

The ultimate use of the switchboard came one day when the long distance lines in our area were accidentally cut by some road construction workers. Two major towns in our part of Tennessee were instantly rendered incommunicado. Neither of the repair crews on either end of the problem could get in touch with each other directly to start dealing with it. (This was long before the era of cell phones.) In a flash of inspiration, one of the Bell Telephone linemen remembered that anyone in Summertown could make a local call to either of these two towns, and The Farm had a switchboard. Could I call Columbia and get the other repair crew on the line? All well and fine, but the conversation is a little difficult with me trying to relay between two phones like a shortwave radio operator. Wait a minute. Throw open the two out-

side line switches on the switchboard and effectively give the two guys a direct connection. Oh, oh. That closes the board to access by anyone else. Grab the spare phone that hooks into the switchboard to answer the routine Farm calls trickling in.

No system this evolved could survive without a crackerjack crew to keep it going. My undying gratitude goes out to the hard-working guys who fashioned low-tech, quick fixes to any electronic crisis Beatnik Bell presented them. The system worked surprisingly well considering the amount of circuit-clogging dust our unpaved roads coughed up every summer. So what if you didn't always get a dial tone every time you picked up the phone. Or you dialed and were left dangling in phone hell. While I was still on the phone crew, I made a trip into New York City for a few days and discovered the phones there didn't work much better. A vindication for backwoods hippie technology.

Maintaining Beatnik Bell wasn't much different from nursing along a twenty-year-old VW van. You knew its quirks. You salvaged for spare parts. A well-directed kick was sometimes just as effective as a careful turn of the screw. And heaven forbid you should try and deal with finicky relay circuits if you were in a sour mood. Remember, this IS sensitive electronics we're talking about here. The human mind is composed of millions of minute electrical exchanges. So was our phone system—and the system itself often took on a personality all its own. You just couldn't treat phone equipment like it was a brick wall. It was responsive to your vibes.

Nicholas was the anchor man for our repair crew. He quickly acquired the nickname "Polecat" from his ability to scale phone poles and anything else that held up a phone line. Polecat was a perfect candidate for the rugged job of braving any element in any season to keep the phone system afloat. He was a mountain man electronics buff, sort of a Johnny Weissmuller meets Steve Wosniak (the burly cofounder of Apple Computers). My lasting impression of him will always be Polecat standing in the hallway next to the phone lady's booth with shorts on (regardless of season), his tool belt diagonally strung across his bare chest like Pancho Villa (regardless of season), and dirty blond hair exploding every which way. Polecat was not what you'd call a polished individual, a lady's man, but that's not what we needed. Keeping Beatnik Bell running was like continuously patching a boat that was doing its best to sink. There was the emergency birthing phone that had to be installed in the middle of the night, the bank of switches that had to be busied out so the whole system wouldn't go down, the miles of uncooperative phone line that had to be strung through the briars and brambles and blackjack oak, and hundreds of requests for, "Can you add another phone, . . . line, . . . fix my ear piece, . . ." It took a lot of physical effort to keep up with it all, and since most Farm techies fit the general long-on-brain, short-on-brawn prototype for electronic nerds, Polecat was our ace-in-the-hole. So what if he was a little rough around the edges. I grew up in a neighborhood of boys. I was always the quarterback because I was the oldest, so I figured I could handle Polecat.

Polecat and I managed a number of seasons together, making the day-to-day decisions of what to do when and where, but eventually the community more than doubled in size. The phone lady crew itself grew to six or more operators; the repair crew was Polecat and several other guys. Polecat's strength was fixing phones, not the public relations skills needed to distribute meager phone resources to a growing community. Sorting out the daily list of what was broken and had to be fixed right away, what new installations had to be made no matter what, and then who was going to do it and how, took a total "in-the-trenches" management person. Philip was chosen to be arbiteur par excellence and top trenchman. He had a personable style and his background in rock 'n' roll gave him the hippie technology he needed to grasp the electronic subtleties of telephones.

When the days of our communal experiment were over, there wasn't much support for keeping Beatnik Bell going. It took constant attention to maintain, and no one could begrudge our techies for wanting to make good money with their talents instead of performing guerrilla repair duty seven days a week. And though some of us hated to admit it, the advantages of having an outside line you could have access to anytime by just picking up your phone far outweighed the personal connection you made with the phone lady every time you needed to contact the outside world. We negotiated with the local Bell phone company and eventually got them to run phone lines all over The Farm.

Slowly Beatnik Bell was phased out. It didn't go down easily. As we disassembled the system, parts of it mysteriously continued to work, like a body taken off life support that refused to die. There had been a lot of electricity generated over those lines all those years. Many intense conversations. Difficult sort-outs. People falling in love. Life and death situations. CBS News. In a mysterious way, the phone system captured some of that human lifeforce and used it to survive its imminent demise for just a while longer.

Cynthia Holzapfel (a.k.a. "Ma Bell")

WUTZ 88.3 Community Radio

I first flashed on the idea of starting an FM radio station on The Farm one day while talking to Albert about his days growing up in Japan and how he used to have his own pirate radio station when he was in high school. So, with my interest piqued, I asked what it would take to start a station here. He said we would need a license from the FCC if we were going to broadcast, but we just needed a transmitter to start a "carrier current station."

Carrier current stations are common on college campuses. The signal is carried on the electrical system in the dormitory so that radios in the dorm rooms can pick it up. It wasn't designed to get out more than a few feet from the electrical lines.

This was way before anyone on The Farm had anything as advanced as electricity in their homes. But the Beatnik Bell phone system did make it to every bus, tent, and building on The Farm. The common point for the phone system was at the phone building at the Head of the Roads, and that building also had electricity—something which we would need. So we pulled an empty school bus out of the back of the motor pool and up to the phone building, borrowed a mike from Bandland, found a couple of old turntables and a funky transmitter somewhere, and began broadcasting as WRFB, Radio Free Beatnik!

It didn't take long for these media-starved hippies to come crawling out of the woods eager to spin disks or chat on the microphone. It turned out many people on The Farm had great record collections stashed under their beds just waiting to be heard. So folks started bringing their records to us. We even got two or three copies of some great titles. When we did, we would gather up copies of the triples and not-so-hot doubles. Mr. Kaputi and I would then scam a vehicle and take these records to the used record stores in Nashville and Memphis and trade them for titles we didn't have. It wasn't long until we were convinced we had the greatest collection of rock 'n' roll, blues, jazz, and acid rock on the planet.

While this was going on, we were also busy getting our paperwork together for the FCC. We faithfully followed the guidelines set forth by Lorenzo Milam in his excellent manual *Sex and Broadcasting*, subtitled *A Handbook on Starting a Radio Station for the Community*. It is still the best book on the subject.

Community radio had already established a grand tradition. By 1975, it had been over twenty years since the first community station, KPFB, went on the air in Berkeley, California. Inspired enthusiasts in many parts of the country followed their lead. These were noncommercial, nonprofit stations, run mostly by volunteers. These stations were, and still are, islands of enlightenment in a sea of commercial radio babble.

We toned down our name from Radio Free Beatnik to Radio Free Broadcasting for our license application. We naturally wanted WRFB for our call sign but, as it turned out, these call letters were already taken. So we started asking around for suggestions for our new call sign. When I approached Stephen (freshly back from a run to our base in Guatemala) with this dilemma, he thought for a moment and then pointed out that "utz" means "good" in Cakchiquel (a Mayan dialect). This flashed us on W-U-T-Z which rhymed with the frequency 88.3 (FM) that we had applied for. So now we had a name, which the DJs soon twisted into WHAT'S as in "What's happening radio!" and similar slogans.

WUTZ continues to rock on today as a voice for alternative radio in middle Tennessee. Demo tapes and CDs are welcome!

Jeffrey Keating

Enchiladas for Fifty from Scratch

I lived in a house called the Long House because that's what it was, a long, two-story, many-roomed house that was home to fifty people, twenty-six of them aged nine and under, and ten of those the children of single parents. The day-to-day running of a household that size resulted in huge logistical challenges. The women had to divide up duties—baby-sitting, cooking, cleaning, and the everyday tasks of store runs, along with the twice-a-week mammoth laundry run. We would set up a schedule a day ahead of time and make sure we had four able-bodied (not nursing or sick) women on duty during the day.

One woman took care of the little kids and another would take care of the older kids. One woman would clean the house, and one would cook. Usually a first priority was to listen to the "all-points" messages for that day on our internal, Farm-wide Beatnik Bell phone system—The Soy Dairy will have soy milk and tofu by noon. The Bakery will have bread ready by 2 p.m. The store will have matches, toilet paper, sugar, oil, and margarine due in around 5 p.m. The clinic needs shit sample bottles returned right away—please wash. There will be no more propane until next week, so conserve. The Farming Crew needs people to plant sweet potatoes, meet at the Tractor Barn—stuff like that.

Occasionally the household duties would blur, kid herding might merge into food prep. One morning Barbie took all of the older kids, eight or so, and walked them down to the fields to pick tomatoes so we could have enchiladas for dinner. Now remember, we are talking dinner for fifty without anything like packaged tortillas or Prego spaghetti sauce. So Barbie combined playing with the kids with the picking of four bushels of canning tomatoes. Then they flagged down a passing truck and got themselves with the tomatoes back to our house, a few miles from the fields.

Barbie then washed all of the tomatoes in the kitchen sink and started cooking them in big pots on the stove while trying to stay out of the way of the lunch lady who was cooking lunch for all those hungry kids, plus whoever else was home that day. After a half hour or so, Barbie dipped out all of the steaming, red tomato mush and strained it through a hand colander, which netted one big fifteen-gallon pot of tomato purée, ready for several hours of slow cooking, while she began mixing her first batch of tortilla dough. Sometime during this process she also started a pressure cooker full of beans (after sorting them and removing the pebbles).

Back to the tortillas for fifty people, she had to roll and cook on a hot griddle at least eighty tortillas. When this stack of tortillas was steaming under a damp towel, she seasoned the pot of tomatoes into a spicy enchilada sauce, mashed the cooked beans, and started assembling the enchiladas with the help of whomever was around—and into the oven they went.

By this time it was late afternoon, getting toward time to eat. When the first pans of enchiladas were done baking, all of the kids were called to dinner first, because even though we had a huge table, no way it could seat everyone at once. The kids were first routed through the bathroom where one of the adults would supervise hand washing. Having done battle with giardia, shigella, hepatitis, and old-fashioned diarrhea, we were very aware of germ theory and made hand washing a ritual. Each kid had to use the soap, get a lather, then rinse and dry their hands. Sometimes if we weren't able to supervise the ritual directly, we would perform a sniff test for soap on the kids' hands.

Finally, with the kids sitting in long rows on either side of the table, the enchiladas were served. We didn't pray over the food or chant mantras, we just got them to the place where nobody was screaming or otherwise pouting. (This was central in Farm parenting—no rewards or praise or treats until the kid "showed you a good one.") Then it was time to eat. Our food was not fancy or varied, but the kids did get warm, wholesome meals every day. And on this night, even though the kids did not realize the amount of preparation that had gone into this meal, they declared it yummy.

Then as the adults trickled in from their various duties, two or three more sittings at the enchilada table happened, but the grown-ups definitely recognized that this was not your typical beans, greens (if we were lucky), and cornbread meal we sometimes grew tired of, but, in retrospect, was wholesome peasant fare.

With the day's duties done, the bedtime rituals began. Parents took over their own kids and waited their turn in the bathroom getting them bathed and ready for bed.

Usually volunteers were attacking the incredible pile of dishes, pots, and pans, but sometimes the dreaded Dish Schedule came into effect whereby couples would each be responsible for the night's kitchen clean-up.

Once a meal such as the enchiladas was finished and cleaned up, boom, what did you have staring you in the face, but the next meal for fifty! Breakfast always on the horizon. There was never time to catch your breath.

As the kitchen slowly faded from its central place in the Long House's daily life, and after the kids were all or mostly put to bed, the adults would find themselves in the living room where we kicked back and talked about our day. Except, of course, for the breakfast crew who had to be up at 5 a.m. or so, starting the whole thing all over again.

Joan McCabe

There Had to Be a Positive, Spiritual Spin on Everything We Did

The whole basis behind the "sort-out" and "getting straight" with another person was that we were all going to be living together for a long time. You might as well come to an understanding with whomever it was you didn't feel "cool" with because you were going to be interacting with them over and over again. Plus the longer you waited, the more weirdness, anger, etc. would build up over what was originally perhaps a petty misunderstanding or slight. Which was all good, sound mental health—staying current, constant communications. The "teachings," if administered with the right spirit, were mostly dead-on advice concerning how to live with each other.

Late in the first summer, Kathy and I went peach picking with a busload of folks. The peach grove was down almost to Alabama, and as we passed this deep valley of huge, green vines, some with purple blossoms, all the California people started saying, "Oh, wow. Wild grapes. What a beautiful countryside. We'll stop and pick some on the way back!"

Kathy and I couldn't stop laughing when we heard them. "It's kudzu," we said. "That's the biggest pest plant on the face of the earth. It's horrible, has no fruit, eats up whole farms, kills trees. Everybody in the South hates it!"

There was kind of a silence for a moment, but then they all turned on us for being such glib messengers. "Hey, I kind of see that as bad vibes, hating a vine," one person said. "No green growing plant is a bad thing," another agreed. "Yeah, it's really kind of a low-juice rip-off trip for you to act like we're dumb for thinking that valley was beautiful because it was."

So then we were deep into it. And from there it got around to how I had a habit of getting ego hits off perceiving myself as smarter. Which led to—folks had noticed me being smug a lot, as if in silent judgement, instead of just joining in and letting my "thing" down.

It got deeply serious, at least for me, real quick. I had to "consider" the information and be careful not to get defensive. I had to take residual guff for the rest of the trip, for weeks afterwards. And certainly I could not revert back to the material plane issue of, "But look, it really is kudzu, and kudzu really is a bad weed, and it really was funny that you all thought it was wild grapes." It was past that point in an instant, it was into the vibes, and from there, no escape, my friend. No saying, "whatever," like we all do now to something patently stupid. Oh, no. And no eloquent defense of yourself was allowed either, for that would be "conditioning" the group head to watch out, don't mess with me because it's going to be a hassle every time. And once you got a reputation for being a "hard copper" (someone who didn't easily give up their ego), it was but a short hop to the status of full-blown "tripper." And that you did not want.

We were, if not the inventors of Political Correctness, one of its early refiners in that there had to be a positive, spiritual spin on everything we did, said, or thought. Just listening to the radio in the Motor Pool could bring on a crisis. We'd turn up the local Nashville rock station as loud as possible to pump up some energy, but then here would come an inappropriate song. That first Steely Dan song, "Do It Again," had a great intro, and we were all dancing around to it, but the first line is, "In the morning you go gunning for the man who stole your water . . . " So it was like, click, off with the radio. This kind of "herd mentality" took "positive manifesting" to unhealthy levels in that by suppressing anything negative, we never got a chance to inspect it for what it was.

I have friends now who spend good amounts of money and time doing "anger work" with a therapist, and when I tell them that on The Farm, anger was pretty much not permitted, I am regarded as a head-copped idiot or worse. Never mind we were supposed to ideally take that anger and get current with whatever had caused it, it's beyond explaining. It's from another time, another place.

Rupert Fike

I Would Do Anything for a Horse

As a child I worked on The Farm Horse Crew. I was fifteen when we took a trail ride on horseback to the Smoky Mountains. Even though most of our parents came from cities, we kids were growing up in the backwoods, and I guess you could say that we were kind of innocent. I mean, we weren't concerned with our clothes or things like that, and we didn't have a lot of money or put much attention into getting things. What we really cared about was horses.

It would be hard to explain how much the horses and ponies meant to me. I can only say that I loved them. I loved them so much that I wanted to be with them and take care of them all the time. I would do anything for a horse.

The community owned twenty-six horses, half of them ponies. We had a horse crew, and the kids who were on it got to take care of the horses and to ride them. The more time and work you put into the horses, the more you got to ride, including rides off The Farm. You also got more responsibility for their care, particularly when they were sick and needed special attention. Personally, I spent a lot of my time walking sick horses and organizing the other girls to help. That was my work and I loved it.

Everyone on the crew had at least one barn day a week. On that day you had to go to the barn early, before school, and make sure all the horses got fed, and if you had time, brushed. Some horses and ponies had specific kids assigned to them, but all the others were the responsibility of that day's barn crew. Later in the day, you would have to help clean the barn. Cleaning the barn was especially important in the summer because of the flies. Sometimes we had projects like bringing in the hay or making our own riding equipment.

Caring for the horses and ponies in the summer was fun, but in the winter it could be a real drag. Things just generally got more difficult. The pastures, which had been eaten down the summer before, had little for the horses to graze on, so we fed them hay and grain. The water hoses would freeze and the tether ropes would be frozen to the ground. The horses got ice balls under their feet, and often they couldn't be ridden. The winter was the test of a young girl's true love for horses.

It was in the midst of this winter struggle that our original idea of going on a long horse ride came to us. A group of us girls were in the Horse Barn, sitting around the potbelly woodstove. We couldn't get the fire hot, and we were feeling wet, cold, and miserable. Kidding around, I suggested we ride down to Florida to get warm and see my mother. But Dawn, who was the adult in charge of the horse crew, said we should think of someplace closer. So we talked about where we could go and came up with the idea of going to the Smoky Mountains in the springtime. It would still be a long ride from our farm in southern Tennessee, but we would have a few months to prepare ourselves and to get the horses and ponies ready.

I thought we were only dreaming and we could never actually do it. But that is just what we did. Twelve of us girls rode from rural Tennessee to the Cherokee National Forest in the Great Smoky Mountains. It was a six-hundred-mile journey altogether, and we made the whole trip on horseback.

Katherine Correa

Uncle Bill Changed The Farm's Perceptions of Old Folks

Kissing Tree was what we called our house because of the two tree trunks that grew close to the point of almost smooching out by the road. There for nearly ten years, a core group of five to seven families created a scene with various single folks, teenagers, pregnant women on sanctuary, older folks, trippers, and visitors from all over the planet. It was an extended family of forty to fifty, always in flux, but relatively stable by Farm standards.

Several of the school's teachers lived there as did the community's lawyer, Book Company honchos, painting and carpentry bosses, a nurse/midwife, and even the occasional radio operator on Greenpeace's Rainbow Warrior. Obviously just keeping the place clean and getting that many people fed, ten to twenty of whom were children, made every day a production. Still, we all usually got along quite well. There was rarely a call from us to the housing ladies demanding an immediate shake-up in the chemistry, which was a normal state of affairs for many households. Not to say we had any special magic, we just seemed to get along.

Since our house was one of the more substantial on The Farm, (it had no canvas rooms or additions,) we became a logical host for the community's forays into elder care. We had several old folks come through for short periods of time, but it was Uncle Bill who truly made his mark on The Farm.

William Axlerod was Lois's great-uncle. The Farm "sprung" him from a nursing home in Florida where he had been stashed after a lifetime in Brooklyn working at a deli and being a cantor at his synagogue. Roberta and Joel were his main connections, and as soon as he got to Kissing Tree Roberta gave him the run of the kitchen, since he was quite proficient at food prep from his years at the deli. At first he used a walker, but eventually he settled into getting around in a wheelchair.

Uncle Bill changed The Farm's perceptions of old folks because rather than just being taken care of, he actively made a difference, "took on more," which was one of our motivational catch phrases. It happened that the summer and fall he came to us, there was a bumper, make that a double bumper, crop of cucumbers. We tended to overplant some things, underplant others, but that summer through a convergence of rain, good cultivation, and an abundance of visitors to man the harvest, there mounted up a colossal pile of "cukes" outside of the Canning and Freezing building.

What to do with them? Uncle Bill to the rescue with his tried-and-true bulk pickling recipe, which, with the help of Robert, another New York City Jew, turned that pile of cucumbers into a winter's supply of soft, very tasty dill pickles that saved many an otherwise drab meal of soybeans, sweet potatoes, and cornbread. Ditto with his recipe for pickled eggplant. From that point on, The Farm looked upon Uncle Bill as a full-fledged trucker, pulling his share of the load, kvetching around Canning and Freezing in his wheelchair, his stocking hat on, directing the pickle operation, "No, no, not so much. The other barrel, the other vun!"

The men at Kissing Tree rotated each night taking care of him. When he needed anything his cries of, "Man, man!" could be heard throughout the house. Our bedroom was downstairs near his room where we could be quick with Pierre, the bottle he peed in at night.

One very cold night we put him to bed, cranked up his woodstove to red-hot on the sides, lay some extra covers over him, and went to bed ourselves. Not long afterwards the cries of, "Man," filled the air. When I opened the door to his room, a blast of superheated air hit me in the face and almost took me to my knees. It was so hot and dry in there, you could barely breathe. But there was Uncle Bill under the covers saying, "Cold, cold." It was hysterical and sad in a way that makes you laugh so you won't cry. He had poor circulation so sometimes we massaged his legs and feet. When you went in to him at night, he always asked you who you were even though he knew us all quite well. I think he liked the Jews among us. He was all the kids' grandfather.

A lasting image of Uncle Bill is his sitting at the Kissing Tree kitchen table cutting onions or something else for "Boita," his surrogate daughter/friend/companion. He loved pickled eggplant and herring from town, the greasier the better. The Passover seder became a big deal at our house during those years, with The Farm being roughly a quarter Jewish. Uncle Bill helped me see my Jewishness in a new light, seeing ourselves as Jewish rastas or a hybrid of Zen and Judaism—Jubus, they're called now. But mostly Uncle Bill was a grandfather to hundreds of us kids, most of whom he barely knew. I can still hear him using his favorite expression as he sat contentedly among us after a hard day's work, "I am the happiest man in the voild!"

David Friedlander

Sheriff T. C. Carroll

T. C. Carroll probably weighed about 270 pounds the first time that I met him. This is not to say that he was fat. He wasn't fat at all. It's that his children weighed between ten and fourteen pounds when they were born. We were sitting in my school bus on the Martin Farm when we first landed. T. C. and his deputy were both wearing those little cloth caps with a shiny black bill and a little button on top that Southern cops used to wear. They filled up their side of the bus. I could see that I had no rapport with the deputy, but I felt like Sheriff Carroll was an honest man. I thought I should tell him about it like it really was. I said, "Sheriff, I can't be without a sheriff. You have to be my sheriff too. If I need to call the sheriff, I need to feel like you would come just as much as if it was any one else in Lewis County." T. C. took me seriously. I feel like we became friends, and it has lasted twenty-six years.

I had occasion to talk with him many times over the next few years. T. C. had such a vital body field that when I would lean down to talk to him when he was in his car visiting The Farm, the proximity would make the hair stand up on my arms. Long after he retired we met at the post office one day, and as we were chatting, he told me, "Looking back on my life, I think you were one of the best friends I ever had." I told him that I felt the same way. Our friendship never wavered, even when he was the arresting officer who sent me to the penitentiary up in Nashville in 1974.

While the cops were walking around the Martin Farm, I noticed that T.C. was carrying an M2 carbine which is a five and a half pound army rifle that shoots 550 rounds a minute. I thought to myself, "T. C. sure is overgunned for us peaceful hippies." Just at that moment, as if he had heard me, T. C. looked over his shoulder at me and said, "You might not be afraid of these rattlesnakes around here, but I sure am!"

I voted for him for sheriff after that and every time he ran. When he was county executive, he married me and Ina May in his office in Hohenwald. I wore my wide striped black and white prison coat from the walls to the wedding.

One time T. C. told me that he had to argue forcefully with the county commission to get a new car. His old car was a fairly new model, and I asked why he needed a new one. He said that was what the commission said too, but he had explained to them that he had torn all the door handles off the old car chasing moonshiners through the oak trees.

While I was going through my appeals from prison, I had a hearing in Hohenwald at the county seat. T.C. came to transport me from the walls to court. When he picked me up, I was turned over to him in handcuffs, but as soon as we were in the car he took them off. He said, "I guess you know that ain't anything going to happen at this appeal." I told him that I understood that and that it was part of a larger strategy by our lawyers. He said, "Well, at least you get a drive in the country, and if I make good time, there might be time to stop by The Farm and let you visit your family."

I soon saw what he meant by making good time. His car, like most county sheriff vehicles, was a big four-door V8 with some speed and handling options. Anyway, it really hauled. He went into every corner under heavy breaking and when he came out of the turn, he stepped on it until the four-barrel carb and the passing gear kicked in. We were making eighty to one hundred on the straightaways. It was his county and he was the sheriff and he knew every turn. It was one of the fastest and best cross-country rides I ever had. T.C. was a master. I was never afraid; he had everything under control.

When we got to The Farm, my family came up to the Gate and we got to hang out together for a good while. I was always grateful to T. C. for that ride, for the thrills as well as the kindness.

Stephen Gaskin

We're Throwing Out Large Amounts of Ego

Once after services, I was standing near an interesting conversation. Larry and Marie had moved into the Schoolhouse Singles tent to "integrate the group head." Lucy and Donald were to follow them. Marie was reporting how it was going so far, and she said, "Some of the single men are worried that you are planning to throw them out when you move in. What should we tell them?"

Donald replied, "Tell them we are throwing out large amounts of ego. If they ain't attached to their ego, then they can stay."

Patricia Lapidus

Earthquake Relief Central

In 1976 a devastating earthquake struck Guatemala, killing 23,000 and leaving a million people homeless. That's when we decided to launch Plenty into the great unknown of international disaster relief. Word went out through our network of satellite Farms and city centers resulting in a huge shipment of medicines and medical equipment which included seven tons of army field hospital equipment that had been sitting in a warehouse in Boston. We got much of the transport donated, and in a few days the shipment reached Puerto Barrios on the eastern coast of Guatemala.

Priscilla spoke fluent Spanish and worked in the Farm Clinic, so the two of us flew down, wide-eyed, tie-dyed hippies in a plane out of Miami. The plane also carried some preachers with wooden crosses around their necks and handle-bar mustaches, clutching ostentatious Bibles as they headed down to save souls that had been presumably humbled by 7.6 on the Richter scale. There was also a festive gang of elderly orchid lovers on their way to Panama for an orchid convention.

The Boston shipment had preceded us, gilding Plenty's credentials, so we were met at the airport in Guatemala City by a government-issue Mercedes Benz and a retired colonel of the infamous Guatemalan army. From there we were whisked away to Earthquake Relief Central in a cavernous, previously vacated railway station. It seemed as though we had been time-capsuled back to Allied Headquarters before D-Day, except everyone spoke Spanish. There were rows of scuffed-up hardwood desks with old-timey phones ringing off their hooks and Olivetti typewriters clacking away, huge maps filled with colored pins covering the high walls, and people scurrying around everywhere.

Incredibly, no one noticed we were hippies (or let on), and they kept treating us like foreign dignitaries. They assigned us to the Terre Moto Comité de Civil y Militar, and we spent the next week buzzing around the highlands in military trucks delivering food and other supplies to outlying villages. I became the assignment photographer for the Comité because I had a real live 35 mm camera, and I got my first glimpse of patronizing charity as crew leaders pointedly organized photo ops of grateful Indians being handed boxes of food by uniformed officers.

We were overwhelmed by the destruction from this, the greatest natural disaster in the history of Central America. But we were even more overwhelmed to meet the Mayans. Who were these beautiful, stunningly attired, graceful people? Slowly it began to dawn on us. These were the people who had always been here, yet they appeared so poor it was as if this terrible earthquake was but the latest in a long line of indignities.

Back with the Comité we began to get restless. Half the men in our meeting were packing firearms. We were peaceniks, draft-dodgers for God's sake, and we were there to help. We

were also uppity gringos. "What's with the hardware?" The last straw was when we were picking up some medical supplies Plenty had shipped and we announced to the Comité that we were taking it to the civilian hospital in Guatemala City. "No, no," they protested, "We want to give it to the military hospital." We said, "Sorry, we have decided not to be on your Comité anymore, adios muchachos."

It was only two weeks after the earthquake, and aftershocks were still rumbling through the countryside. When we stayed for a night in a hotel in Guatemala City, the shocks would roll through the city like subway trains, closer and closer, then WHAM! Cracking the hotel like a whip, rattling windows and steel. People we talked to described the night of the BIG ONE. It struck on February 4th at 3 a.m. when most people were home in bed, in adobe-walled houses, under roofs made of tiles and timbers. The earth moved in three-foot waves, toppling everything with its relentless, tidal fury.

We returned to The Farm completely mind-blown. We had been shaken by the scenes of destruction, but we had been transfixed by the Mayan people who we felt drawn to as if through an aged kinship suddenly revealed. We made our report to The Farm on a Sunday morning in the meadow after meditation. We stressed the need for housing. Tens of thousands of Mayans were homeless, and the rainy season was fast approaching.

Within a week, three of our best carpenters were headed south, carrying their tools in backpacks, with no set destination other than Guatemala. One was from Venezuela and spoke Spanish. Within days of their arrival someone suggested they visit the Canadian embassy, as they had heard the Canadians were planning to engage in reconstruction. Once at the Canadian Embassy they learned that, in fact, a Canadian freighter loaded with seven hundred tons of building materials was on its way. However, the Canadians had no idea what they were going to build with these materials.

Dennis, the lead carpenter, asked for a piece of paper and proceeded to draw a model house and school that could be constructed with the pressed board, 2 x 4s, and laminated roofing that was on the freighter. The grateful Canadians hired our guys on the spot, and so commenced a four-year relationship with the government of Canada which became Plenty's most generous supporter. This relationship resulted in the construction of twelve hundred homes in the village of San Andrés Itzapa, and twelve schools in the surrounding neighborhoods. We also built clinics, community centers, water systems, a soy dairy, and the grand Municipalidad Indigena for the Cakchiquel people of Solola with its rococo ironwork and tile and the first and only Mayan-owned and -operated FM radio station.

More than two hundred Plenty volunteers served in Guatemala over the years from 1976 to the end of 1980 when we pulled out. Guatemala provided Plenty with its post-graduate education. It's also where we lost our innocence. We lived in tents in villages and shared everything with our Mayan neighbors, including their parasites and viruses. We invited people who were having a hard time to live with us. We adopted kids who were orphaned by the earthquake. Our camp was turned into a twenty-four-hour clinic. People died in our arms. We saw the brutality of poverty and the enforced suffering of indigenous people. We identified with Mayan culture and adopted much of it. We dressed in traje (traditional native clothing) and learned to speak Cakchiquel. We threw ourselves into this work with a passion, grateful to be there, and, in retrospect, very lucky we didn't lose any of our volunteers in the process.

Peter Schweitzer

The Mayans Seemed to Us Like Distant, Long-Lost Psychedelic Cousins

When I talk to folks about my years in Guatemala, I always think of it as a peak experience—one of those times that shines as tasting life at its richest and edgiest. I went down with my wife in 1978, two years after the earthquake that had decimated the countryside and killed thousands of people. Together with our kids, a two-year-old girl and four-year-old boy, we went headlong into an adventure that we feel blessed to have been a part of.

By the time we arrived, the initial shock of the quake had subsided, but the country was still rebuilding. There was a feeling among our crew that this was a chance to really help out and make a difference.

The first crews that Plenty sent to Guatemala did construction, rebuilding San Andrés Itzapa, a village that had been wiped out by the earthquake. During Plenty's days of building houses in Itzapa, our crew, somewhat by accident, started an underground medical service providing care for those who were brought to us. We had considered people with medical skills to be an important part of our own essential personnel, and their presence attracted the many in need. Several times, sad mothers from nearby villages brought us emaciated babies ravaged by malnutrition and dehydration, problems that were caused by poverty, not disease. Using soymilk as our formula, we were able to save some, and two of the children were adopted by Farm families.

Plenty had to back down from our unlicensed medical practice when it started to compete, or more correctly, to reflect poorly on the local medical authorities, who really weren't deal-

ing with the problems of the people in the villages. We left Itzapa for Sololá by Lake Atitlá. That also meant leaving behind some unfriendly vibes and getting a chance to start over—a chance to take on projects that would get more to the root of the problems facing the local people there.

Our Camp, about forty or so Plenty volunteers and assorted semi-adopted Guatemalans who had come to stay with us, moved from Itzapa to Sololá. Itzapa was hot and dusty, poor and oppressed. In contrast, Sololá was further up in the highlands and much cooler. The town overlooks beautiful Lake Atitlán and its surrounding volcanoes. It is the capital of the region, both for the Ladino Spanish government and for the Cakchiquel people, the indigenous Mayans of the area who are known for their strength of community. The road to Sololá passes through the magic mountain gates of Las Miradador (The Overlook), a vista of the deep Lago Atitlán Valley, and Los Encuentros (The Crossroads). It is a beautiful mountain pass that fingers out toward the different ancient Mayan kingdoms.

In Sololá, our community base was a huge house on a hill, El Molino Belin (the Beautiful Mill), located in the Aldea San Bartolo, a small village or neighborhood a mile or so outside of Sololá proper. It had been built many years before by some Europeans who had attempted to use the stream below to power a grist mill. Long abandoned, the home's thick adobe walls with twelve-foot ceilings were filled with cracks from the earthquakes. We felt okay about using the building for our community center, but at night we slept away in little sheds and outbuildings lest a big quake come in the wee hours and tumble it down on us in our sleep.

I went down as the ham radio operator, and my wife Deborah as the lab technician specializing in parasites, a critical part of the puzzle for our survival in the Third World. We were immediately plugged into the ongoing scene; so much was happening. Each person from The Farm was considered part of the crew and filled some need with a skill.

When we arrived, most of the Mayan men in the region still wore their traje, the hand-woven clothes that identified their particular home region, as well as showing their family's pride and artistic skills. Created on backstrap and foot looms and filled with religious symbols and spirits, these rainbow-colored fabrics crafted by delicate hands brought alive for us the culture of these incredible people. The Mayans seemed to us like distant, long-lost psychedelic cousins, aunts, uncles, and grandparents.

Filling the Niche with Water for All

We had the only running water in the village, in fact the only clean water at all. It came from a covered spring far up in the hills behind our house. The local people were getting their water out of streams and struggled continually with parasites and sickness spread by the unclean water.

Feeling in our hearts we had to help out who we could, we let our immediate neighbors (and that could stretch pretty far) come and get water from our tap. The path to it went behind our house past the lines where we hung our laundry. After a while we noticed that along with the continuous stream of people coming for water, some of our towels were disappearing from the lines. We soon found out that towels from the rich American hippies were prized as diapers among the young mothers in the village.

While we could sympathize, these towels had come down with us from the States and were prized by us too, not something easily replaced! The solution was obvious but also a challenge: How were we to get clean water for everyone?

Working with the village elders, who were also becoming close friends, we searched for another spring. We found one with a pretty good flow about a half mile away, higher up in the mountain hillsides.

Everyone who wanted water had to help. We had a huge line with thirty men digging the trench to bury the pipe. Others hauled sacks of cement and gravel up the mountain to the

spring, where we encased it to keep out groundwater and insure its purity. Down below on a ridge top above the village, others worked on El Nacimiento, a huge storage tank.

It wasn't long before we had a steady stream of water filling the nacimiento, and you could feel the excitement building. Quickly, plans were made on how the water would be distributed. The whole thing worked by gravity. There were no pumps or moving parts to wear out or break. Pipes went down through the village, tap-offs going to each house or family compound. At last the lines were open, and at various valve points, water spewed high in the air like glorious fountains! It was a happy day.

The Plenty Band

Although our original purposes for working in Guatemala were reconstruction and relief efforts, there was another way that we communicated with the Mayan people that was less obvious but still very real. As full-blown hippies, we were obviously not a part of the American government, yet we were doing very strong and important work. The hippie culture cries out for peace and personal freedom—a loud signal against the repression so prevalent throughout the world.

Music was a part of The Farm wherever we were, and it was only natural that a band would blossom in Guatemala. The faces changed as different groups of us went back and forth from Tennessee to Guatemala, but "La Banda Plenty" kept going for over three years, inspiring massive free assemblies and a tendency to let loose with the hippie-hippie shake.

Our band was also a major part of our own home entertainment. Many nights we jammed in the living room or on weekends out on our lawn for ourselves and the neighbors.

Since none of us had personal money for travel, the band became a ticket for us to visit other parts of the country. Our price to come play was gas money for our big flatbed truck and a case of soda for us to drink during the gig. But you didn't just get a band, you got a mini-Woodstock. Most of our camp would pile in the back of the truck with the speakers and other gear, and sometimes twenty or thirty of us would show up somewhere to dance and help set the mood. We had the luxury of playing music not for money but for its highest ideals, as a communications medium with an unmistakable message.

Birth of the Soy Dairy

Juan Salvajan was a Mayan grandfather who had been nursed back to health from near death back in Itzapa. He stayed with us for many years both in Guatemala and Tennessee. Inspired by the healing nutritional powers of soy, Juan Salvajan worked with our farmers growing many different varieties of soybeans.

At the same time, other Plenty volunteers from the camp were going directly into homes and teaching families how to make soymilk and tofu. We ground the soaked beans by hand on a mataté, the same stone pedestal that has been used for centuries to grind corn for making tortillas. The beans were first pulverized into a mash, then added to a pot of boiling water. Before long the soymilk could be strained out. By adding a little vinegar or lemon juice to the soymilk, we got tofu. These folks knew what hunger was about and appreciated the goodness of soy.

We took this all one step further with the construction of La Lecheria, the Soy Dairy. We were able to get the funding to set up a state-of-the-art system for producing soymilk, tofu, and the one soy product that truly crosses cultural boundaries—soy ice cream.

Our new water system provided a dependable source of clean water for cooking and cleaning. Local masons were hired to construct a cinder block building. I installed the electrical service. Plenty and The Farm back in the States lined up equipment—stainless steel cooking kettles, industrial blenders, and a brand new soft-serve ice cream machine.

When the equipment arrived by ship, we used the plywood from the storage containers to expand our housing. Because it never went below freezing outside, we were able to build little uninsulated cabins to give us more bedroom space, an added bonus that came with the construction of the dairy.

Our "ice bean" was an instant hit. The regular ice cream sold in the markets tasted like water with chemicals. Ours was rich and creamy and flavored with local fruits like blackberry or lime and, of course, there was dreamy chocolate as well.

The dairy was designed to stay low-tech wherever possible. The mill for grinding the beans to a pulp was the same kind used in town for grinding lime-soaked corn into the masa used to make tortillas. Our cauldrons for cooking the beans were fueled by sawdust waste from the local sawmills, eliminating the need for propane. This same system also heated water for cleaning. The cooked milk and bean pulp flowed by gravity to a lower level where the milk was strained and then turned into tofu.

We had La Lecheria up and running for only a couple of months when our time in Guatemala came to a sudden end. When the 1980 election ousted Jimmy Carter for Ronald Reagan, the political climate immediately changed. The very next day there were more soldiers on the streets, roadblocks at the entrance to towns, and killings by death squads became a daily occurrence. Helicopters flew over our camp every day headed into the mountains in search of guerrillas, armed insurgents against the state. Our members often had to go to government offices in Guatemala City as part of our relief work. These offices were the site of various assassination attempts and bombings.

But closer to home, the local people that we worked with were starting to come under threats. One man went home to find a death squad had just been there looking for him. People started

coming to us seeking sanctuary in our home. We gave money to some so that they could attempt to relocate anonymously somewhere else in the country. Others we managed to get out of the country and up to Tennessee with student visas. It got to a point where we felt that we were endangering our friends just by being there. The hit squads knew that to kill an American could stir up bad press. Instead, they sent a message to organizations like ours by murdering their friends and coworkers from the indigenous community. We wanted to leave before that happened.

Everyone was very sad during our last days in the Land of Eternal Spring. We tied up loose ends and tried to pass on as much as we could about running the dairy and maintaining the

many different water systems that we had installed. Our plywood cabins were rapidly disassembled and absorbed into the local community.

Miraculously, the dairy has survived. Plenty has been able to stay connected and has helped with funding to keep the it in soybeans. The dairy is operated by a small community association and is managed in a way that provides employment for a number of people. Even through the turbulent years of the 1980s, there was still enough tourist action to create a demand at some restaurants for tofu. The dairy now has an expanded product line, producing tempeh (a fermented soy product), roasted soy "nuts," and even has molds for making ice cream on a stick. Nearly two decades later, La Lecheria de San Bartolo continues to pump out high-protein food. You can see the difference in the kids around the village. They are bigger, stronger, more energetic, and bright-eyed.

I still think about going back to live again in Guatemala. I pray that the peace agreements take hold and that the beautiful Mayan people can have a chance to take their rightful place in our planet's future. Like so many other developing nations around the world, much of the challenge now is to survive the onslaught of Western values and maintain their identity—the centuries-old magic that has allowed them to endure for thousands of years.

Doug Stevenson

That's the Farming Crew Meeting Over There

First I remember the sound of a conch like an inland fog horn echoing softly just before dawn. Then from a nearby ridge, the harmony of another conch—time to rise. It was April 2, 1972, my second day on The Farm.

I was living in a 16 x 32-foot army tent with sixteen other single men. We all slept stacked next to each other on a large platform that wrapped around two sides of the tent. There was a rough wood floor and a woodstove in the middle for heat. In the summer, we would roll up the sides for ventilation, but it was spring in Tennessee and the nights were still cool.

Stepping outside in the refreshing morning air—the sky was just turning orange and pink—I felt anxious to begin my adventures on The Farm. I headed for the Community Kitchen to eat breakfast and get "plugged into a gig."

When I arrived at the Community Kitchen, a woman said, "Do you have a gig yet?"

I said, "No"

And she said, "What do you want to do?"

I said, "I want to farm."

She said, "That's the Farming Crew meeting over there."

I took my hot cornmeal cereal, sweetened with Farm-made Old Beatnik Sorghum, over to the benches where the Farming Crew was meeting and told them I wanted to farm. They were all delighted and by the end of the meeting I, along with one other guy, had accepted the challenge of figuring out how to irrigate what looked to be almost endless fields that stretched from the Community Kitchen to the tree line five or six hundred yards away.

The view from the Community Kitchen was a panorama of fields bordered by mostly oak, hickory, and dogwood. Some of the trees had put forth their first green leaves, and the dogwood blossoms were just beginning to appear. Walking out in the fields with their first blush of spring I felt so free and open. With true beginner's mind, I saw the possibilities were unlimited. My partner and I also immediately saw that the area that had been dammed for holding irrigation water was too shallow and of not much use. We drained the area and moved on to another assignment

I had come from California where I had a small garden that I loved. Once I had the sheer delight of tasting the first fresh vegetables from my own garden, I was hooked. I wanted to do more. I wanted to feed people, work the earth, really farm. My "first cause" for coming to The Farm was, like everyone else, to live in a spiritual community with like-minded people. That I could actually get to farm was a real bonus.

There's an old joke about a farmer who won the lottery. When they asked him what he would do with all the money, he said, "Oh, I'll probably just farm until it runs out." Some people don't get his joke, but if you've ever farmed you understand the irony and the truth in it.

In the first few years, the farming crew was responsible for figuring out a lot of their own funding. When spring came and we needed extra money for diesel, seeds, tractor parts, etc., the whole crew would do odd jobs until we had enough money to proceed. This often took the form of working temporary jobs for Manpower or our own temporary employment service called Farm Hands. Whenever we showed up for Manpower, they were delighted to have this sober, well-integrated crew of hard workers with tools and skills.

The morning I joined up, the Farming Crew was about thirty men and women. That first year we cultivated sixty acres and planted thirty-five different crops. We were also partners with several neighbors on 140 acres of sorghum cane. By 1976, the crew had grown, along with the community, to about 110 full- and part-time farmers.

You might think that a bunch of hippies coming from the Bay Area might be a laid-back bunch, but that was not the case. Up at dawn and home after sunset was the rule for most of the crew. In the beginning, we worked five days a week. This eventually went to six days in the spring, summer, and fall.

All of the crews on The Farm had their camaraderie, and the Farming Crew was no exception. Our "togetherness" stemmed from a love of working with the soil. That special feeling you get from watching things grow—watching life take hold in a freshly prepared field, sprout, and come to fruition. Then there was also the fact that feeding other people was definitely a right livelihood.

Being farmers also made us a part of a larger community outside the Gate. Even though we looked different and mostly were not from the South, farming itself was a common language. We shared the same fortunes from the weather, we discussed implements, blight, hydraulics, and farming methods. We hung out at the co-op and tractor dealers swapping stories. When the locals saw that we worked hard and loved farming, they accepted us and began to give us advice.

Another binding factor was our fearless, charismatic leader, Mojo. To say that farming was in his blood was an understatement. One day as we were talking about how much we loved our gig, Mojo said, "Well, learning to farm is like becoming a doctor. We're raising food to feed hungry people. They have to eat to live. Once you know how to do it, why would you want to do anything else?" We didn't.

Everything you do in farming is timed to the rhythm of nature. Farmers are always looking for ways to mitigate the randomness of weather via greenhouses, irrigation, cold frames, etc., but overall, being in tune with the seasons is the way to grow food.

For the first two years, I worked almost exclusively doing hand work in the fields—planting, hoeing, staking, and picking. This was all hard work, but something about being out in the fields in all kinds of weather at all times of the year, working your own land, growing food for your family and friends made it very rewarding. It could also be very interesting.

The farming crew was the main place visitors were sent to be "plugged into a gig." Most of the visitors we got were sincere, helpful seekers. They worked hard and for the most part participated fully in Farm life. But over time we became well known as a place where people with all kinds of difficulties could come for sanctuary. As a result, the crew sometimes took on an interesting edge.

One day I was in charge of a crew that was supposed to hoe the corn that was about waist high. On this particular day the crew was made up of almost all visitors. Usually this would mean interesting, lively conversation about their lives, questions about The Farm, discussions of philosophy and religion, and a general good time. What was unique about this particular crew was that there were two people who had recently been released from mental hospitals and had independently decided that morning to quit taking their medications. And of course, as fate would have it, they ended up right next to each other about the time their last meds were wearing off.

I immediately noticed that their conversation was dissolving into non sequiturs. They were talking to each other but their ideas were not accessible to anyone not operating on their plane. There was, however, a definite communication in the vibes that was clear, yet at the same time inscrutable to everyone in the field. Several of the visitors were quite intrigued by the exchange and had put down their hoes to try and join in on the disconnected, rambling conversation. I saw that the attraction to this magical exchange was escalating quickly, and certainly no weeding was getting done.

I separated the rambling talkers by several rows and actually succeeded in getting the crew back to hoeing, but after about fifteen minutes the discussion resumed across the rows. This time, because of their separation, the whole crew was between them and became even more involved. I realized my only hope to get any work done was to take my new friends aside and talk it out with them for a while under the trees. As soon as I decided to be unattached to getting any hoeing done myself, we had a pleasant and lively discussion. The field did not get

finished, but the vibes were preserved and a good time was generally had by all. In our way of thinking, the most important things were accomplished.

Michael Cook

Sonny Jones Was Our FBI Man

Sonny Jones was our FBI man. I don't mean he was staking us out. He was the man from the local FBI office in Columbia. If the Feds wanted to check us out, they would ask Sonny to come see us. The thing about Sonny was that he was not from Washington, D.C. He was a Tennessean and he knew all about us just like all the other Tennesseans did. He was always honest with us, and we came to trust him and he us.

He checked out our Plenty project in Guatemala and reported that we were not gunrunners or political revolutionaries. He reported that we did not take deserters and that runaways had to call their folks to ask permission to be with us. I felt that he was a friend and still do.

Later on, when Albert Bates, one of our lawyers, took the FBI to court to get our FBI dossier under the Freedom of Information Act, I got to read Sonny's reports on us. They were so sweet and honest that I could send them to my mother.

One night, after T. C. Carroll had retired and we had a new sheriff, I was called to the Gate because the cops were there. When I got there, the sheriff was there with an FBI man I didn't know. There was also another man who turned out to be an off-duty cop working as an out-of-state child stealer in a messy divorce case and had come to try to get the kids of a woman who was on The Farm at the time. I had to take him down on The Farm and let him talk to her. On the way back up to the Gate he said, "You reek of pot!" and I said, "Yeah, and you ain't a cop in this state either."

Things were a little strained when we got back up to the Gate. I said to the sheriff, "You know, you are new and maybe don't know that we have had a good relationship with the sheriff's office for years. This was not a way to treat us. This guy could have walked up to our Gate without your help. I don't say that we could make the difference, but you wouldn't want to start your next election about eight hundred votes down." Then I turned to the FBI man, and I said, "This child stealer didn't need the FBI either. I want to tell you that you are blown on The Farm. No one will talk to you anymore. It would be a waste of time for you to come here. We won't talk to anyone but our own FBI agent, Sonny Jones."

Some weeks later, I ran into Sonny in the supermarket where we were both doing our shopping. After all the "Hey Sonny, how are you?" and "Yo, Stephen, how's The Farm?" Sonny looked at me a little funny and said,

"You know that fellow you barred from The Farm?"

And I said, "Yeah?"

Sonny replied, "Well, it was a little embarrassing for me."

I said, "How come, Sonny?"

"Well, you see, he was my boss."

Stephen Gaskin

Tantric Monks with a Boom Truck

Kathy—After my first child got old enough to be in a kid herd (what is known in the outside world as a "play group"), I looked around for a gig and settled on trying to help "manifest" the bakery. Some large industrial ovens were already in place, and I soon found out that a monastery in Georgia had offered us a large bread dough mixer almost a year earlier. I made some calls, got in touch with Brother Vincent, the elderly monk/baker at the Monastery of the Holy Spirit outside of Conyers, Georgia, and he said, "Come on down, it's out in the yard wrapped in plastic waiting for you."

The next step, and always the hardest, was getting a vehicle. Just scheduling a trip to one of the local towns through the Motor Pool dispatcher was difficult enough, and even then sometimes you got "bumped" at the last moment by a higher-priority run. But a trip to Georgia to pick up a five-foot tall Hobart mixer, that narrowed down the field of possible vehicles quite a bit.

Luckily though, The Farm Band was in need of an equipment truck for their upcoming tour, and a likely candidate had been found in Atlanta at the Mayflower Moving depot. Tex was in charge of that project, which had a little more push to it than mine, so we combined runs—Tex, Rupert, and I would drive down, buy the truck, and pick up the mixer—perfect.

Rupert—Still, we had to get a vehicle. The Bronze Van seemed the obvious choice, but it, as usual, was on a nonstop succession of runs for the Print Shop or to pick up relatives at the Nashville airport or to get emergency tractor parts in Huntsville, etc., etc. The Bronze Van was one of those fairly together vehicles that, once its owner signed the vow of poverty, immediately became an overworked vehicle hammered nonstop by an unending string of tag-team drivers. Plus it had an excellent CB and an AM/FM radio. Never mind it was only a shell, no sooner was it back from Miami than boom, there it went to Memphis, and once it pulled into the Gate, it was not unusual to see the next set of drivers sitting on the porch, waiting on the Bronze Van. They'd hop in and ride the incoming folks down to their place so there would be no dilly-dallying around with the transfer. Then they'd tsk-tsk about the way the others left the van strewn with soda bottles and wrappers, but in a few hours they'd have it right back to the same place, empty cans rolling across the floor every time you turned a corner.

So anyway, we were on the list for the Bronze Van, but a few more Print Shop runs got squeezed in ahead of us until finally Tex and I went up to the Gate to snag it for good the next time it came in. That was around eight in the evening. So we loaded up and drove all night to Atlanta, hitting the big city morning rush hour in a pretty much dazed state.

We test drove the truck, kicked some tires, checked the maintenance records, and decided it looked like the one. The poor truck never knew it was immediately going to get the top of its cab torched off, then have the front of an old Econoline van welded on, thus making it a double-decker, cab-over, cross-country companion for the Scenicruiser. But that's another story.

Next we drove out to the Monastery of the Holy Spirit, a real turnaround from Fulton Industrial Boulevard. The monastery housed an order of Trappist monks, who, having founded it way out of town in the 1940s, were now feeling Atlanta's encroachment on all sides, especially overhead where jets slowly paraded, waiting their turn to land at the airport about thirty miles away. Still the place was lovely—tree-lined, granite buildings, a bell tower. The monks baked Monastery Bread and distributed it to the city's supermarkets where it was a popular item. They had recently upgraded the bakery, which was why they had an old mixer to give away.

Kathy—We went to the gift shop/ office, announced ourselves, and a call was made to my contact, Brother Vincent. The gift shop/gatekeeper cupped his hands over the phone and said,"They've got a woman with them." Actually it was me—the woman—who had written to Brother Vincent, so he said,"Send 'em back." He met us back in a kind of quadrangle of living quarters and workshops that is usually offlimits to the public, and certainly to women. Nobody said anything so we all trooped back into the private area where we were surprised to notice the monks actually talking to each other and the younger brothers looking quite normal in pretty much everyday work clothes and sporting trim mustaches.

Brother Vincent was a quite elderly, chatty monk who was more than happy to answer all of my questions about the bakery and the mixer, except he addressed his answers to John and Rupert even though I was asking the questions. He told us that they had originally tried to sell the mixer to a neighborhood organization, but that price bargaining was so alien to them they jumped at the chance to give it to us, a spiritual community. My letter had arrived just before a meeting about "what to do with the mixer." The arrival of my letter settled the question. We had presented them a way out, he beamed.

Gradually he loosened up to me, forgot or overcame the fact that I was a woman, and while Rupert and John helped with the loading of the mixer, Brother Vincent asked if I would like to see his bread recipes down in his office. As we walked to a nearby building he occasionally shook his fist at the low-flying 747s. He was very interested in The Farm and how we managed communality, which to him seemed a bit of a bother, especially with "the women and kids on our backs."

"And if you want to go to town for some personal things, or if you have a doctor's appointment," he said. "You have to schedule a car ahead of time!" I nodded. "And sometimes they'll say it's too bad and they're sorry, but something's come up and you can't even use the car you had reserved! Can you imagine?" I said I could imagine and that "Things were very much the same at . . . ," but he was going on. "And when you get back, you can't calmly get out and unload your bags; there's somebody impatiently waiting to use the car!" He shook his head at the sad state of affairs in the Monastery of the Holy Spirit. He had been born in Ireland in much simpler times.

Brother Vincent kept asking if I wanted coffee, and I kept refusing, thinking it an imposition. It was only after I left that I realized I was his excuse for an extra cup of coffee. So we stood there by his altar and discussed the similarities and differences in our "orders."

The most memorable thing about his office was a simple yet beautiful altar he had created in a corner. It was an altar to St. Theresa, the Little Flower, complete with plastic flowers. I began to ask him questions about Catholicism, partly out of simple curiosity and partly because this was an area of communication that was obviously a kosher way for us to exchange energy. He seemed so hungry for communication with someone who was not a Cistercian monk just for a change.

Rupert—Tex and I drove the Bronze Van around to the back to their garage which was the neatest little scene we had ever seen. It was a four-bay garage with absolutely nothing laying about—no oil spills or dead batteries or old tires or blown transmissions. In fact, the only thing out there was the Hobart mixer wrapped in plastic and rope, waiting for us to take it away and make the yard perfect again. The thing was much larger than I had imagined, all stainless, about five feet tall with a forty-gallon bowl and a huge, 220-volt motor. It looked immensely heavy. Tex and I wondered how we were ever going to get it in the van.

No problem. The brothers had already swung into action. From somewhere came the crispest, army-green boom truck we had ever seen. "Old Yeller," our Farm boomer, was a monstrous, bashed-in, counter-weighted, junk-strewn thing that we used as a battering ram and seat snatcher more than as a tool for lifting heavy objects. In contrast they called their boom truck Saint Gabriel. All of their trucks, it turned out, were named after saints.

The monk driving Saint Gabriel, which actually had a working muffler, quietly followed the hand signals from another brother who had skillfully chained the mixer at its exact balance point and was now holding the cable's hook while directing the truck backwards. Tex and I, who had been prepared to lift, grunt, holler, yell "whoa" a hundred times, all the things we did everyday on The Farm to move something big, stepped back in awe.

Once the cable was hooked to the mixer, we were directed to back the Bronze Van up to a certain point, slowly, then his hand went up—stop right there—we stopped. The back doors were opened, and again we stood back. I was waiting to hear how their PTO and winch sounded but it never came to that. Once the mixer was hooked, the truck simply backed up as if on rails until the cable tensed, then slowly pulled the top of the mixer over so that when it eventually touched the back of the van, it was already halfway in. Then through some signal I did not even see, maybe six inches of slack in the cable was winched out, the monk on the ground unhooked the cable, and he with another helper effortlessly tipped and slid the mixer straight into the van and shut the doors before Tex and I could even move.

On The Farm we threw around the term "tantric," usually in reference to sex, mostly nobody ever understanding it, but in a general sense we used it to mean the smooth exchange of energy or being able to do something easily in just the right way. This certainly was the most tantric thing I had ever seen. We had a great laugh over how that operation might have gone at the Motor Pool, and indeed, the next day when we backed up to the bakery, the cry of "Monkeys!" went out, and there ensued a great discussion about where to put it and how to get it out of the van. Except it actually went pretty fast, because two guys from the Print Shop were antsy for the van to get unloaded because they were heading to Chicago with a load of books.

Kathy—For years afterwards, Brother Vincent and I exchanged letters. Each time I wrote to him, I would receive a three- or four-page letter before I thought my letter could have arrived. He always began, "My dear Kathy." Gradually it became more of a holiday greetings type thing, and then when he did not answer a letter of mine after two weeks, I knew something was wrong. Soon I got a note from the monastery that Brother Vincent had died several months before and that they all missed him greatly. They said they were sorry not to have

told me when he died, but (and I can see a few monks gathered around a table drinking several cups of coffee, deciding just how to put it) "We just didn't know about you."

Kathy Fike, Rupert Fike

Energy Shakes

When doing psychedelics there's a phenomenon known as "energy shakes." It's like having the jitters. Your whole body shakes as if you were freezing cold, but you're not cold. It's like being surprised and getting a chill up your back at the same time, except that the chills keep coming. Before living on The Farm I only got them when I was tripping on a strong psychedelic. But I remember on The Farm getting them in regular day-to-day activities, without having taken any psychedelics — well, maybe smoking some grass.

One early memory is sitting in the small sentry booth at the original Gate. We'd be on security watch, three of us, squished in this six-sided booth, meditating. If we had a joint, we probably smoked it. And I would get the shakes. I felt tons of energy moving through my body. It felt good in a way, but in another way I felt very self-conscious. I was often the youngest one there, both in age and in psychedelic experience, so I figured I was the only one who couldn't "handle the energy." And that made me get even more self-conscious. In time I learned how to "relax into it," so instead of actually shaking, I focused on the tingling warmth come up my back. But even years later, sometimes the shakes would still happen.

It was a common belief on The Farm that we were all connected by some kind of energy web, that we could all feel each other's energy if we were paying good enough attention. For example, if several people were all feeling good, and then someone came into the room who was confused or scared or angry, then everyone would feel that without a word being said.

So I remember that when I got around certain people on The Farm, I'd often get the energy shakes. One person in particular, I'll call her Grace, did it to me almost every time I was around her. The prevailing opinion was she had heavy energy, heavy spiritual vibes. She was very psychic. She could see through you. She was so subtle that she could feel any uptightness you had.

Now understand that my nickname was Rhino, and of course the thick-skinned Rhino was full of uptightness, so no matter what situation or place I was in head-wise, when I was around Grace I felt bad that she was going to have to put up with feeling my uptight vibes. So I was always trying to be on my best behavior when I was around her, and that's when I'd get the shakes.

Years later I thought that maybe Grace and some other people were caught up in their image. That perhaps it wasn't me generating the uptight, but Grace herself was uptight, and my nervous system was reacting to hers. I remember occasionally thinking that she carried herself aloof, that it seemed like she really thought she was hot shit. Those thoughts would invade my head every now and then, but I'd fight to beat them back quickly. She was very telepathic so she'd know what I was thinking, and, after all, we did call ourselves a mental nudist colony. So I'd try to quash those thoughts . . . and get the energy shakes.

Gary Rhine

Stepping Into a World of Uncharted Territory

In our first few weeks of visiting The Farm, we hooked up with a friendly couple who took us under their wing in order to show us the wonderful, amazing spiritual advantages to becoming part of The Farm.

Jacob was convinced that Stephen was an enlightened being and that life on The Farm was the truest path to help change the world, to create an ideal community in which each individual could reach his or her full potential.

We hung out with them for a few days, taking it all in, and there was a lot to take in, this whole alternate world that was The Farm. This was in the midst of a Tennessee summer, heat, humidity, the works, so one afternoon we all decided to go down to the creeks to get some relief in the cool water. We were walking through the woods on a narrow path when, without any warning at all, Jacob, who was walking a few steps behind me, decided to jump on my back. Literally. This 170-pound guy, almost a stranger, leaped on top of 100-pound me and held on saying nonstop, "Look at how strong you are. See, I just want to show you that you are much stronger than you ever thought you were."

I was pretty much mind-blown, but I managed to carry him a few steps in shock and disbelief before he hopped off. That impromptu Zen teaching did not turn on any major light bulbs for me, but it did reinforce my belief that I had indeed stepped into a world of uncharted territory where anything could happen and often did, where teachings popped up, and were expected to, at the oddest moments. It was nothing my sheltered, suburban existence had prepared me for, but that shouldn't have been much of a surprise—I was 18 years old.

I was very susceptible to the "energy shakes," an unconformable, trembly place your body went to when you felt you were in the midst of people who thought they had a higher consciousness than you did.

Another place I got them was in the early days when groups of us would sit or stand in a circle and eye-vibe, which is exactly what it sounds like—no talking, just deep, meaningful stares that hopefully express your spiritual openness, but most of the time became amazingly uncomfortable. No one wanted to be the first to look away or break the silence, but everyone wanted the silence to end, for laughter or smiles, something, anything. Especially before meals the tension would get unbearable as we held hands with the food out in the middle of the circle, everyone staring across to whomever, breaking off to switch to another pair of eyes, hopefully friendlier, the food getting cold, but no one wanting to be the one to break the spell because maybe that meant you were low energy or exhibiting a "scarf" (gluttonous) vibe. The longer these circles went on, the tighter my stomach got from the anxiety and paranoia of wondering, "Oh, no. Somebody's going to get into my thing,"and then there would come that fear that you had some kind of astral BO that everybody else was picking up on. And you'd say to yourself, "Why can't I relax like everyone else?" but actually everybody else was probably in the same boat, only I couldn't quite be sure. So I ended up with the energy shakes.

Debra Heavens

The Adobe was An Orphanage of Sorts

It was an apartment house made of mud up to the window sills and a patchwork of salvaged building materials above that. Besides the six families living in the Adobe, there were two other families in an adjoining, more conventional two-story building. And there was the Bunkhouse a few yards away where the teenagers lived. All together the population of the Adobe scene was about seventy. The household was defined by the Adobe's kitchen, which served them all.

Not all The Farm's teenagers lived there, just most of the orphans and feral youth of the day. Wanderers and throwaways and left-behinds, not actually the children of dead parents. I was eighteen, but if you were younger they either wanted you to get in touch with your parents and work it out so you could stay or you had to leave the community.

My sister Winnie was sixteen but she had no problem getting to stay. The Farm had separated her from the menace she had arrived with, and our mother couldn't have been happier or more grateful to have us both there. There were whole families of kids at the Adobe. Parents came and went; they came with kids and went without them. Some of this came about

because of the midwives' offer to take care of the babies of unwanted pregnancies. Some people extended this to older kids. Many of the teenagers living at Adobe were, like me, just wanderers separated from their families. We somehow found The Farm and thought this looked like a nice place to call home because The Farm people looked like us. Like children finding their lost tribe.

Winnie and I had both long since turned wild. She'd been chasing around the country with a very bad guy twice her age. I came from a street life in New York City. I had started much too young, hitchhiking around the country, then moving around with a girlfriend. We lived in Gainesville, Boulder, and Austin and succeeded mostly in staying alive. Winnie did too, but not much else. She found The Farm by way of *Spiritual Midwifery*, Ina May's book. So, I heard from my sister that she's at this vegetarian commune and they got rid of the bad guy she'd been kidnapped by or got him away from her. I was bored, had broken up with my girlfriend, and ended up working in a boat factory cutting vinyl for upholstery. I left the next day. When I arrived, the Gate sent me to the Adobe to live.

Some of the Adobe kids were informally adopted by the resident couples. These were always girls who attached themselves to one couple or another and helped mom out with the kids while she was busy with important Farm business: Annie with Beth, Rain with Priscilla, and Winnie with Mary. This gave these girls some authority, as I would find out later. Boys were appreciated for splitting firewood and stoking fires and had no authority. It seemed a little chaotic at first, everybody whirling around, babies crying and toddlers and teenagers, but it was highly disciplined, really.

It took a lot of organization to make two hundred meals a day. At dinner everyone lined up, first to take a turn rolling a tortilla, then cooking and filling it themselves before they could eat. The fillings were usually beans, margarine, and nutritional yeast. All food ingredients were essentially optional, though, as anything might be unavailable at the moment, except beans of one kind or another. Margarine was especially precious. Fruit and fresh vegetables didn't exist most of the year. Cleaning up went well into the night and breakfast got started very early. Some of the teenagers were grimly serious about all this, working very long hours.

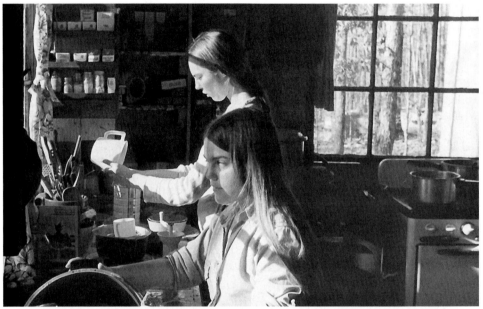

Schedules were tight and rules were many. No cigarettes was one rule. I smoked one cigarette a day for the next twenty days. Every time I did, somebody would smell it and start announcing the fact loudly. They never did pin it on me, though.

I did get into trouble for having an opinion on how to cook hash browns, something I am pretty good at. For this I would experience the collective wrath of this strange new house for the first time, my offense being trespassing on the girls' turf—cooking. Or maybe it was just being a smartass about it. They were making lousy hash browns.

For awhile it seemed like what I was really good at was collectively pissing these people off and making myself the center of impromptu pecking parties. It seemed like "get Piggy" in Lord of the Flies or maybe a tie-dyed Cultural Revolution. I was saved by somebody newer coming along. There was culture shock for many kids who came there from a life without rules, where wits counted for more than cooperation.

The bunkhouse was not finished. It had been built out of salvaged materials by the teenagers shortly before I got there. They'd torn down some building first. Big holes remained in the floor and an upstairs wall. The stove, therefore, served only to create a convection current that brought in more cold air and only heated the room directly above it. Nobody complained. We did laugh about it while all wrapped up in our sleeping bags. We were fed and happy.

The bunkhouse population changed constantly; it would rise in the summer, then fall in the winter. Mark and I were the only boys left that winter to chop all the wood and start fires in a dozen stoves. Mark had been brought to the Adobe by his mother on remand from a Florida court. He's the one that took my place as the new camper with an attitude to trim.

We did a lot of kid stuff like hiking off aimlessly through the woods doing our best to get lost, hanging around listlessly listening to Grateful Dead tapes, and skinny dipping with the girls.

I had wanted to be recognized as an adult by the adults, but they weren't listening. I'd been on my own for five years in the street and on the road in strange cities, surviving against vicious rednecks, police, and all kinds of thieves. I thought I was an adult for all that. They had made up their minds though; I would be a kid. Except I was too old to go to The Farm High School. I would have to work. It was a compromise. I got some remedial parenting, to be safe and carefree for awhile. They taught me about hard work and got back the benefits of my efforts.

In many ways my experience at the Adobe and on The Farm prepared me, gave me the confidence and competence to do whatever I set my mind to, an attitude without barriers to success. And I found out what was really involved in being an adult—not just surviving, but also being productive and taking responsibility. But mostly I had a lot of fun at the Adobe. I gave in and got to be a real kid.

Richard Lanham

The Great Scam

Many people saw The Farm as a way to further their own ends. One day we were approached at the Gate by a group of men who claimed to have a lot of money and power. They said that they were going to really fix us up. All they wanted us to do was file to incorporate as a city.

They explained their plan to us and said they would pay for everything. They would pay for us to have a police station, buy the equipment, radios, and a police car. They would pay for all filing fees and all lawyer fees. The clincher to the deal was that we were to get a bonus of a hundred thousand dollars.

Then came the pitch. After we were a city, we were to annex a certain piece of property and arrange for it to be leased to these guys to install a solid waste dump. We didn't let on how offended we were. We just let them go on and tell us the whole plan, which was to circumvent the people of the county and put a waste dump here for money, right next to our neighbors. It was interesting to see that they never noticed that we weren't with them. We told them that we had to work it out with The Farm and they left.

As soon as they were gone, we called the local environmental organizations and our county officials and told them what we had been offered. Some of the papers sent reporters and interviewed us.

The next day the headlines read:

"The Farm Turns Down $100,000 to Put in Waste Dump in Lewis County."

The neighbors thought it was funny. Their attitude was that those guys should have known better than to hit on us with such a moldy scam. They weren't surprised about our attitude, though. They knew that we wouldn't do a thing like that to our neighbors. They expected no less from us.

Stephen Gaskin

Attention Equals Energy

Why were there so many "trippers" and mental patients on The Farm? This is a child's question, one we were usually too busy to answer. Busy trying to chase down a hyperactive teenager in the woods or busy trying to put someone's clothes back on or busy trying to keep the clinically depressed resident upstairs at the Gate from putting his arm through the glass window again.

The actual answer traces itself back to Monday Night Class in San Francisco where Stephen often hammered at a simple equation—attention equals energy. A common example was the removal of a crying child from a room of adults—without their attention (juice), the baby's energy (crying) would run down.

From there it was but a short hop to realigning someone's psychic energy by gaining their attention through love and compassion. The Haight was brimming with case studies—acid casualties who were basically sane, good-synapsed college drop-outs, who had been overwhelmed by chemical- or cactus-induced experiences. They'd signed up for a little ride and gotten the big one that wouldn't quite go away.

At Monday Night Class, Stephen put their predicament into a spiritual perspective—these confusions were the same ones that young sadhus (holy men) had been experiencing since the beginning of time. It was all just a case of receiving too much information too fast, and once you grounded out a bit, learned how to breathe and truly pay attention, you'd be fine, realized, crisp, and in control.

These teachings really worked, on some faster than others, but plainly people changed and got better because their attention had been corralled. This, however, was a rather skewed control group—almost entirely alert, college students from loving families who'd stumbled into a spiritual crisis they were only too eager to figure out.

Which is not the case with most mental patients. But never mind that. These accumulated case histories led to a certain conceit on The Farm's part which stated that if you could get somebody's attention, and if that person wanted to change, really try, there was no mental illness or psychic disorder that could not be reversed, made ten times better by real (not sentimental), caring love.

Such mental health "social work" was not originally a major goal of the community, but it soon became a holy duty, because if you possessed the skeleton key to sane consciousness, you had a moral imperative to share it.

Due to the open-Gate policy and referrals from families who'd seen the improvement in young adults they'd written off as acid casualties, there was soon no shortage of projects. The Farm first took on out-patients, then in-patients from a society whose mental health institutions were little changed from the days of Dickens, except that psychotropic drugs had replaced chains. Forget what their inch-thick chart said or what medications their cerebellums were swimming in. Get someone's attention, show them love, and with a little co-operation, their energy would change.

Which was all naiveté. Certain successes with middle-class dropouts in a spiritual crisis was in no way a qualification to take on the major league mentally ill. Still The Farm tried, nobody ever coming right out and saying, hey, this is a hopeless drain. But as the years passed, it was certainly thought.

As in many of The Farm's misadventures, the brunt of this came down on the Gate crew. To say that anybody was just too hard-core a case would be to admit that the community's assumptions around energy didn't really work, and that could not be done.

Perhaps hubris is a useful term here. Hubris is the Greek concept of presumptuous pride that leads to trouble, if not an outright fall from grace. It was prideful to imagine working changes (first-class, real-deal miracles) on certain people, yet The Farm never recognized it as such. Responsible, competent members were removed from their productive jobs and turned into "tripping buddies" (24-hour baby sitters).

There is one mention in the Gate logs of Walter abandoning his regular job to be a tripping buddy for an uncontrollable, good-sized man. The subtext to that story is that Walter had invented and was the sole operator of the pumper truck, a large vehicle that went around to overflowing outhouses and did what the name implies. In a community where shigella, giardia, and other feces-based diseases were a constant problem, keeping the outhouses sanitary was a super-high priority gig. Yet Walter parked the truck for a few weeks to "trip" with one of our sanctuary cases.

Not that there weren't successes, lives changed, turned around, attention actually captured, mental energy actually refocused. There was a teaching to the effect that if you can make a difference in one life, then all this is worthwhile. And certainly that happened, but meanwhile psychic train wrecks kept piling up at the Gate. Vast resources were poured into every tripper. To give up on wild-eyed bipolars and send them back to a mental hospital was a defeat no one was prepared to accept. So year after year, more and more energy was poured into the effort.

Gate Logs

Be Careful About Kidding Around with Someone Gone Vibrationally Outlaw

—Looks like S. will be here for awhile. Beth, one of her night tripping buddies, is a bit blown out by S. We're working it out. John ended up sitting with her most of the night. We didn't really comprehend how heavy S. was tripping, tended to Gate business without checking in with her. She got real nice when I brought her some food, but went nuts when Nancy went up to be with her. Threw her plate at Nancy, then put her hand through the window. Thomas and Gary came to stitch her up, but she refused. Gerald, Kay Marie, Priscilla, and Marilyn came up, plugged in deeply, got her to take two lithium, which she was supposed to be taking regularly. Also valium. We all worked with her for rest of the afternoon. Realized how smart she was; saw the power of love working on her. She got loud and dramatic again waiting for second dosage to come on. Fell asleep at 8:30 p.m. after shower at the House.

Looks like she might sleep the night after being up three days and three nights. Stay in close touch with S.—it really matters.

—D. came in from Central State Mental Hosp. He's on Prolixin and Cogentin. Says he's into quitting them, going cold turkey at the Gatehouse. He's hanging in there, shaking a bit.

S. is sleeping in the upper room. Slept all night except 3-3:30 a.m., took her meds again, went back to sleep. Did two-hour shifts with her through the night. Stephen came up in afternoon and tripped with her. She feels good.

This guy M. returned for another visit. Pretty schitzy, says he took thirty acid trips in two weeks in his Indiana home town and everybody turned on him. Didn't feel like Visitors' Tent was the one, so he'll stay here for the night and try to house him tomorrow. Felt more grounded by the time we left.

Wavy Gravy stopped by the Gate on the way out. Had a good time. He drove off "into the sunset" leaving a donation of about $250,000 in funny money and some Dracula teeth.

—Walter came up and tripped with R. who is just out of Central State. Also just off Thorazine and Melaril so he needs a buddy. R.'s helpful and friendly, just kind of childlike and spacey. He got sent here by his old social worker who said this place might be his only chance. He could stick if he digs the trip. J.'s medicine dosage—laxative, Cogentin 8 a.m. and 8 p.m. R. gets Coricidin every three hours for two days.

—R. tried to sleep all day. Called Jeffrey who said he should NOT sleep all day He should be going to a household three times a week to help out and do it with kids or housework until he gets well enough known and liked to get into a household.

Seems we need continuity about our psychological therapy crews.

B. is always ornery when told to do stuff. Question—Who is noting and covering the progress of B. and R.? It's only my second day at the Gate, but they feel kind of on the shelf.

—Jim visited from the President's Commission on Mental Health. Went down for a cup of tea with Stephen. Later W. weirded out, threw flashlight at Ben. Got him some cooled, but then night crew made mistake of jiving around with W. and supporting his trip. Got to be careful about kidding around with someone gone vibrationally outlaw.

—Last night R. came in hitching, a runaway from Cleveland Psychiatric Hospital. Been in and out of there for four years. Says car accident messed up his head. On Tofranol and Prolixin for seven (can that be right?) years. Been here once before. Gets into fights. Just quit cigarettes. Comes on wild-eyed sometimes, but so do Holy Men. Will take him for a few days, talk to Leslie, see if we can help. Not making any waves so far.

—Two visitors from Germany hitched in and an hour later two more from Germany arrived. Action then got thicker. Lady came in from Canada drinking beer and toting a huge Great Dane. We hipped her about us, beer, and dogs. She tied up the beast and cut loose of the beer. Had to back M. out of her juice. He seems to zero in on visitors for the opportunity of an intellectual discussion, usually with ladies, usually about evils of "sexual repression." Definitely good to keep him plugged into something real and not let him run his b.s.

—Pretty wild day. There were probably as many folks on downers up here as there were straight. Worked it out again with M. about hitting on ladies. Gradually found out dosage and where medication was for about five people. Perhaps we could have a sheet where it's all down in one place because there's lots of other stuff to integrate.

Got a family of Mom and Pop and eight kids stop by on their way to Penn. Heard about us thru Hey Beatnik! Lot of heart among them. They even found room for a visitor to get a ride to Knoxville, one who had just been dropped off by a semi full of cattle, driven by a trucker whose handle was Naked Nigger. Whew. Where do they all come from?

—(Later note) 4:15 a.m. almost full moon.With all the people I have done Gate with—night men and couples and single ladies and visitors and trippers and everybody including myself, I am struck strongly with the concept and feeling of brotherhood tonight, brothers and sisters.—Wonder Wally

—L. is back, on downers and pretty trippy. Talked to Stephen about him. He said L. could stay if he really wanted to do it. Need to watch him to see if he needs a tripping buddy. He argued with Ruth and Jeffery about his medicine, then went into S.'s purse in back room to get some of hers, lied about it and how many he took. Found them in his pocket. Talked to Stephen again. Walter to be his tripping buddy starting tomorrow.

—Guy called in from Tony Kidd's store saying there was a deaf and dumb visitor out there trying to get here. We picked him up, then on the porch we started signing to him and he copped to not really being deaf. Things got so nice and open he started talking—amazing the healing energy of the Gate. Turns out he's been so backed off by life in city, he'd tried being deaf and dumb for a little armor.

J. came up kicking and screaming. Scratched Nick pretty good in face. Nick gets the Gate's Purple Doorknob Medal for wounds received in action. Then J. hid out under the front porch all day. Had to explain, or try to, her hissing and such to visitors who thought it wild. B., an orbiting tripper kept whizzing by, making faces, smoking ciggies. Corralled him, escorted to highway. Also put M. on the road for uninterrupted, two-day uptight. Italian and French visitors. Folks back from La Paz and Homestead.

—(Note from night Gate man) It's late and I must say, the rat problem cannot be over-stressed. We need traps, poison, perhaps a BB gun. The kitchen reeks of rat piss. They are fighting under the sink. I've retreated to the doorway by the steps and plan to make my stand here. We can't lose the living room to the rats or it's all over. Send reinforcements soon. We're doing our best to try and make it through the night and hold our position. The kitchen has fallen to the rats, I repeat, shortly after midnight, the rats gained control of the kitchen. Mayday. Mayday.

—Tripped with E. We had a couple of nice organic, crunchy type visitor couples and he started messing with them. He got pissed when the night Gate man told him to back off. Matthew woke me about 2 a.m. E. very uptight, wired, shaking, shouting, and stomping in and out of the Gatehouse. He had a vial of pills in each hand. He said that the white ones were downers and the pink ones were uppers. He kept stomping and rattling the pills, waking the visitors. Their eyes were wide as saucers. Finally during the mellow end of a mood swing we talked him out of the pills. Not too long afterwards he wanted them back and said he would kill for them. When I refused he pulled a knife out of nowhere, a big one, threatened me, then himself, all of which felt pretty unreal and melodramatic. But then he got violent and smashed the woodstove fence, which made Matthew and me hold him down for a short. He continued to trip heavy for an hour or so, but didn't get violent again. He gradually ran down, we all drank some camomile tea that he had with him, and he eventually crashed on the couch. E. decided to split in the morning. I gave him back his pills (Haldol and Cogentin) and he felt pretty good, though he did threaten to sue us for $40,000 for the loss of his knife which we found after he left. Quiet day after that.

—J. qualifies as our latest tripper. Told us soberly that he communes astrally with the Dalai Lama and ten thousand saints in Nepal. Dalai Lama told him to come to The Farm, so here he is. He raps about incarnations and does magic tricks. Nice vibes, not a terrible rip-off so we've been gentle with him and are keeping him up here for observation. All else in order. Upstairs here is full as is The Farm.

The War Comes Home

In 1975 the United States was finding out that even though the Vietnam War was officially over, the fallout in refugees from that country was just beginning. Some of us on The Farm decided to look into the possibilities of helping a Vietnamese family assimilate itself into the U. S., and since I had soldiered in Vietnam in 1968, I was feeling like that might be a way for me to make some good out of a decidedly bad situation.

With the help of Peter Schweitzer and the local Catholic church in Lawrenceburg, we managed to hook up with a refugee family who would come live with Karen and me. The deal was they would stay with us until they could make it on their own. At that time we were living in the Park Tent on Second Road, a 16 x 32-foot army surplus tent erected on a wooden platform floor. Such was the housing for many of us in those days. In the summer you could roll up the sides, but in the winter they were mostly gloomy, damp, and cold.

We tried as best we could to spruce up the home scene for a few weeks, and then one day they arrived from their temporary home at a Florida air force base. There were seven of them—a grandma and grandpa, their daughter, and her husband who had been an officer in the ARVN (the South Vietnamese Army). The couple had a teenage son and two-year-old boy. A young man who was a close friend of the family came in the deal, which turned out well because he was the only one who spoke any English.

Right away they let us know that our scene was not acceptable. They begrudgingly settled in, but being Catholic they insisted on seeing the priest right away. We got a car from the Motor Pool dispatcher and hauled them to Lawrenceburg where they handed the priest a list of complaints about their "accommodations." On that list were things about the tent, the outhouse, no private bathtub, all the dirt, and finally, that their hosts were "naturalists." That word made me feel like some kind of lowlife or degenerate or worse.

What happened was the priest rolled over and told them he would start the process to change things for them, but that such matters took time. That seemed acceptable to them so we went back to The Farm, and in the months that followed we made a life together. They bought fifty-pound sacks of white rice because they ate it for nearly every meal. They were so adept at boiling rice in a four-quart pot that there would only be a delicate golden brown crust left on the bottom and edges of the pot. This crust was like a dessert and a sweet treat.

The grandma swept the earth around our tent so it would look neat, much as she might have done back home in their fishing village. Sometimes after dinner the three younger men would sit half on top of each other with a guitar in our one stuffed chair and sing songs. It was, of course, an unusual sight to see guys be this close. When we started having English classes, I learned to appreciate this quality as we only had one book, but the men crowded up around our little, low table shoulder-to-shoulder and leg-to-leg while we studied. They had no subconscious in being this way. It was natural for them. Later one of them told me that at the air force base in Florida there had been a bulletin written by other Vietnamese about what life was like in America. It said that in the United States, American men always stand three feet apart from each other and never touch.

I took the men (but not grandpa) to work at a house one of our construction crews was building behind the store. They got the hang of banging nails right away, but unlike us, if they dropped a nail it was retrieved, and if a nail was bent, they took the time to straighten it. This was no small task considering that we were using oak. There was also the matter of the scrap pile which they eyed curiously. In Vietnam I don't remember seeing any scraps. Everything was utilized.

Sundays we took them to Mass in Lawrenceburg, and afterwards they put pressure on the priest to get them off The Farm. The initial good relations I thought we were going to build up never quite seemed to exist, and this was a bit hard for me to accept at times. Another thing was how they disciplined their two-year-old boy. On The Farm one of our main tenets was talking "real" to our children, expecting the most from them, accepting zero complaints or whines, and most of all not rewarding such behavior. There was pretty good, universal agreement on such matters. But when their two-year-old began winding into one of his usual late afternoon tantrums, the grandparents appeased the kid by throwing cookies to him. This was such a contradictory response to what the community practiced, we could barely handle it. But since it was just not possible to "work it out" with them so they would understand and "cop," all we could do was quietly fume.

Because we could not realistically provide for their many needs, we made a couple of trips to Nashville to a bank that would cash in some of their one-ounce solid gold Asian currency. They'd get approximately three hundred dollars for it, and we'd go home. God only knows how much of it they had. After a few long months of this, the Catholic church finally came through, and they left for Baton Rouge never to be heard from again. We were all quite glad that this episode had run its course.

Thomas Heikkla

Fallen Yellow Mastodon

By 1974 we were going wide open on our farming operation, involving our newly founded satellite farms by sending members of our more experienced Tennessee Farming Crew to Florida, Wisconsin, and other locales to build a grid of the revolution as we saw it. The Homestead, Florida, scene was going to grow green beans, tomatoes, and wintertime veggies while the Wisconsin Farm was going to do potatoes.

At this time I was part of the Motor Pool/Trucking crew, so when word came down from Wisconsin that they needed The Farm's potato harvester pronto, we swung into gear. Obviously it would have been simpler for them to just buy a potato harvester up there, but they had not been able to find one, a freeze was coming, so okay, we'll load it onto a flatbed trailer and haul it up. That was the thing about The Farm—you could wake up all mellow way back in the woods, and by nightfall you'd be on some crazed mission out on I-65 a hundred miles away, a mission you'd had no notion of twenty-four hours earlier. And now it was imperative to get this piece of machinery up to Wisconsin or else there would be a crop failure—no potatoes. Make that no potatoes for anybody for years, a potato famine, we'd all go hungry—somehow it was quite easy for us to whip ourselves into those kinds of frenzies.

Now a potato harvester is one funny-looking, off-balance contraption. It has a main body that digs the spuds up to the surface, and then they get loaded onto this long conveyer belt arm that reaches out to one side and feeds them into a truck running alongside in the field.

Our method of loading farm equipment onto trucks was via this inclined plane of dirt that was shored up on the sides with wood so that at the top of the dirt you were level with the beds of most trucks. From there you just drove whatever it was onto the truck, boomed the thing down, and away you went.

The potato harvester was a little more complicated to load than some other equipment because it was pulled by a tractor. This meant we had to back it up the ramp and onto the truck. Plus it had been raining steadily for about three days, and the mud ramp was as slick as a greased pole. John P. was driving the tractor, and he was good at it, but nobody had more than a couple of years experience around heavy equipment. Whoever did it was going to need the steadiness and precision of a surgeon because the flatbed trailer was less than a foot wider than the potato harvester.

The trailer was being hauled by our flagship semi, a '64 Kenworth. As I drove down the road from the Motor Pool to the Farming Crew ramp, the rain was coming down in buckets. Lawrence and Rudy, the potato crew guys on the Tennessee end, were having a hard time getting the money together for the trip. This usually had the effect of making us more frantic and attached than ever to get whatever it was done. Never mind that the *I Ching* description for this trip might have been Difficulty, changing to More Hassle Than It's Worth. We were going to get on the road with that funny-looking thing, were going to talk to other truckers on the CB about it, have a great experience, and that was that.

So I got down there and backed up the trailer to the ramp, hopped out and started helping guide the tractor drivers as they tried to back the spud digger up the ramp. Because the mud was so squishy, the digger kept sliding from one side to the other. Plus the conveyor belt arm sticking out to one side was making the thing tilt wildly when it angled out too far over the edge of the ramp. The rain was coming down so hard it was difficult to see, but the trip money had come in, we all had visions of the open road (Cokes and candy bars) — we were going for it!

Somehow Rudy got the digger up to the top of the ramp, over the crest, and onto the end of the trailer even though the tractor's big cleated tires were spinning in the ramp's spongy mud. We stopped at that point and agreed we just had to back the thing straight back — which might not have been so hard, but remember the tractor was still on the incline. Rudy tried it a few times, got the harvester a little crooked, decided to go forward, straighten out and try again, but during that maneuver, the harvester's mud-caked tires just started sliding on the truck bed, skidding sideways instead of turning. The conveyor arm tilted and bobbed, aggravating the slide, and the harvester continued its slow drift to the right as if pulled by some force (gravity actually, the bed was slightly tilted that way). And then it was slow-motion clear to all of us that there was nothing we could do to prevent that thing from falling off the trailer and crashing to the ground below. It lay there in the downpour like some fallen yellow mastodon.

It was a mess. The conveyor arm was bent all the way up, the axle raked to a near forty-five degree angle. We felt pretty defeated, although self-defeated was more like it. Had we waited until the next day in the sunshine, it could possibly have happened, but when you're fueled by that heady drive of "the world is depending on you, all our kids were going to go potato-less for years" — we did dumb things like pressing on, trying to make a way when there was no way. Plus, if we'd waited till the next day, the money might have been gone or the trip cancelled, and that certainly wasn't an option.

We stood there wordless and looked at the wrecked implement in the mud. There was just flat no taking this baby anywhere. Nothing to do but go up to the House and call the guys in Wisconsin and tell them what happened. "Oh, that's okay," they said. "We don't need it anymore. We just found one three miles from here we can rent."

John Coate

How I Got to Be a Part of Johnny's Family

I was having trouble getting pregnant and hoping that I might be able to take care of a baby that was left with the community under The Farm's midwife agreement: Don't have an abortion. You can come to The Farm. We'll deliver your baby for free, and you can leave it with a family there. If you ever want the baby back, you can have it. The midwives were trying to inspire my body to do its thing by having me help them at birthings. At one birth we were sitting around talking about what a busy day it had been. This was the fourth birthing in twenty-four hours — four boys — the greatest number in one day that had ever been born on The Farm. Pamela mentioned that the woman who had given birth at her house that morning had come with the intention of leaving the baby here, and the thought that there might be a chance that a baby could come my way left me pretty excited.

Several days later, I got a call from Pamela saying the mother of the baby was still set on leaving him with someone in the community and would I be interested in having him. Would I? I was there in a flash. Johnny was a beautiful, healthy boy, big brown eyes and dark hair — the very picture of the baby I had dreamed of for years. His mom was very sweet. She was young and felt strongly that her baby would do better with someone who was older and committed to raising a child. She came from a very large, closely knit Catholic family and had never considered abortion an option. Her first priority was her baby's long-term welfare. It was a very difficult and unselfish decision on her part. She was grateful to have discovered The Farm because she didn't want this baby to totally disappear from her life.

It was an amazing experience to become a parent overnight. I fell in love with this little boy immediately and completely. I felt some wariness lingering in the background, however, like a little elf sitting on my shoulder, reminding me that I was just a caretaker. At any point, Johnny's family might come to take him back. And, in fact, his maternal grandmother showed up at the Gate about a month after he was born and wanted to see him. I was racked with fear. I knew this day might come, and I was terrified at the thought that she might want to keep him.

I walked into the Gatehouse with Johnny in my arms and passed him to his grandmother to hold. She was a little hesitant, as if she wasn't sure she had a right to be so close to him. "You have to understand, this is very hard for me," she said. "My own youngest child is only six." (Like I said, a very large Catholic family.) I got this strong sense of what it would be like for my mom if she was coming to meet a baby I had left with strangers. I said the only thing I could think of at the moment, "Well, don't think of this as losing a grandson. Think of it as gaining a daughter-in-law." That worked for her. It set the tone for the wonderful relationship Johnny and I have had with his mom, his grandmother, and their whole family ever since. Their love and acceptance made a place for me in Johnny's family.

Cynthia Holzapfel

If You Love, There Will Always Be Someone There Needing That Love

Michael and I were married in the summer of love, 1967, and our daughter Kerri was born that December. All this was not in the Haight but in New Jersey where I worked for Dow Jones as a programmer/analyst and Mike taught in the Jersey prison system. So with two incomes and flower-child sensibilities we soon found ourselves wanting to do more for others. We'd drive around picking up hitchers, feeding them even, that sort of thing. After five years of this we heard about The Farm and knew this was the place with access to people in need.

From early on we'd dream about our future family. Mike had had a son out of wedlock before we were married that he and the mother had given up for adoption, but that was unchangeable. In our dreams it was always six kids. It turned out that we couldn't have any more babies after Kerri, who was so precocious she really needed a brother or sister. Remember, this was the early 1970s when you couldn't adopt if you were of mixed religions (Mike was Catholic) or didn't make a certain amount of money. So The Farm midwives' invitation worked out perfectly for us.

At first we had a couple of babies "given" to us, then taken back after an emotional roller-coaster-ride of attachment. It was tough, but that's foster care. Here one day and gone the next. A few months later we got a four-year-old boy with Opitz Syndrome. C. was born with a cleft palate, his feet went out at a wrong angle from his legs, and he stood on his head a lot because his head was so big he felt out of balance otherwise. He even played that way. It was wild. His teenage father had taken him from his mother and was in way over his head. He was working at a local horse farm and had to leave his son in the car all day. A woman on our horse crew visited that stable, saw the situation, and pretty soon we were giving C. a home while his father tried to get his life together.

The father never came back for him. It was taking me and Mike everything we had to fix up this kid while covering our regular jobs. When we first got him, C. had food in his hair and was dirty everywhere. He didn't understand baths. He was like a wild animal. C. didn't talk, he mainly ranted and raved, made animal noises. If he was happy, he'd make a clicking sound with his tongue, but mostly he had no presence.

After a few weeks he began really responding to us, which was quite gratifying. Then a woman named A. showed up at The Farm and had her baby. She came to my office one day (I was a "Bank Lady") and said, "Linda, will you adopt my baby?" This was very tough since we had C., to whom we were now committed; there was just no way. It wouldn't have been fair to either of the children. Even though this was something we wanted so badly, a newborn to adopt, the whole situation wasn't just about us. But things worked out for the baby because another Farm couple adopted the little girl, and she was raised to adulthood in the community.

Maybe eight months later we heard from C.'s mother for the first time. We sent her some pictures which captured his quite angelic aura. She saw the pictures and said, "I can't believe this is my C. I want to come get him." That was rough on Mike and me, because what the heck were we going to do with ourselves? We'd need two kids to replace C.

No sooner had we said that than M., a nineteen-year-old junkie, showed up at our front door with A. and M., who were three and one. M. was in a bind because she needed to get into Synanon to kick heroin, but they demanded that she terminate any parental rights beforehand, which was something she did not want to do. So she came to The Farm for a visit and was staying with us when C.'s mother came to take him back. The way it worked out was that M. observed us with C. for about a week, and then when his mom drove up, C., who would never go to anybody but Mike or me, immediately went straight to his mom, laid his big head down on her shoulder, and started clicking away happily. She looked exactly like him.

I had thought, "Oh my God, how are we going to give C. back?" My heart was breaking. But as soon as we saw C.'s mom, we loved her as much as we'd loved him. It was instant meld. She was quite grateful, saying it was a miracle what we'd done with him and that she hated to take him. That was what happened, though, which was per the agreement. M. witnessed the whole process of giving him back with no strings, and a few weeks later when she was leaving, she asked us to take M. and A. because she knew we'd give them back at some time and not make her feel bad in the exchange. Again, I was at my office, so I took the boys, put them in the car, rode out to Mike's job site and said, "Guess what, honey? We have two sons." This became our core family—us, Kerri, A., and M.

One day Joel, the community's lawyer, told me he had been writing to this woman, S., who was in jail and pregnant. The father was in jail too. Her sentence was going to run thirteen months after the birth date, so she wanted to know could somebody on The Farm take her baby, keep her, send pictures, etc., then give her back. I said, "That sounds great." The State of Texas sent us tickets, and we flew into the Dallas airport the day after the baby was born. I recall walking around wondering how were we ever going to find these people when we saw this roped-off section that said, "Police Area." Ahh, that's our spot. So we met the prisoner mom, the social worker, three cops, and the baby, who S. immediately handed to me. And I'm thinking, "Oh my God, a day old. So small." Then we're on the next plane back. We flew out in the morning and came back in the afternoon with a new baby. Whew!

We all just loved T. Kerri and the boys loved her as much as we did. We sent pictures and wrote to S. and G. (the father) regularly. They even came on a work release furlough one time to visit the baby. All was bliss until just before S. was due to get released. That's when G.'s folks decided to take T. because S. had already had two kids removed from her custody for abuse or neglect. G. got out a month before S., so he and his parents came and took the baby when she was thirteen months old. T. was gone.

That was a rough one. We cried and cried and cried. Tiara had never known anyone else as family but us. Still, Mike and I kept saying to each other, "We've got to be strong within ourselves because if we're all tripped out, the baby is going to feel that, and it'll just be harder on her." We had learned from C.'s leaving that if you loved, there would always be someone there needing that love. Once again, it wasn't about us, it was about the children, their needs, their love. They did not need us blithering all over the place.

During these years M. was always showing up, staying for months, still trying to get her act together, drying out, whatever. She was like one of our kids herself, and on one of her visits she met a man who was also living here on "sanctuary." We had a policy that "sanctuary does not mess with sanctuary," as each case had problems enough on its own. But there was this prisoner from California, A., who had gotten out on good behavior and was remanded to The Farm for the duration of his sentence. As soon as I saw him I knew that if M. ever met him, it would be all over. They were like two peas in a pod.

So I reminded M. about "sanctuary doesn't mess with sanctuary," but as soon as his time was up, off they went to Puerto Rico. They wound up getting pregnant and having A. down there. Soon she was writing that they were both clean, were moving to Newark, and would be picking up the other two boys, who were now school age, on the way through. Oh well, what can you do.

Soon after M. took M. and A., a woman dropped off her two-year-old boy, J., with us. That turned into a very involved custody battle with the State of North Carolina, his grandparents, social workers, trips back and forth, and court appearances, but finally it was apparent that J. was part of our family. (After being taken away once, the first time he saw us again he said, "I knew you'd come.") So he came home to The Farm.

We got a chance to go to Boston for Thanksgiving. We thought, "Great, we can visit M. and A. on the way." When we got to their place in Newark, M. came stumbling out looking terrible, and inside, the baby, now nine months old, was screaming and crying; he was hoarse from it. He was covered in poop, and his plastic bottle was sucked to the point of collapsing. All that was left was curdled milk. Obviously he had been in there alone for some time. I picked him up, started cleaning him up a little, and at that point M. and A. came busting in from school. "MOM!" they yelled as they threw their little arms around me. I felt like I could have died. We had a little visit, and then we had to go. There was just nothing else to do. I gave M. the phone numbers where we would be and told her that if the situation was not working (which it obviously wasn't) to call us and we would take the kids back.

After we got back to Tennessee, A. called us on New Year's Eve and said, "I'm coming home if I have to walk, and I'm bringing M. and A." M. and A. had not been home in a couple of days, they didn't have any food, and A. had beaten up M. in front of the kids. They were

shattered. So we were scrambling trying to get a flight up there because by the next day everything might change. But the schedules were not working out, so we called Jerry and Kathryn at The Farm's Bronx Center. They drove in the middle of the night into an unbelievable ghetto scene in Newark and, like two archangels, they got the kids. The next day Mike flew up, brought all three brothers back, and again we were all together.

M. called us several months later saying she was over three months pregnant and had OD'd on heroin. She was in the hospital where they were about to abort the baby. The doctors said that the chances of the baby's being normal were next to nothing. So on the phone M. was asking me for one last shot of help. I'll never forget that moment—it was six other women and me all holding each other while I talked to M. on the phone. We saved S.'s life in that moment. It took that much energy, all of us crying and M. crying. She didn't want to have a baby that was handicapped, but having seen us work with C. years before when she first came to visit, she said, "I remember you loved that little boy who was not normal, so I know that if this baby is not normal, you'll still care for it and love it." At that point she promised that when she had the baby she would have her tubes tied. No more babies. And she did.

S. was due to be born at the end of April, but since we had little A. too, our big project was to get A. walking before S. came. We were in deep flux, having moved into a just-built two-story house with twenty-five kids and twenty adults, which was fairly typical for a Farm home scene. And then J.'s mother, D., showed up and took four-year-old J. to Arkansas after cursing me out for "stealing" her kid. Never mind the custody battle from Hell we had gone through that she could never have won herself.

A few weeks later we got a call from some people in Arkansas who said this kid, J., got dropped off to be baby-sat and nobody had ever come back to get him. They were about to call the police, but J. kept saying, "Please call Michael and Linda on The Farm." So we borrowed the Painting Crew van which had lacquer thinner spilt in it and took off. We were pretty light-headed by the time we got to Little Rock and picked him up, but we got J. back home again with us.

Right up until S. was born M. kept saying, "I can't just give this baby up without bonding. I've known all my other kids since birth." So I said, fine. It was obviously her call. S. was born prematurely and had to stay in the neo-natal unit for two weeks, which was hard on M. and me both. M. finally said, "I can't just go in there, get the baby, then hand her over to you. You're going to have to go get the baby."

I said, "M., I am not going to be able to walk into the hospital and walk out with that baby. Come on. You're the mother, the only person that can go get her. You go get the baby, and then you can give her to me. That's the only way it's going to work."

So here we go again. Mike and I fly to New Jersey, rent a car, and follow her directions to the apartment. It's the middle of the night, but in Newark that's like mid-afternoon: lights, parties, guys on the corner. We get to the address but no M. We wait and wait, then decide to go to my mother's house and arrive just as the sun's coming up on, what else, Mother's Day. Both my grandmothers were there, so we were in the middle of telling them some version of the whole story when M. called and said, "Where were you? I was here." Boom, back to Newark and into this very dark apartment where there was this tiny, little baby lying on the bed sucking her thumb, curly hair, big old dimple. I thought, oh my God, she's barely five pounds. And there's not a sign of baby stuff . . . no formula, no bottles, no diapers, no nothing.

I came in, picked the baby up, and said, "Okay, well, we're going to go now." And M. said, "Oh no, wait. A. and I have been making payments on this crib. We've got to go down to the store, get the crib, and then you can go." This time I had custody papers for all four of her kids, so I said, "Fine, you sign these papers, and we'll all go get the crib." We drove over to the store, and in a minute M. came flying out screaming and cursing, "That son of a bitch, A. He put the last ten dollars down, took the crib, and now he's buying fucking dope, that son of a bitch."

That's how we left her, on the street screaming. Back at my mother's house, one of my grand-mothers was crying her eyes out at the sight of S. She couldn't believe that someone would give her up. I was happy as can be because the papers were signed, and I had me a brand new little girl. My mother took pictures, my grandmother was still crying, "The poor little thing," my brothers came over, and then the phone rang. It was M. She had changed her mind. A. hadn't taken the crib after all. He had paid it off, brought it back to the apartment, and was now flipping out because he couldn't believe his baby girl was gone.

M. said, "We're meeting you at the airport to take her back."

I told her, "No way, absolutely not. Thirty minutes ago you didn't even know what was going on, didn't have one diaper. I'll give you a month to think it over. But I ain't giving you the baby back right now. I can't in good conscience do that." We changed our reservations to fly out of Philly, and off we went home with S.

So life goes on from there because now we had the kids. As far as The Farm was concerned, we just became "The Brady Bunch—Gavin-style." But it wasn't like that. We had five seri-ously disturbed kids. We got very little acknowledgement for taking on all these troubled kids and parents, which was one of the unstated, yet very clear goals of The Farm. We raised five kids whose mothers could not take care of them, and the kids, of course, didn't understand why. I mean, it was all fine when they were little—just line them up. They all ate at the same time, did homework, and went to school together.

The first year S. went to school was after The Farm's change-over, so she went to school in town, and when the bus brought her back that first day she got off with a sad little look on her face. I said, "What's the matter, S.?" And she said, "A boy called me a nugget." She knew the feeling was bad, but she had never heard the word. I said, "No, honey. He called you a nigger, and probably you're going to be called that sometimes. A. is called that too because you're both half Puerto Rican."

I tried to explain about racial history and that because she was mixed race, she was not go-ing to be accepted by either race. To the black community she was white, and to the white community she was black. So along with the rest of the problems these children had (such as not knowing why their parents didn't want them), now they were ostracized because of their skin color.

Our kids all had a rough time in school because of the racial prejudice. Also, nowadays at-tention deficit disorder is more recognized and can be helped. None of them except K. and J., both white, excelled in the social aspects of life. They were troublemakers in the eyes of others, wouldn't pay attention, wound up in and out of special ed classes at different schools. One year I had all five enrolled in Summertown schools, and by the end of the term I had one kid, J., still there. There were racist teachers. It was so oppressive for A. he started picking at himself, making big sores on his body, things like that.

All of them were healthy, good-looking, strong, smart, personable . . . but mentally strug-gling. They'd say things like, "When is the pain going to stop?" I don't know if it's from the

mental makeup of attention deficit disorder, or the fact that their parents did not want them, or all of it together. But to see these kids grow up and then start suffering—it really affected me.

I got to where I was afraid they were going to end up in a boys' home, but gradually they all left, with friends or to go visit M. (which was basically running away). The three brothers ended up in Gainesville, Florida, where they broke into the courthouse, rifled through the district attorney's office, and took state's evidence: general big-time mischief. They went to jail but somehow lucked out doing very little time.

It kept getting worse as they became older teens. The Farm had restructured, which meant the adults were all scrambling for paychecks in town, leaving the kid and teen scene definitely up-for-grabs. Some of the other teenagers even had their own house. Their parents were able to be accommodating in a permissive way that I just could not possibly match or agree with, because my kids—except for Kerri—were not mine biologically.

Even J. changed, dropping out of high school in his last year after doing so well. He had grandparents whom he visited in the summer and relatives juicing him; he was more together in that respect than any of our other kids. But he was turned onto psychedelics, had a complete personality change overnight, and pretty soon he was down in Florida with A., M., and A., his "brothers." S., at this point, was the only one left in Tennessee, and she was saying things like, "Why can't I go down there? I want to leave this house and be with them," never realizing the hell they were all living in and going through. So she stopped cooperating in any way, shape, or form, this little baby we rescued from neglect in Newark. She was fifteen, A. sixteen, and neither of them were past the eighth grade. There was just no way they were going to finish school. I had to basically take her to M. because that's what S. wanted.

So there we were, Mike and I, still trying to make a go of things and trying to be the center of the family so there was one place for them to all touch base. And that place was me. Although they all did touch base at regular intervals, none of it was ever good news. None of it was something you could even handle. It was all so sad, so out of our control. I was beginning to fry. I was crying all the time. Things were terrible. No more family. We went from a six-kid household, having all this fun and activity, to having nothing. It was all gone except that they were calling up saying they were totally miserable. What can you do?

I looked for counseling everywhere for the kids. And the irony is, there is this Plenty project, Kids to the Country, that brings city kids to The Farm for the summer, but I had these kids already here who needed serious help. The Farm didn't realize that if you took on certain kids, they were, in most instances, going to be troubled. They needed help. And at $100 a session for counseling, . . . no matter how much money we made we couldn't afford that for as many kids as we had. We made too much money to get aid and not enough to get psychological help for every one of the kids. So we ended up watching them deteriorate.

Here's what I'm saying about that whole agreement: The midwives put out a generous, heartfelt offer and made agreements, but after that, there was no support group. When there were problems, the community wasn't supportive of the people who had backed up the original call to come have or bring your baby here.

Emotionally it's been very hard for all of us. I've had to harden a heart that was very soft. I had to consciously withdraw, begin not to care, and basically change my nature. It just hurt too bad to try to process so much of other people's pain, especially when you love them so much. It would have been nice to get some support from the community whenever there was a problem with the kids. Instead, Mike and I were always painted as the wrong ones, and the support went to the kids, no matter how off-base that was. The kids have told me what folks have said. It's sad, because Mike and I have tried really hard to dedicate our lives to service.

On a final, lighter note, I can report that each of the kids is pulling through. A. is still in Gainesville. M. is in California near Kerri, who just had a baby of her own. J. is in the National Guard, and S. and A. are back here with us trying to get their GEDs. And remember in the beginning of the story the baby boy Mike had to give up for adoption? Well, after searching for him, he was located on his thirtieth birthday. He said, yes, he wanted to know who his biological father was, what's his phone number. So he called; we've met him and his beautiful children. Our family continues to grow, and I have high hopes for everyone.

Linda and Michael Gavin

When Something Belongs to Everybody, It Doesn't Belong to Anybody

My first job as a mechanic in the Motor Pool was to replace the rear leaf-springs on the truck that hauled all The Farm's laundry and diapers into Summertown. It was a two-and-a-half-ton, six-wheel International from the mid-1950s, and the leaf-springs which held the truck's axle to its frame had obviously never been touched. The nuts to the U bolts were so rusted and I was so inexperienced that it took me two days to loosen four nuts.

By 1975 we were responsible for over one hundred vehicles. There were the dispatcher's cars for general town runs, pickups, trucks, and buses for the work crews, utility trucks like the water truck and outhouse pumper, midwife and medical crew jeeps, and semis for long-range trucking. You never saw a more ragtag fleet because most of the time there was very little cash. So, in the case of the leaf-springs, once I had the laundry truck's broken ones off, then I had to go out in the woods and take a set that fit, or was close enough, off a bus that was someone's house.

Early on, an NBC News crew was in the Pool taping part of what turned out to be an eight-minute segment about The Farm on the national news. When they showed up the job at hand was pulling an automatic transmission from one of the town-run cars, which isn't that big of a deal with a good floor jack. But we didn't even have one of those, so we monkeyed the Buick over the pit, a five-foot-deep hole in the shop floor, four  of us climbed down and went at it with the cameras rolling. And there we found out what a heavy hunk of aluminum and steel the thing was. I happened to be the guy in the very back, and right at the crux moment, somebody in front loses his grip, the whole thing tilts back to me, and about a half gallon of transmission fluid roars out of the rear seal onto my shirt and pants. So much for looking sharp on national TV.

We started out with one guy who knew what he was doing, Jose. All of the mechanics were basically trained by Jose who was a product of Puerto Rico and New York City. "Hey, take your hands out of your pockets and do something with them," he'd holler with that rare ability he had to shout in a spiritual community and not be resented for doing it. Mostly because he wasn't mad.

The Farm soon realized that having reliable, or even semi-reliable, vehicles was a must for us to survive. Thus, we needed a stable maintenance crew, so Jose was given first pick of ten men at a seminal men's meeting held one afternoon at the Horse Barn. Before that meeting it was pretty easy, accepted even, to drift around from one crew to another, changing your vocation to fit your perceived spiritual needs. ("I need to get in my bod more, I'm joining the farming crew," or "I need higher standards on the material plane, think I'll be a carpenter for a while.") Soon though, it was realized that to get any real work done, buildings built, crops raised, machinery fixed, we had to start sticking to one occupation.

Our main town-runner fleet consisted of a few Fords and Chevys that newly arrived members threw into the pot or else they had been bought for a few hundred bucks when somebody went to see their parents. These cars were "dispatched" by a much stressed-out "dispatcher," whose job was a twenty-four/seven nightmare of logistical juggling, explaining, cajoling, and occasionally "bumping" scheduled drivers for something "more priority" that had come up.

The dispatcher's cars were placed in constant service for runs into the local towns, and even Nashville, usually for medical appointments or picking up relatives at bus stations or airports. Every run contained a full load of adults and kids. The stress and strain on these already used-up vehicles was staggering. There was no auto insurance and almost never working seat belts. That there were no fatal accidents during this period could make a strong case that optimism and good vibes create a strong connection with Divine Intervention.

It was quite common for a car to limp home from a town run and head straight to the Motor Pool with muffler dragging, charging light on, and a hissing from the radiator. Or the brakes might be soft, or they had to jiggle the battery connections in town to get going, or they barely made it back up Rockdale Hill (a steep grade that was the final climb before reaching Summertown).

Then, while you tried to do triage on all this and determine if the Caprice was roadworthy, there'd be Amy the dispatcher asking when it would be ready because she had it scheduled, and then there would be the next crew of drivers, pumped and raring to go, always saying

that whatever you were trying to fix was not that big of a deal, and that they would get the needed parts in town in return for giving them the green light to hammer it back out the Gate. A common exchange was, Mechanic—I'm sorry, but the brakes are grinding metal on metal. Hopeful Driver—We'll buy the brake shoes in town. Mechanic—But that doesn't change the fact that you're driving around on shot brakes. Hopeful Driver—I'll be tantric.

The first act of any repair, especially if it involved working on the inside of the car, was to remove all the accumulated snack wrappers and soda bottles that were rattling all over the floor. Then when the afternoon run commandeered the car, the floor debris just developed

another layer. This underscored a common communal problem: When something belongs to everybody, it doesn't belong to anybody.

I can remember regularly filling two shopping bags full of litter out of town runners. It could, of course, become discouraging, but getting disheartened was an unacceptable, and even countersurvival, attitude. The sanest way to look at things was to see it for the comedy of errors that it was and try to laugh about it.

In 1974 after the entire community embarked on a "grass fast," our drug use shifted over to a more common substance—caffeine, and that spawned the great age of the "town run." These jaunts were often just to one of the little markets in Summertown or near the junction of Highway 20 and Drake Lane. One place, Larry's, did so much business in Coke and candy bars that he was able to finance the construction of an entirely new building on the profits from The Farm's mammoth snack-habit. Every day it was one vehicle after the other, all day, hordes of sugar-starved, caffeine-jonesing hippies in their beat-up, dusty vehicles. And the thing about Larry's was, you didn't even have to have a license tag or blinkers because you never had to get off the county road. Eventually we tried an experiment with wholesaling Coke and Dr. Pepper to ourselves to save money, gas, and borderline lying. (In the Motor Pool we would always tell the Gate man that this was a "test run.") That plan was abandoned when we learned that Larry was then unable to make his building payment.

After awhile, a large segment of the Pool gradually moved from straight mechanicing to going out in the surrounding counties to salvage scrap metal and old cars, for fun and profit as they say. But it came down that several of us were to come back and fix cars. Jose got to continue scrapping as he was getting a bit burned out mechanicing, so the weighty mantle of Motor Pool boss was somehow deposited on the broad shoulders of Frank, a quiet Minnesotan, who was already head of the community's welding shop (which was a shed really). We were all stunned, most of all Frank, whose nonexistent management style was far removed from Jose's.

Frank did alert us to the fact that since we were an official auto shop we could get free trade magazine subscriptions, so here came all these glossy publications, half shiny trucks, half shiny girls, but in Fleet Management, which we always got a roar out of, there was a monthly cartoon about a fictional, nothing-goes-right, two-bay garage, The Kaputi Shop. Boom, that was us. Frank was Mr. Kaputi and remains Mr. K. to this day.

From that point on, we sunk into an arcane subculture of The Farm, playing touch football at lunch complete with bitter arguments, selling scrap radiators to rent a color TV for the Daytona 500, secret handshakes, practical jokes, the Order of the Golden Bolts which you entered by committing a massive and costly mistake—the more spectacular the better—buying and drinking near-beer even though some of us hated it. The Farm was changing no matter what we did, but certainly we gave things a push, and then on Sunday morning, there we all were, scrubbed clean, in our meditation clothes.

And if you had been walking by the Pool in the mid-1970s, this is what you might have seen. "Stand and Salute! The Potentate is passing! Stand and Salute for Mr. Kaputi, Grand Potentate of the Loyal Order of the Golden Bolts." DD is in his signature greasy herringbone coveralls, long ponytail covered with maroon stocking cap, hanging out the right rear window, summoning the faithful.

John Coate

The Mat

Debra—Our household of four families, a single mother or two, some single men plus twelve to fifteen kids, at least eight in diapers—this group generated a lot of dirty laundry. For the first year or so we'd all pile in a truck (sometimes an old Nabisco Cracker truck that had zero windows or ventilation in the back) for the ten-minute ride to the Summertown laundromat. This was a bad plan for many reasons, community relations not the least of them.

But eventually we built ourselves a laundry, even though the drainage problem never quite got addressed. The area behind the "Mat" was called the diaper field and smelled kind of ripe, especially in the summer. Still, even with our very own coinless laundromat, there were logistics. The first step was how to get this huge pile of laundry bags and diaper pails up out of the meadow, a mile or so up to the Mat. I remember borrowing a wagon from a more affluent neighbor and pulling my family's individual load up through the muddy ruts. If you were "well connected" (Farm-style), perhaps a midwife's truck from next door could drop it off for you. Another plan was to get the bags and pails up to the road, then holler "Whoa!" every time a truck or horse wagon passed.

Kathy—I was on the "run" that took the Big Pickup down to an army base in Georgia to pick up these twenty or so washers (our first) that were going into the new laundromat. Sara had gone to an auction down there and bid on them while the man she had come with was in the rest room. She really wanted some washing machines for us, and nobody else wanted them so the price was right. If you looked closely on the prospectus, the machines were listed as "parts." Obviously after the army gave up on them, who wanted them? Well, it turned out we did.

So we showed up, three long-haired men and myself in this monstrous, cut-off school bus, and of course, the MPs with the white gloves and all that, they're like no way are you getting on this base. They make us pull over, we show them our bill of lading, receipt, papers all in order. Then on the way back with the machines, two times we got pulled over on the highway

and had to show our papers. The second time I think the police were more interested in the Big Pickup than anything else. One guy in north Georgia wanted to buy it on the spot. Anyway, when we got back and unloaded the machines into the Sorghum Mill, it was determined they were pretty much junk, but since they were all the same model, Hobie and Mark Thomas were able to get a few of them going. This whole trip had been, like many other Farm enterprises, long on adventure and short on bottom-line results.

Debra—There was a whole strategy for getting in line to do your laundry. If you had other plans for your day, it was best to go in the very early morning, say 4 a. m., or even in the middle of the night. Once there, you got on "the list" and waited your turn. Waiting to get up there until 7 a.m. or 8 a.m. could easily result in waiting for three or four hours. Eventually this plan evolved into a new incarnation of "the list" which was more efficient. Starting precisely at 5 a. m. you could call the Laundry on our Beatnik Bell and put your household's name on the list.

The drill was to set the alarm, wake up, and start madly dialing. Jumping the gun was frowned upon but sometimes worked, depending on who the poor soul was who was up there doing their laundry and happened to answer the phone. Anyway, the phone was usually busy, but you just kept at it. When you finally got through, you would find out what number you were and then give the approximate number of loads you had to do. Key questions to ask at that

point were, "How many machines are working?" and "Who's ahead of us in line?" Then you could gauge when you needed to get up there.

Since we only had a few dryers working at any one time, they were reserved for diapers only. They smelled like it too, a hot, borderline poopy aroma that made you really not want to dry your clothes in them anyway. So once you washed your laundry, you had the pleasure of dragging it back home wet to hang up on the line. In the winter you wrestled rock-solid frozen clothes off the line to bring in, a few items at a time, to thaw out by the woodstove.

Kathy—Another strategy for getting your house's laundry done was to not get in line behind one of the larger households. You might be third in line for that day, but if it was the Long House and Schoolhouse Ridge in front of you, forget about it, until late in the afternoon that is.

One particularly hectic day our number was next, but the poor, overworked machines were dropping like flies. The Philharmonic Hall "family" (thirty or so people) were finishing up, so it looked promising, but just as Barbara and Ellen were loading their last bag, they began talking more, loading less, then standing up with hands on their hips, speaking forcefully to each other with great eye contact. Their laundry was half in the machine, half out, but now it was clearly forgotten. They were in the grips of a major "sort-out."

One of them said, "This affects the entire future of our relationship." I was sorting my loads out on the floor, but when they said that I just stopped. Other women caught my eye and we kind of traded looks, but what could you do? There was absolutely no way anybody was going to go up to them and say, "Hey, why don't you put those last loads in, then go outside and discuss things?" Reasonable as that might sound now, it went head-to-head with one of our major agreements—sort out the vibes (the subconscious), right now, not tomorrow, not this afternoon, not in a few minutes. Nothing was more important. And if you even thought about putting some minor material plane "priority" ahead of the vibes, then there would be an even bigger sort-out about that. So there in the Laundry that day, all we could do was watch and wait as Barbara and Ellen eventually sat on the pile of dirty clothes in front of one of the remaining few working machines and "figured it out."

Debra Heavens and Kathy Fike

Dan Rather Meets the Wolfman

When the news hit that CBS was coming to The Farm for a segment on 60 Minutes, we were ecstatic. That is until we heard that they only wanted to talk to Jack Wolf. The angle of their story was "The Hippies, Ten Years Later—Where Are They Now?" CBS had dug back through old footage of Haight Street and identified three flower children they'd interviewed back in 1967. Now they'd traced them down for a follow-up. Jack Wolf was one of them. That he lived on The Farm was secondary.

Jack had stood out even in the mass of freaks at Monday Night Class. He was over six feet tall with dreadlocky hair, a head-bobbing walk, and heavy-lidded eyes. Kathy recalls working in the Diggers' Soup Kitchen at the Boys' Club with Peter Coyote, Emmitt Grogan, Richard Brautigan, those guys. And one afternoon here came barefoot Jack with a bushel of mutant turnips from Lou Gottlieb's Morningstar Ranch out in Sonoma County. Dirt clods, leaves, worms hung off the turnips while Jack kept ranting about free food for the people, stuffing more mud than turnips into the Boys Club's nice refrigerator. It took them the rest of the day to clean up the mess.

Jack was still pretty much the same when he showed up in Tennessee, unreconstructed. That first year or so we were all big on reinventing ourselves, if not becoming Southerners at least not scaring them. The future of the community depended on it. And in a large measure, social position, that non-existent staple of Farm life, flowed early on from your ability to shed Bay Area traits.

Inside the Gate we could be beatnik spiritual students raring to get up in somebody's thing, fine. But when we went to pump gas at Tony Kidd's or Dunn's or Jim's Cash and Carry, we had to say, "Howdy," and once we got good at it, try something like, "Think it's gonna come up a storm tonight?" We had to translate "stoned" into "down-home." Not that Jack didn't try. I did the Gate with him a few times, but he kept saying "ya'll" too much.

We were concerned that the image CBS portrayed of him would color the world's perception of The Farm. Certain individuals like Jack found themselves stuck with the identity of being "spacey" because of their demeanor, in spite of the fact that they were dependably holding down important jobs. Jack was first a regular on the Farming Crew, then he worked the Compost Truck, going up and down the roads emptying those smelly pails. Each responsibility he handled lead to a greater one, and according to the teachings, that's how you got smarter, gained respect, got prettier even—by "taking on more."

Still, the Wolfman could never shake the community's perception of him as a tad slow. And even though one of our basic teachings was "Don't hold someone to a place," many times we did just that. There is a wonderful picture in Peter Jenkins's book, *A Walk Across America*. It also appeared in *National Geographic*. A woman is struggling with a cultivator behind Belle, one of our Belgian mares, while wild-haired Jack rides the horse. They were taking turns at the tough job, but when the shutter shut, there was Jack, looking like he was goofing off.

Eventually Jack decided he wanted to be a mechanic. That put those of us on the Motor Pool crew into something of a bind. We were not great mechanics and were barely keeping our "fleet" of old beaters going, so the idea of letting the Wolfman loose with a tune-up or brake job just didn't seem like the one. Then it came to us—put Jack in charge of the tires, one of our biggest headaches. Wolfman the Tireman—he took to that gig like he had all others— tubes, tubeless, bicycles, wheelbarrows, he whipped them out on that antique manual tire changer over in the corner. And that was his job when CBS showed up—tire man.

Since Jack was working in the Motor Pool, the CBS trucks gave notice they would be parking there. This led to a massive cleanup. Dead cars got hauled to the back. The Welding Shed got straightened out. Junk transmissions were lined up in formation. The unlucky acres of middle Tennessee scrub oak that had become the Motor Pool were made to look as tidy as possible. Even the old tires got stacked, Jack's tires.

Cleaning up the Pool was one thing. Jack Wolf was another. Lee and David, The Farm's PR crew, swung into action. We were picky about our image, like one of the Third World countries we were intent on helping. We hated it when visiting press zeroed in on outhouses or sagging horse wagons. So Lee and David prepped Jack for two days, spin-doctoring every possible question he might get. Plus he got a makeover.

The day of his interview, Jack was transformed, almost unrecognizable. And somehow his hair had been, well, if not tamed, contained. That rasta mane was creme-rinsed, pulled back tight. A white cotton tunic shirt fit him perfectly. And new tennis shoes! Going through channels with the Petty Cash Lady could be a tedious trip, but now, magically, Jack had new shoes without even asking.

When he showed up that morning, we couldn't help staring at this new scrubbed Wolfman. We knew we shouldn't, but we couldn't help ourselves. Then he went into the studio van to answer Dan Rather's questions. Lee and David were left outside with the rest of us where we paced like expectant fathers, wondering what he was saying, hoping it wasn't a bunch of inappropriate "y'alls."

Only on viewing 60 Minutes months later did we hear this exchange:

Rather: So, Jack, how does your life on The Farm compare to what you were doing before you lived here?

Jack: Well, back in San Francisco I was mostly just going door to door saying I was the prophet Ezekiel.

When they came out of the van, Dan Rather began looking around for some "exteriors." He approached us. "Boys, when we drove in here yesterday, a group was pushing that bus in here." He nodded to an engineless International Harvester school bus. It was true, the cry of "MONKEYS" had gone up just as the CBS crew was pulling in. Fifteen or so of us had "hy-aed" the bus into the open-ended garage. We remembered. We eyed each other and scuffed the dust with our sneakers. We knew what he was getting at, a major Farm taboo.

Dan Rather, even though he was a well-known newsman, was at this time by no means the celebrity he is now. Walter Cronkite was the network star, and in all fairness, if Uncle Walter had been there asking us to push a bus, we likely would have done it.

"So that would make a great shot, you guys pushing the bus in here again," Rather said. "Let's see, Jim. What do you think of setting up over there by the tires, and . . ." Somebody had to say it, but nobody wanted to.

"We don't pose," I said, hoping that was enough. We had good agreement on that one—if some reporter or film crew saw you doing something and shot you, fine. But if they said, "Now could you hold that tomato in your hand like you're really proud of it?"—well the answer was, "No." There was a definite loss of dignity there. Plus in this case it would be a bunch of work. We'd have to holler "MONKEYS" to push the bus back out in the yard, and then we'd have to uphill schlep it back. Rather was not used to hearing "No." He kept talking to his cameraman about the angle of the shot.

"We can't do that." I said it louder. "The bus is already in here where we need it, and . . ." I tried to think of a new way to say it, but couldn't. "We don't pose."

Dan Rather now understood perfectly, and he did not like it. "Boys," he said. "Now look. We're trying to show The Farm in the best light here, and this is a powerful image. It's cooperation, working together, the bending of backs. It'll stick with the viewer. I know it's a little extra work, but the shot is definitely worth it."

We all recognized he was making sense, but nobody wanted to be the one to say yes, even though if anybody had said, okay, we probably all would have done it because we all wanted to be on *60 Minutes* like the Wolfman. But here's the thing that stopped anybody from saying yes. Long after the CBS vans had pulled out, word would go up and down the roads, and maybe even get brought up at services, how so and so agreed to pose. And that's what made us hold fast—the fear.

So Rather threw a little fit there in the Motor Pool driveway telling us we were only hurting ourselves, but then he gradually got over it and called for Jack again. They wanted a shot and interview combo of Jack working.

We were prepared for that. It didn't seem right to just have Jack over in the corner patching a tube. Perhaps a bit of guilt was creeping in over holding him to a place of being incompetent. We'd arranged for the Wolfman to change the oil on a van that was over the pit. Jack had been rehearsed on oil changes, and a fairly clean pair of coveralls had been found for him.

Okay, okay you're saying, well, wasn't that posing? No. We had it all worked out, justified. The van DID need an oil change, and we HAD discussed giving Jack some small mechanical jobs which he was always asking about, so NO, it wasn't posing, even though it's true Jack would have had a hard time getting use of the pit on his own.

So they all climbed down in the pit—the Wolfman, Dan Rather, the camera and light guy. The sound man stayed up on the floor holding the boom mike while Jack began undoing the oil drain plug. It actually went quite well. No, hot oil did not spill all over Rather. Jack caught it in the bucket like a pro. The filter change went okay as well, Jack answering Rather's little easy-toss questions about life on The Farm as he did it.

But then as Jack was tightening the oil plug, Rather tried to slip in a fast one as a good interviewer often does. "Jack," he said in a slightly different tone of voice, as if this were a new, serious side to the conversation. "Jack. We've seen you on Haight Street. You followed Stephen and the buses out here to Tennessee, The Farm. You've worked in the fields, now you're working on vehicles, but Jack . . . " Instead of locking eyes with him, the Wolfman kept on working with the oil plug, making Rather repeat his name. "Jack . . . is there anything different you would have done with your life if you could do things all over again?"

"Well," Jack said, giving the underside of the van a last look with the drop light, "I guess there is."

Rather looked so excited I felt happy for him, while at the same time I was worried about the answer, which the Wolfman was in no hurry to produce. "What, Jack? What would you change if you could?"

The Wolfman turned to Dan Rather and drawled with his new-found down-homeness. "I reckon I wish I would have taken auto shop back in high school." The heightened color that had filled Rather's face drained like the oil from the van. End of interview. A wrap. Into the vans they all went and out the Gate, and, to their credit, they ran the pit interview uncut.

Jack Wolf is now a family practice physician in North Carolina, or, as he says, "a snot and piss man."

Rupert Fike

Cowboys and Indians

As a child, I was always the youngest kid in my crowd. My birthday was late enough in the year that I just made the cut-off date for school, so all the kids in my class were older than me. The older crowd was the Lloyd brothers and Oakley. Oakley was a tall redhead with a fiery temper and hyperactive tendencies. The Lloyd brothers were as close to a Farm version of the Mafia as I could imagine. The ringleader was Tony, the middle brother. Tony was tall, handsome, and very personable. His younger brother Nicky was Tony's shadow. Nicky was close to my age, and we were chums. The oldest brother Jed was the shy and quiet one of the group. All of these boys provided me with a lot of my early information as a youth, information on important stuff like sports, school, break-dancing, and things of less significance, like girls.

One day as the gang and I were walking down Second Road, Tony said, "Let's play cowboys and Indians." The site of the festivities was the yard behind the Lloyd brothers' house, next door to the Adobe, where I lived. We descended the hill behind the Lloyd's to the site of the war-to-be. There was a creek nearby which provided us with fresh water to drink and to play with. We would take our socks and shoes off and wade nimbly like elves in the creek, trying not to step on the magnitudes of black-speckled snails dotting the creek bottom. Invariably we'd end up getting wet, so Nick and I quickly built a fire. This was the first of several rituals that were part of our usual playtime routine. It was taboo on The Farm for kids to make fires, and we felt like grownups by lighting a small fire to dry our clothes next to.

Next, we would find creek rocks and paint each other in "Indian war paint." Only the "Indians" would be painted. Creek rocks were composites of mud, chert, and other materials that had settled down into the creek eons ago. We used them as an abrasive against larger rocks to make paint. By grinding the two rocks together, the softer creek rocks would leave a powder called a streak. When added to water, this powder would make perfect face paint.

After the war painting was done, we'd get down to it. We would start off slowly with games of hide-and-seek and a game called freezetag. Freezetag was a variation of tag—you're it, using teamwork as a part of the game by the people who were not IT. Then we would begin the motions of chasing each other through our jungle. Cowboys chasing Indians, Indians hiding and retreating, and then an all-out front of Indians chasing cowboys, etc. Lunging and running and laughing hysterically, we all had a wonderful time.

TV wasn't very accessible to us back then, so this sort of play was our entertainment. Not having TV meant that you were either going to be bored off your butt or very creative. We were rebellious, so we were not going to be sitting on our butts. Living in rebellion as a young child meant doing things your parents would not have completely agreed to. They were very concerned about us being drawn into violent play, getting toy guns and stuff. But, heck, we were just typical kids. We were fascinated by heavy artillery. There's a fine line between being naughty and being creative. We were being creative.

We knew our parents wouldn't let us buy toy guns at Wal-Mart or even squirt guns at Krogers. So we built our own AK-47s and rocket launchers. Hidden out behind the Lloyd's woodpile was a collection of handmade toy weapons ranging from Huck Finn-style slingshots, to dart and blow guns, to PVC pipe rocket and missile launchers. We had it all. Our parents would have put us on kitchen duty for years if they had seen all this stuff. Any other kid in any other neighborhood would have been jealous of the artillery à la Farm kids.

Our parents didn't need to worry—we were really pacifists at heart; we just had a lot of creative energy and nothing else to do out in the woods. To us, these toys were more than just instruments of war. They were for survival as well. They represented homemade tools with thousand of uses such as walking sticks, garden and weeding tools, back-scratching devices, and many more. We could have written a book, 1001 Uses for Scrap Lumber and Old Moldy PVC Pipe. And we had unspoken rules about not hurting each other with these creative tools. No pain, no explanation to somebody's mom. No feelings hurt. No egos unleashed. We passed down these rules of conduct from one "generation" of kids to the next. That's how we got started with the face paint. It was something an older kid showed us that had probably been shown to him. I know I'm going to show my kids my method of war painting.

As an adult, I reflect back to these games as my earliest battles of young adulthood: how to have fun and not get lost in violence and ego. When I say we didn't need weapons, that is precisely what I meant. We were not out to hurt each other. We were out to feed off each other's energy and to learn from each other. Violence to us was just not an option. We knew what it was and looked down upon it as not the direction we wanted to head in. Being violent, to me, meant being out of control. And being out of control meant you didn't earn your war paint.

John Schweri

Birthing the Bronx Center

In the heady days of the mid-1970s, we figured we could move out and change the world just by starting various Farm "centers," being "cool," and initiating needed projects in our new communities, rural or urban. Our nonprofit relief organization, Plenty, was getting out with projects all over the globe, so when a couple moved to The Farm and turned over their assets, which included a house in Alexandria, Virginia, it became clear that this was going to be our "embassy."

Precisely at the same time, it was becoming apparent that I would have to decide between trucking and staying married, so I chose to stay married. Anyway, the agreement among us trucker guys was getting a little stale after so many years, and my wife Tish was having her ups and downs too as she tried to cope with having her small health food business absorbed into the bigger game plan of Farm Foods. All the signs were saying it was time to move on. Not that we wanted to leave the larger community, but the thought of staying on The Farm proper wasn't that attractive to us, so we opted to move to the new D. C. Center. Tish was pregnant with our third child at the time, which meant we could only stay in Alexandria a few months (in the living room) before heading on up to the Bronx Center where there was more of a medical scene and a midwife.

The Farm's Bronx Center came about after we read some newspaper accounts and saw a TV show about how the Bronx was burning and hopelessly bombed out. It had the worst health care in the nation, the fewest doctors, nonexistent emergency services, etc. It was truly a Third World country in the middle of the richest city on the planet—exactly what we were looking for—the perfect place to begin a free ambulance service for the community.

There was, at that time, a movement called "sweat equity," whereby you could work on a trashed-out abandoned building and build up equity in it. By the time Tish and I arrived, there were already twenty-five or so Farm people living in a small four-story building. Since there was zero rent, only a few guys needed to actually hold down jobs to support everyone, which meant the rest of us could spend the day fixing up "our" building and cruising around the South Bronx looking for stuff in abandoned factories and warehouses. Real urban scrapping.

It wasn't long before we realized we needed a bigger building. We took a liking to one down the street that was much larger than ours and in better shape, except for the cast iron drain pipes that had been scammed out of it. Plus it had a rotted-out section on the roof.

Fine, it was ours. We bought some new drain pipe and ran it up the building. To fix the roof, we did something that amazes me still. We went up to the roof of the adjacent building (also abandoned), and cut out the part of that roof that would repair "ours." Then it was down the steps and up our steps next door and presto-chango, a solid roof. Anyone from New York City knows how beautifully made those old Bronx apartment buildings are, with fine tile foyers and elevators. But let me tell you, it doesn't stop there. Those rafters were 4 x 12 heart pine, twenty-four feet long! And here go these hippies, moving them from one building to the next right in the middle of America's war zone. The police station known as Fort Apache was only a few blocks away.

About a week later, this guy in a snappy suit walks up and says he's the city councilman for that district, and what were we doing with that building of "his" next door? Turns out he had his own designs for that place, seeing as it was right across from Crotona Park and all. He made a deal with us that if we laid off his building, he'd help make our "acquisition" of the building we were already in "official."

The Bronx was very tough, incredibly so. People would park cars and vans right in front of our place and strip them for parts. You had a feeling that there was a lot of violence around us, but not too much in our little neighborhood. We somehow believed that we wouldn't be taken as just another bunch of "whiteys," and that did hold true. During the time Tish and I stayed there, the Plenty Ambulance Service had not yet started, but we were laying the groundwork. I think the neighborhood sensed something good was going to come from so many people working as one. Maybe it was because of the church across the street, I don't know.

On April 4 we had our baby right in our bedroom. It was a Sunday morning, and for the entire delivery it was as if peace had descended on the whole area. Everything went perfectly. Church bells rang out across the street at just the right moment. It was joyous.

Hustling a New York City birth certificate, though, was another matter. Carol, our midwife, had to get a doctor to sign for a birth he had not attended. It took a few tries, but she got it.

John Coate

It's All Relative

Sometimes great lessons come at the most unexpected times, in ways you never could have imagined. One of the teachings we held central to our spiritual path on The Farm was the idea of nonattachment. This was also expressed as nonpreference for any particular form. Praise and blame arise together. Sometimes your point of view can shift in an instant, and what was an extreme problem one moment may suddenly become a source of joy. To help people see things from a different perspective, we often talked about "getting relativity." This could involve anything from listening to someone else's point of view, to changing jobs, moving to a new house, or leaving The Farm for awhile. Sometimes relativity just sneaks up on you when you least expect it.

I was fortunate enough to be able to work with Plenty, The Farm's relief and development arm. While living on a "satellite farm" in Homestead, Florida, we decided to develop a project in Haiti. We were very aware of the situation there because of the large Haitian population living in and around Miami. We also realized that, as the crow flies, we were closer to Haiti than to The Farm back in Tennessee. I went to Haiti with my wife Margaret and our two children, five-year-old Christopher and two-and-a-half-year-old Emily. We were accompanied by another family, Michael and Mary and their two children, five-year-old Jeremy and two-year-old Dan. We were working with Mother Teresa's order, the Missionaries of Charity.

In the first phase of the project, we brought seeds and tools to put in a garden. This was expanded to include teaching soy technology. Back in Florida, we packed large kettles, grinders, beans, etc., and shipped them to Haiti for the second phase of the project. We all flew down to Port au Prince to meet the boat. However, when the boat docked, the supplies were not unloaded, and the boat set sail for another tour of the Caribbean.

As it turned out, this was not a problem. There was plenty of work to do. Margaret and Mary worked at the free clinic, and Michael and I worked at the Home for the Dying and Destitute. We would all take turns having one of the adults stay home, take care of the children, and cook while the others worked with the sisters.

We learned some Creole (the clinic basics—Esque ou gagne pici penicillin du foi? Have you a had a penicillin shot twice before?—daily greetings—Coma ou ye?—How are you? Pas pi mal—Not too bad, and basic commerce—Coca glace, si vous plait, cold Coke please). It was hot. We also learned some wonderful lessons.

One day Michael and I arrived at the Home for the Dying and Destitute and were greeted on the front walk by the ever jovial Sister Aba. She was from India and had been raised in a small rural village. She always had a big smile and a kind word. On this day her smile was larger than usual. She began to tell us about her morning, and as she started, she really cracked herself up. She was slapping her knees and laughing heartily as she told us the tale.

It seems something was wrong with the water system. The water in the city was only turned on for a few hours each day, and the sisters had a tank to store water in for the times in between. Running water was certainly a necessity for taking care of ninety or more truly sick people. Somehow, the water to the tank had not been refilled, and they were out of water. Sister Aba was in charge of the whole scene, and to her this was like a little personal joke from God. She was also delighted that we were there to help out, share the experience, and maybe have a good laugh too. I am not one to panic easily, but this would have normally brought out my more serious, concerned side. But the whole atmosphere from all of the sisters was so "Let's just do it" that we just jumped right in. It had rained that morning, and they had plugged the holes that normally drained the rainwater from the second-story balcony. So throughout the day we formed bucket brigades to haul down water for cleaning, flushing the toilets, etc. Eventually the plumbing was repaired and things returned to what we had now come to think of as normal. Sister Aba had really shown us the value of humor in the face of adversity.

After about a month, the boat returned with our supplies. With the sure-handed experience of the Sisters, we worked our way through customs and brought the equipment to the Home for the Dying and Destitute. The time we could afford to stay was nearing an end, the last pieces of the project were falling into place—then we hit a major hurdle.

First, Margaret and Mary came down with dengue fever (also called breakbone fever), a mosquito-born disease. It is characterized by an extremely high fever, fatigue, muscle aches, and loss of appetite. Then Michael came down with it also. This meant I had no time to do anything except take care of the children and three very sick adults. As they began to feel a little better, we decided the best course of action was to send everyone but myself back to the States, and I would move into the Home for the Dying and Destitute. That way I could be close to where I was working, and finish up the project.

We packed up everything and went to the airport. Michael was still very sick, and we had to prop him up until it was time to board the plane. When they were all safely aboard, I went back to the apartment and prepared to move the next day. I fixed myself a simple dinner of cooked canned beans and went to bed early.

About three o'clock in the morning I woke up. I wasn't sure why at first until I began to feel my head aching and my heart racing. My body had strong rushes all over, and I realized I was getting sick at a very rapid rate. Panic hit and my first thought was, "Oh no! I'm going

to be a patient at the Home instead of a worker." It didn't look good.

I had seen the others too weak to do almost anything for themselves, lying there with high fevers and headaches. I knew the Sisters would take care of me, but they certainly didn't need another patient to add to the ninety or so truly sick people they were already taking care of. I got up and went to the bathroom.

What happened next was pretty dramatic and very interesting. Without being too graphic, I'll just say I became much sicker and was throwing up and cramping hard. I was in Haiti alone, and there was a lot of physical discomfort. But it was at that moment that I became one of the happiest people alive. These were not the symptoms of dengue fever. I realized I probably had simple food poisoning and would be fine by the next afternoon. So there I was, sick as a dog, alone in a foreign country, and really, really grateful and happy. It's all relative.

Michael Cook

That's Just Art

Art was one of those "strays" that The Farm was forever taking in. He was sixty-ish and what we might today call borderline "homeless," though that designation hadn't really been in use back in the 1970s. Art came into our lives when some of us tried to start a Seattle Farm. We were renting a house north of Seattle in the Cascades near Skykomish—very beautiful. Kathleen ran into Art at the grocery store and struck up a conversation. She learned that he was living

in a trailer along a river. His friend Pearl had recently died and now he was alone.

It was pretty obvious his mind was drifting. There was a sort of spaced-out holiness about Art. He loved the radical-spiritual-revolutionary spirit of The Farm and easily threw in his meager belongings with ours when we gave up on living in Seattle and moved back to Tennessee.

Living in our community, Art had to make a few compromises. For instance, he didn't like to wear clothes, but since we couldn't handle that, he opted for the biggest, baggiest bib overalls he could find so that the cloth barely touched his skin.

Art was an eccentric whose major contribution to our household (because he did little else) was to repeatedly try to convince us of the brilliance of the sine curve. He would drag out a big piece of graph paper and lovingly draw the curve, but most of us had our heads into our self-important everyday struggles, and wouldn't (or couldn't) stop to conceptualize with him over this miracle of mathematical perfection.

Art also was obsessed with his potassium levels and the pH balance of his skin. I cannot shake the image of him walking in front of his trailer on Schoolhouse Ridge in those huge bib tops, bare arms, long gray hair and beard all covered with wood ashes. Because he was low on potassium, he needed to eat a lot of bananas. We were militant recyclers and composted everything we could, but since compost piles don't break down banana peels very well, Art would hang all of his banana peels from the limbs of the trees in his yard until they dried out enough to be composted. And as luck would have it, one of our visiting, very uptight mothers was driving down Schoolhouse Ridge and made a wrong turn into Art's driveway. She was treated to the sight of half-naked, sooty Art, hanging banana peels off the branches of a blackjack oak tree with the utmost care. "Oh, my God," she screamed, rolled up her windows, locked the doors, and put the car into reverse, never understanding our reaction of "Oh, that's just Art."

Joan Levin (McCabe)

How I Defended the State Constitution But Lost the Sprouts

When I first got to The Farm in the fall of 1972, one of the first jobs I had was handling the Supreme Court appeal of Stephen and three other men arrested for growing marijuana on the Martin Farm. After those appeals were exhausted The Farm once again had little use for a lawyer, so I worked at various jobs: horse-farmer, mason, scrap wrecker, flour miller, book salesman, typesetter, graphic artist, off-the-Farm day laborer, whatever came along.

In the late 1970s I found myself back before the Supreme Court for Plenty and the Catfish Alliance, fighting TVA's nuclear power plants. Then one day Stephen came to me with a letter he had received from the county registrar of voters which stated that his voter registration had been revoked and he needn't bother to re-apply.

Apparently there was a new Tennessee law stating that because of his felony conviction, Stephen was forever disenfranchised in the state. This law purged the rolls of more than 180,000 voters state-wide, and you didn't have to have broken a Tennessee law—an infraction in any state would do. The whole situation appeared to me to be retroactive, or "ex post facto," with the state placing an additional punishment on top of what the courts had applied. However, a challenge had already been brought against Tennessee in federal court testing this issue, Collins v. State, and the state won, mainly because federal doctrine says that state regulation of the ballot box is not punitive, just good government.

The Collins case seemed at first glance to doom Stephen's constitutional claim, but never say never. In the state archives I found a little known section about voting rights in the state charter enacted in 1870, when Tennessee was a military-occupied zone and the Union Party elected all officials. Anyone who had served in the Army of the South or had voted during secession had been stripped of their vote after the war. A constitutional convention was called and the delegates, many of them disenfranchisees, inserted a clause that read, "The right of suffrage . . . shall never be denied to any person entitled thereto, except upon a conviction by a jury of some infamous crime, previously ascertained and declared by law." Normally, the phrase "previously ascertained and declared by law" would have given the state a way to say, "Well, we've just decided to pass a law adding a punishment to your sentence—you lose." But because of what had been done to Civil War soldiers, the law had a special meaning. The U.S government retroactively disenfranchised Confederate soldiers and the soldiers, in amending the state constitution, said in effect, "Never again!" We had our case.

When the day came for arguments at the state supreme court, my biggest problem was getting to Nashville. Stephen, who always had a car, was away on a speaking tour. I had been given, or acquired, a succession of vehicles from outside donors for my anti-nuclear work, but their fate fit a pattern. When I was not using my car, it got dispatched to the community at large, and usually within a month it was totaled—hit a tree while someone was experimenting with hand controls for a paraplegic and the accelerator stuck; rolled down an embankment when the emergency brake was left off; the engine blew because no one checked the oil. The legal crew's current car was in the Motor Pool, waiting on parts. None of the rest of the crew was available to come with me, so I was on my own. I arranged for the use of another vehicle which was to be waiting for me at 8 a.m. at the Head of the Roads, ready to go to Nashville.

At 7:30 the next morning I had my "law suit" laid out: a nice denim, three-piece that Suzanne had made for court cases. I called it my Suit of Lights. My briefcase was packed, my arguments memorized. I had a few household chores still—rinse the sprouts, take out the compost and the recyclables—then I could go.

It was with the sprouts that the unimaginable happened, a "rapid disassembly" as they say in the nuclear trade. As I put the sprout jar back up on the drain rack, the rubber band holding the cheesecloth broke, spewing alfalfa sprouts all over the floor. Aaaaarg! Not only would there be no sprouts for the next few days (one of our major "condiments" for soybean tortillas), but now I had to clean up the mess. Plus take the time to start a new batch.

When I got to the Head of the Roads, panting, my suitbag over my shoulder, it was 8:15, and the car was gone. Whoever was next in line for it figured I didn't need it. I remember standing there and doing a "Farming Crew Salute." (The palm of the hand strikes the forehead in a brisk, curving, upward motion, like "I walked three miles to get to this field and forgot my hoe.")

I lucked out and caught a ride to the Gate, arriving by 8:25, ninety-five minutes before court began, which was seventy-five miles away. I had at most twenty minutes to find a fast ride, but hey, here came two guys from The Farm Ambulance crew on their way to work with the neonatal emergency team at Vanderbilt Hospital in Nashville. While we drove, I put on my suit. The crew dropped me off on the sidewalk outside the Supreme Court building with fifteen minutes to spare. They knew how to drive.

Inside, there was my name on the printed docket, first in the line of oral arguments. In some of our other cases I had had a full support crew, the Farm Band bus, printed news releases, press conference on the steps, radio techs scanning the news crews and police frequencies to get a feel for the city, not to mention a gallery full of tie-dyed supporters. This day was much different, and even though I was just as happy to play this case low-key, it had become an inescapable fact that the halcyon days of our youthful exuberance were past. The rest of our legal crew was out tree-planting to make the basic budget. I didn't even have lunch money.

I took my seat at the appellee table where usually there would be several lawyers seated, perhaps some paralegals directly behind with boxes of papers. I opened my briefcase and removed the slim appellate briefs. A black man dressed in a white waiter's jacket entered, said "All rise," and the five elderly white male justices in black robes filed in and took their seats. The black man presented a large ledger for each justice to sign, walking from one to another in order of seniority. Then he took up his position by the door of the chambers, and the senior justice called for the first case. "Gaskin versus State," the clerk announced.

The attorney general arose from a group of several men in black suits seated at the appellant's table and moved to the podium. Amazingly, it sounded to me like the state really had no serious argument, apart from an emotional one asserting that prisoners, being undesirable characters, should not be allowed to vote. But—it ain't over 'til the fat justice sings.

When I got my turn I gave the justices an analogy. "Suppose Mr. Gaskin had been a bugler boy in the Confederate Army," I said. "Here he is in 1980, 126 years old, and the state legislature, in its infinite wisdom, decides to once more punish Confederates by removing their vote. How is that circumstance any different, in a constitutional sense, than what the legislature has just done in stigmatizing all felons? If the crime did not carry disenfranchisement as a penalty 'previously ascertained and declared by law,' it cannot have it imposed later."

We won a unanimous decision, and afterwards I told friends I could barely believe I had won a case by wrapping myself in a Confederate flag and whistling "Dixie." It was the first time that part of the state constitution had been challenged in more than a century, and later the inmates of the state penitentiary invited me out for an award ceremony and presented me with a plaque as a token of their appreciation. Over the years more than a quarter of a million Tennesseans have had their voting rights restored by that decision.

But that afternoon as I rode home with the ambulance crew, my exhilaration soon gave way to concerns over how I would face the folks in my household and explain why there were no sprouts for dinner. They really wouldn't care about what had happened in Nashville. What would matter is that I blew the sprouts.

Albert Bates

Visiting

I visited The Farm during a low point of my life in that I was drinking heavily, not being a good husband. If you were charitable about all that, you could say I was grieving for my lost youth or something, but for whatever reason I was in a messed-up place. A good friend of mine had visited earlier that summer and came back to Montgomery pretty enthusiastic about his experience, so I just took off one day, didn't say where I was going, and in about four hours I was there.

Immediately at the Gatehouse I saw that this place was totally different from what I expected, which was a free, no-rules Woodstock without the music scene. I recall two immediate run-ins with the Gate man—one, he smelled beer on my breath, and being a smartass I offered him some, and he said, really, you've got some beer? So I took him over to my truck and opened my cooler, and he said we were either going to have to pour it all out, or I was going to have to turn around right there and leave. In a way I was happy to get rid of it, and while I was doing that we started talking and it came up I was married. "Where's your wife," he wanted to know. I mumbled something about we were having difficulties, expecting such an admission to put an end to it, but oh no, he wanted to know more. Then he was telling me I needed to get straight with my lady, so I went in the Gatehouse and called home. I must have answered that question about where my wife was ten times in the two days I was on The Farm.

I spent a good bit of the afternoon up on the porch of the Gatehouse talking to various Farm people. Some were real friendly, others were more probing and serious. There was one guy running around in and out of the doors, talking real loud and acting crazy. At first I thought he was part of the Gate crew, but just kind of eccentric. Then someone told me that he was a "tripper," which I took to mean he was actually tripping on LSD or something because that would have explained his behavior. Later I caught on that the term meant somebody who was on their own uncontrollable trip. He was from some mental hospital I think. Everybody knew his name.

There were a couple of other visitors who came in right after me. The Gateman said they had attitudes. By that time I was kind of quiet because I'd gotten up early, had drunk a few beers on the drive, and now I had a headache. But I think they figured I was mellow, so later on I was allowed to go down to the Visitors' Tent, while the people who came in after me had to stay up there and talk some more.

It was quite an eye-opener to see the amount of activity going on in this place as we rode down the road—a lot more vehicles and big trucks than I had imagined. Lots of dust too. But what sticks in my mind were mothers pulling their kids and babies along the road in little wagons with wooden sides. I don't know why, but that just really made me feel I was in some other kind of place. That night at the Visitors' Tent the host couple talked to everybody some more about how this wasn't a commune; it was a spiritual community. I heard that quite a bit. After that, I went out for a walk and talked to some other people on the road. I saw that some people on The Farm were really together, while others, I don't know, you could tell they were somehow faking it. They were just trying to fit in, a bit like I had done up at the Gate. I don't know if it was from answering all those questions about myself and my marriage or what, but that night I woke up and couldn't go back to sleep thinking about my wife and home.

The next morning after breakfast, this guy came by and asked me if I wanted to work on the garbage and compost detail. Everybody else was going out in the fields, which, being from the South, didn't seem too exotic to me, so I said sure and hopped on the back of this flatbed truck with all these fifty-five-gallon drums. This worked out well because I got a complete tour of The Farm, going to places most visitors never saw—all the roads, workplaces, even out to Stephen's. Then we hit the bakery right as some sweet rolls were coming out. I think the driver had that one pegged. We stayed there for a while. Everybody at the bakery and flour mill were really together and nice.

At lunch I found out that this was an "All-Farm Day." That meant everybody, no excuses unless it was really important (like trash pickup) had to go out in the fields on this particular day and pick or hoe or whatever. I talked to one woman at lunch who was kind of resentful about having to go hoe because she was in the middle of trying to set up this soybean lab to make vegeburgers or something. Again at lunch I saw some very bright-eyed, articulate people along with some others who seemed kind of spaced, not totally into it.

I ended up switching jobs at lunch because this other guy needed help, and the trash truck driver said he was through with me. So I got on a half school bus-half tank truck that went around and pumped out outhouses. He gave me gloves and these big yellow slicker coveralls, and off we went. My job was to stick this big hose, say ten inches wide, down through the toilet seat while the driver ran the pump controls. He told me how to do it on our way to the first outhouse, and I was envisioning, you know, having to push the hose way down there, but when I opened the lid, it was like a mountain of shit, with a peak almost sticking up to the level of the seat. I was totally mind-blown, but the driver said they were all like that, and that's why he didn't have to go out on All-Farm Day. The trick was to not just stick the hose totally down into it, you had to angle the opening so it was sucking air along with the poop. The smell wasn't as bad as you might think, but it wasn't the greatest. I asked him what did he do with a full tank of excrement, and it somehow surprised me when he said he drove it into town and unloaded it at a sewage treatment plant. I don't know what I expected, maybe something alternative, but I guess there is no such thing.

We did two outhouses, which he said was pretty good for an afternoon, and all the while I was answering his questions about why I'd run out on my "lady." I kept saying I hadn't run out on her, I was just kind of having an unscheduled vacation. I remember he started telling me about when guys on The Farm were mean or whatever to their "ladies," they'd sometimes get

sent out on "thirty-dayers," which was just that—thirty days off The Farm so you'd appreciate it and your "lady" when you came back. Relativity, he called it, which I thought made it sound like they were trying to talk like Einstein. I didn't understand the concept. I do now, but not then.

Anyway, as we were hosing off, then going to the showers, I saw that what I was doing was a thirty-dayer in reverse—I'd come to The Farm, saw how cushy my life was back in Montgomery, and wanted to go back. Which is what I did, and I'm not saying my wife and I never had any problems after that, because we did. But going to The Farm, for me, was definitely "relativity" in many ways.

John from Montgomery, Alabama

I Had Serious Regrets Then

I was in charge of many of the on-the-Farm construction projects, so I'd get people sent to me from the Gate to work on my crew. Some of these people would be spaced-out ex-mental patients, people with emotional problems or on medications, guys who'd come with their ladies to have a baby so they were kind of preoccupied. Sometimes this all worked out surprisingly well, but always it was quite a challenge.

Anyway, this really sweet guy, Thomas, got sent down to me one day. He was nice, well-mannered, just a bit disoriented. But he stuck around and gradually became a help, very cooperative but a little lost.

Thomas and I ended up getting along well, and he worked with me for over a year. During this time, I got married to Mary who had two children already, so it was like instant family. Since Thomas began hanging out more and more with us, he became a bit like extended family.

He left The Farm for a while, and when he came back he joined my crew again, but he'd returned with an inheritance of thousands of dollars, which he turned straight over to the bank as per the agreement. Very soon after that, Mary and I decided to leave The Farm, then in a month or so I heard that Thomas had left too.

I had serious regrets then, because here was this guy who was emotionally very vulnerable. Not that I'd urged him to throw in his inheritance, because I didn't even know he had it, but I really felt like some of the reason he made that commitment was his looking at Mary and me and our new family in a bonding sort of way. Perhaps he felt a sense of family or was even hoping, like I had once hoped, that he might get married and have a family too. I still have bad feelings about that whole thing, Thomas taking probably the only sizeable chunk of cash he'd ever see, throwing it in the pot, then leaving with nothing. We wrote for a while, then lost touch. I just hope Thomas is okay.

Henry Goodman

Drafted Onto the Construction Crew

When I came to The Farm, I'd just lived in Canada where I'd built a log house, so I was excited about the possibility of doing that in Tennessee. About a month later, Stephen said at Sunday Services that he thought I should go ahead and do it, so that was a green light to go ahead. I'd been working with Eddy on the wood crew, and he knew a lot about the Southern woods, so Eddy and I went way out in the forest to carefully select and cut maybe a hundred nice logs for the house. Then we snaked them out and were getting very excited about doing it until one day at lunch while we were describing the area where we'd cut them, someone informed us that those trees we'd logged were not on The Farm's land. We'd made a pretty bad mistake and taken some quite impressive oak and hickory off a neighbor's property. This temporarily put a stop to the log house business. All of a sudden our new job was to go "get straight" with the neighbor. Fortunately, this turned out pretty well because they were absentee landlords and were pretty gracious about the whole thing.

Once we got the okay to use the logs, we hauled them to the site, but Eddy had gone back to firewood cutting, so there I was, me and the logs. I had no crew and no truck. I did have a chainsaw I'd brought from Canada, but I didn't have any gas for it or money. I wasn't experienced in pulling strings in the community, so I was just walking around all day, telling my story of how I needed this and that. Ultimately, it drew enough attention to me that I got drafted onto the Construction Crew.

I started out on the Dogwood House, where I was the straw boss to a crew of guys, some of whom were on medications or just out of jail. Luckily I'd been working the year before at a school for juvenile delinquents, so I took the four fairly competent Farm members I had and formed subcrews with them as minichiefs, the same system I'd used at the school.

Unfortunately, there was no electricity at all on the site, so everyday here's all these dull handsaws going back and forth, ten minutes to cut a 2 x 4, stuff like that. My attitude was, whatever, I'll try to make this work, but the other crew bosses were saying, I can't believe you're not absolutely losing it. Somehow we persevered and got the house dried in.

Later on I was helping build The Farm's school with pretty much the same kind of crew. By then I was pretty proud of what we could accomplish so I volunteered us to shingle part of the roof. I was very careful, getting everyone to snap off a lot of chalk lines while I kept going over how to keep the roofing straight.

I went down the ladder and made the mistake of talking with somebody for just a few minutes, not long at all. But as I was talking, I got this sudden feeling that something had gone wrong so I went back up the ladder. It was unbelievable how crooked all those shingles were. Just going everywhere. We had to carefully pry them all off and start over again. In the end the school's roof came out fine, no leaks.

Henry Goodman

Battle of Tullahoma

Ed.: *This story is quite atypical of the community's policy of "complete satisfaction guaranteed" on all jobs done off The Farm. Underbid projects were dutifully completed. Mistakes were made right, even if it meant jackhammering up a new slab or agreeing to supplying thirty pepper pickers for a month. This all stemmed from Stephen's insistence that each interaction with neighbors had to be clean, righteous. The Farm's survival depended on it. Sometimes at Services he would break into a neighborly Southern drawl to illustrate the point: "Yeah, there used to be some hippies lived up there, . . . they didn't stay too long. There wasn't much to 'em." This was not a laugh line.*

Each work crew on The Farm developed its own personality. The Farming Crew was huge, supremely committed, and grounded. The Clinic Ladies and Midwives dealt with life and death, so they often had the last word on things. The off-the-Farm crews were a heroic, moral force, footing the bill for our basic needs. The Motor Pool and Truckers, as the following story illustrates, were sometimes "out there."

John—After a few years of asking the Bank Lady for all our parts money, the Motor Pool crew realized that there was ready cash to be had by "surface mining" the surrounding area for scrap metal and hauling it to yards like S & S Steel in Columbia or Denbo's in Pulaski, an operation that specialized in buying whole junk cars.

We were in the right place at the right time—the surrounding counties had hundreds and hundreds of wrecked cars laying in fields or front yards in every nook and holler. Up in Hickman County we found pastures that had twenty or more cars for as little as two bucks a car. "Crashed ever' one muhseff," one owner proclaimed, his thumb hooked proudly in his overalls strap.

I was from California, so Tennessee was already a foreign land to me, but Hickman County seemed almost otherworldly. As we drove up those winding, two-lane roads each morning into the hill country through a morning ground fog, it felt like our little caravan of pickup, boom truck, and flatbed was entering a kind of mythic place removed from the pace of the surrounding country. Mostly there were two last names wherever you went—Tidwell and Barnwell. And there really is a Grinder's Switch, although Cousin Minnie Pearl was actually from Centerville, the county seat. Once, while so far back in the woods I didn't think anyone lived further out, a small gentleman in overalls came walking out of the brush while I was hooking up the boomer cable to an old wreck. I was startled but recovered enough to ask him how he was doing. "I ain't no 'count," he said and headed off through the next thicket down a barely discernable trail.

After a year or so we had pretty much mined out the local counties for cars. We branched out our scouting operations, but other people had had the same idea, and the pickings all over were becoming quite slim. This led us to Tullahoma.

Paul—Gary had gotten himself busted (fired) from the Book Company sales force, so he joined our scrapping crew. Somehow he talked his way into being finder and negotiator for the scrap metal deals we were always after. So Gary found this old junkyard in Tullahoma and made an incredibly awful deal. He estimated it would only take about a week to ten days to scrap fifty cars, then move hundreds of tons of springs and tires.

The first morning there, DD and I stood on the hood of a junk car surveying about five acres of junk cars and tires and old seat springs. "Let me get this right," DD said. "We get fifty cars for hauling out that monumental mountain of springs and tires?" I didn't answer. We just looked at it. It was too late to back out. The rest of the crew was pulling in with a kitchen bus, boom truck, semi with car carrier trailer, and an ancient wrecker. Several of our wives had come along because we were camping out. It was seventy miles back to The Farm, too far to commute.

The next day we got to work pulling out the heaviest cars with the most metal. We needed to get as many as we could on the car trailer for the eighty-mile trip down to Birmingham. Plus we needed to make the load as flat as possible to make it under the low bridges. Our method of crushing the cars was simplicity itself. We'd take "Old Yeller," our boom truck that had an enormous hunk of counterweight steel as a front bumper, drive it about fifty yards up the road, turn around, floor it, and ram smack into the cars which we'd positioned on their sides. Then we loaded them up, six or eight to a load.

After booming the load down, a couple of us would drive it down to Alabama, always an exciting trip. The way to approach a low bridge was to go at it full speed and let the bridge flatten out the load, stopping on the other side to retighten the chains. I don't believe we ever actually got stuck under a bridge, but we certainly left some hefty dings in them, and on one occasion blew out some tires. While the semi was off to Birmingham, the crew would be readying the next load. When the truck got back at the end of the day, it was met by The Farm bank crew who would take the money back to the community less what we needed for the next run's expenses.

We had been there maybe five days when the police came roaring into our camp and arrested DD as a prime suspect in a bank robbery that had happened in Tullahoma. DD was taken in, "identified" by a witness (all men with ponytails looked alike in 1975) and thrown in jail. He sat in the poky for about six hours before they realized he was the wrong guy.

Meanwhile, it was taking us a good two weeks to prep and haul the fifty cars we wanted and get all the scrap money we were going to get. This was like eating dessert first because we still had to deal with that awesome mountain of tires and springs. We wasted a few days trying to haul out part of it, except nobody wanted that kind of junk—it had no value. So there we were, no capital to run on, having given it all to the Bank Ladies, and ahead of us a task that looked like it would take about a year to complete.

What to do with the mountain? Burn it, we decided. We waited till around midnight, took some gasoline, and set the tires ablaze. We stood around all night, and by morning we came to the sad realization that it would take days and days to burn at the rate it was going. The sun was just rising over the hills, and we're looking at a huge column of black, greasy smoke rising up and disappearing over the hill in the direction of Tullahoma.

As we were watching this monstrous thing we had created, we heard something faint, and then growing louder. It was the sound of sirens. Minutes later, all of Tullahoma's half-dozen police cars and two fire engines showed up and they were MAD. We we're guilty of so much—illegal operation, no fire permits, endangering the community. Jose and I were arrested, thrown in this sergeant's car, and driven off towards town in handcuffs.

Cresting the hill that overlooks what should have been the sight of Tullahoma, all we saw was this thick, thick blanket of smoke that had settled over the whole town. Driving down into it was like driving into dusk, soot everywhere—in the air, settling on cars, schools, churches, soot, soot, soot. The chief of police was very angry, as was almost everybody else in town. They locked us up. For our own protection, they said. Lest the town come to lynch us. After a few hours, Jose and I were let out, taken back to the junkyard, and told to "get out of town, pronto."

Luckily it was a Friday, so we were already pretty well packed up to head home for the weekend. The junk pile owner was concerned that we wouldn't just skip off after scrapping out our fifty cars and leave behind the very mountain of crapola he wanted rid of in the first place. So to allay those fears, we left behind our '49 Ford wrecker and Bo Diddly, a strapping eighteen-year-old. Bo snuck out just after midnight.

Paul Heavens, John Coate

The More You're Committed, the More You're Needed

Board Minutes November 30, 1977

(As published in an internal Farm newsletter—"Amazing Tales of Real Life")

At the beginning of the meeting the Board chose two new members and a new secretary. Susan will be the Ladies Director of Personnel. Jeffrey will help represent the Clinic in rotation with a soon-to-be-appointed Clinic Lady. I'm Patti Davidson, the new Secretary—Hi!

We reminded ourselves that those of us who sign checks must always remember that we have been given a two-fold responsibility: first, to the best of our knowledge of the total Farm situation, we spend money as wisely as possible and second, that we explain to any member of The Farm who wants to know, how we are spending the money and sorting out financial priorities. Lots of candid communication will help maintain friendly feelings about how we spend our bread. If anyone has any questions in this area, they can talk with Linda and Bruce who keep track of The Farm's financial situation.

In order to smarten up the bill business, Linda would like it if all of the bookkeepers would turn in their monthly financial statements to her earlier; within the first week of the following month if possible.

Speaking of friendly feelings, we ought to lay a bundle on Daniel when he knocks on our doors selling advance reservations for a week at the Visitors' Tent. Each of us has commitments, but the more you're committed, the more you're needed.

Flash! One thousand people toured The Farm this year as members of organized groups. We welcomed philosophy students, sociology students, nursing students, and high school students.

We're gonna keep on truckin' with Cherokee Trucking Company, at least until we find another way to cover the payments on the Mack and Kenworth. We've got four drivers now, and we'd like to hold that figure steady.

Stephen and Thomas hung out with us for about three hours. During lunch Paul M. put in a request for extra vehicles. He'll need them to haul Spiritual Midwifery books, beginning December 12. Stephen kicked off the campaign by offering his Ford wagon. How 'bout it out there? No one on The Farm is, after all, completely "auto-nomous."!

If there are any folks who can speak any other languages besides English and Farmese, give us a "howdy" or a "bon jour." Folks in other countries have been asking for translations of our books. Some of the translations we could use are in Spanish, French, German, Hebrew, and Swedish. The more books we can translate into different languages, the more teachings we can transmit to other nations. Don't say "au revoir" just because your French grammar ain't 98.8 percent pure.

The Board agreed to a set of Directors for Plenty in an official act necessitated by our impending contracts with AID and other such foundations and corporations. Official grant requests require a current list of directors. These were agreed on: Stephen, Minister Director; Peter, Program Director; Dennis and Mary, Field Directors; David and Michelle, Field Directors. Bruce and Richard were chosen Resident agents for the Foundation and Plenty, respectively.

Paul M. discussed ways and means of transporting Stephen's family and himself to and from Australia. These expenses are being fronted out by folks in Australia. These include: ex-Deputy Prime Minister Jim Karnes along with members of the House of Parliament; our connection with the Down-To-Earth-Festival; officials of the Nambassa Festival; and Mr. Stuart Oldale, an Australian book distributor, who wants to sell our books. Paul will be working a booth the entire week of the Down-To-Earth-Festival. This way he can also transform into a temporary office for Stephen while he trips around Australia. Paul said that it was almost embarrassing to able to go to Australia.

Don't dig any holes without checking with Paul F. or William first. Otherwise, you might get yourself deeper into hot water than you had bargained for by damaging buried plumbing installations.

The Phone Ladies need a cassette tape recorder in order to transmit All-Points Bulletins. Fewer folks seem to be showing up for Canning parties and other boogies when there's no bulletin.

"Casa Construction" is cropping up all over The Farm. We're going to replace many of our canvas roofs with tin ones. There is more housing being built than ever before, and we're all thankful that we're covering it as well as we are.

Before you jump on the Greyhound to deck your parents' halls with holly, please make every effort to make sure your gig will be well covered while you're gone. Many people will celebrate the holidays on The Farm. The astral and the material planes should be kept mellow for them during this special time of year.

The Motor Pool could use some more apprentice mechanics. High Gear is in gear, but could use more trained personnel.

Want to get in on some Board action? If you would like to observe a meeting, contact me at the Ark. I have attended only one Board meeting so far. It definitely expanded my perspective as well as my consciousness.

Lovingly submitted,

Patti Davidson

Honoring Our Dead at the Burial Ground

A young woman of twenty-two, born and raised on The Farm, talked about Patti Davidson, a blind woman who lived with us for a number of years. Melina had lived with Patti for awhile and remembered how, when she was about six, she had asked Patti what it was like to be blind. They were feeling objects together, Melina keeping her eyes closed and focusing on her sense of touch.

"Being blind must be like keeping your eyes closed all the time," Melina said.

"No," said Patti. "It's more like keeping your eyes open all the time but looking at the back of your head."

Melina said this really made her think and got her inside Patti's consciousness.

Ina May pointed out how brave Patti had been to come out here and live with large households in unfinished homes with rough yards and outhouses. Blind people usually try to live in a controlled and familiar environment without too many other people. Patti had to educate large households about how to be with a blind person, how they couldn't set things down in the normal paths of movement around the house and yard.

Patti got caught in the Change-over of The Farm, when our economy changed from communal to private, and many people left, and there wasn't enough energy going around to keep a loving blanket of protection around her. She became depressed, and on one sad day took her own life. At her funeral out here, her mother said Patti had been depressed before coming to The Farm, and that living with us had probably extended her life by several years.

Michael Traugot

The Yellow Canary

Around 1973 or so, Virginia and I decided to move out to the "suburbs" of The Farm. So we cranked up our still-running bus and simply drove out to the end of Third and a Half Road, the Right Fork. There we lived with the rattlers, panthers, and other wild animals. Bradford and Margaret lived even further out Third and a Half in their bus, and past them was just miles and miles of woods, the Big Swan Creek, then more woods.

It was quite secluded and beautiful, but it was also a logistical challenge, being so far from "town." Luckily though, we had a red wagon given as a Christmas toy to our kids from their grandparents. For us it was far from a toy. It became our utility vehicle, hauling everything—laundry, groceries, kids, propane tanks. Often we loaded kids and groceries both on the wagon for the trip back home from the store.

One day Virginia was hauling two-year-old Eugene, one of "the seven hundred snot-nosed kids of The Farm," as Ken Kesey called them. She was also bringing home the oil, soybeans, and flour from the store. Winter was just over so the ruts in the road were particularly deep, muddy, and tricky, which meant you had to really pay attention and keep the wagon on the high ground between the tracks. But on a turn where the tire ruts widened, the high road narrowed, and there went first one wheel, then the next wheel, then the whole wagon, Eugene and all—into the mud.

Precious flour and soybeans went everywhere, and although Eugene wasn't hurt since it happened in slow motion, he did end up covered with flour and mud. Most of our groceries were ruined. At first Virginia wanted to cry, but it was just too funny, so she sat on a dry rut, held Eugene, and laughed, getting flour and mud all over herself too.

This particular episode, though comical, underscored to me the need for our little neighborhood at the end of Third and a Half to have some kind of shared vehicle for store, firewood, batteries, laundry runs, etc. Since I worked in the Motor Pool, I started trying to scam together old clunker trucks so the little red wagons could go back to being toys instead of our lifeline.

There was this one particularly funny-looking truck which we immediately called the Yellow Canary when it came in to The Farm. It was perfect because since it didn't start very well, the Canary had pretty quickly gotten a bad name for itself. No one wanted anything to do with it. I figured it would be a prime hauler for the Third Road crowd. To us it was a good little truck with a six-cylinder flathead engine like the one in my '42 Dodge bus. It didn't use much gas and had a high ground clearance, perfect for the back road ruts. The starting problem stemmed from its six-volt battery which usually just went, "wah, wah, click," but we started it by rolling it down a hill and popping the clutch. I used it often and it was greatly appreciated by our neighborhood.

The demise of the Yellow Canary came one afternoon when Jose, the straw boss of the metal scraping crew, was loading up a run. He began looking hungrily at the truck which had been sitting for a week or so due to a brake line problem. I saw the look in Jose's eye and told him to not mess with it, but after holding him off for hours, Stephen came through the Motor Pool. Jose said, "Hey, Stephen. Robert here is being a hassle."

I gave my side of the story—that the old truck had been a big help for months and that it was just in a little slump. But Stephen told Jose that it was ugly and to go ahead and scrap it. Our spiritual teacher had once again taught me nonattachment. Later that night Bradford could not believe it when I told him that the Yellow Canary had by now been hammered into a small wad of scrap at Denbo's in Pulaski. The next day we were back to the wagon, and if I remember correctly, that was one of the last straws for Bradford and Margaret. They left The Farm shortly after that.

Robert Gleser

We Never Really Considered Leaving

After doing some traveling for Plenty, The Farm's relief organization, we settled into a household called Thunder Ridge. Stephen and Susan were also living there and had a son who was a few months old. Their bedroom was on the first floor, pretty much under the stairs. It was a loud location, and Lee seemed to have trouble sleeping. He cried a lot. We had one of the nicer bedrooms at the top of the stairs, and feeling some compassion for the strain they were undergoing, we offered to trade bedrooms.

It kind of surprised us when another couple took our room and gave Stephen and Susan a bedroom further back in the house. We felt a little bit ripped off and realized once again that not everyone has the same standards for giving and sacrifice. Were we just naive and not watching out for ourselves and our own family?

Life under the stairs got to us after a while. It was a tiny bedroom, and our kids, now four and six, were beginning to need more room. Just as importantly, we needed more space to be together as a family, and our nightly retreat into the cramped quarters just off the living room gave us very little peace and quiet.

This situation was made worse by one of the men in the household who drove semis for the Trucking Company. He had a tendency to cruise through the house very much like a truck, clomping down the stairs in heavy soled shoes. He also had a mouth like, well, a trucker. We tried to talk it out with him but got nowhere, so we did the only thing we could—we moved out.

It had been almost ten years since we'd come to The Farm, and here we were—full circle, living in a school bus. It was winter, a bit cold, but we loved it. Actually the bus was part of yet another household, this one only fifteen people altogether, which was something of a relief after living with thirty or more for so many years. The house itself was a split-level shack perched on the side of a hill. It had begun as an addition off a tent, and then succeeding additions were added on. Like most Farm houses by now, it had a shower, propane water heater, and a connection to The Farm's in-house cable TV system which played videotaped movies on the weekend. We went inside the house for meals and such, and then every night the four of us would trundle out to the bus for some intimate family time. It was just what we'd been needing.

Eventually we moved into a couple of the bedrooms in the main house. This was a difficult time for The Farm. Economically, the situation was sliding downhill, and disillusionment, previously unheard of, was becoming thick. I was commuting to Nashville, working fourteen-hour days as manager of a new business, the sale and installation of satellite dishes. Deborah was working at the Clinic's lab and missed my help around the house.

After peaking at around fifteen hundred, our population was beginning to decline as people became fed up with the poverty and lack of control in their lives. Finally, in a desperate move to save the community from bankruptcy, the "Change-over" took place. This placed economic responsibility on each individual or family to care for their own needs plus pay a fixed amount of cash to The Farm every month, initially about $130 per adult. The previously all-things-in common community businesses became privatized, owned by their managers or small group partnerships. Coworkers, in some cases, became employees. The whole thing sent massive shock waves through the system, and residents began leaving in droves.

At the time of the Change-over the population was about seven hundred. In three years it dropped to two hundred fifty. Deborah and I and the kids were now living in a house all by ourselves. It was, however, built almost on the ground and was literally rotting out from under us. We couldn't see putting any money into this shack that was already too far gone, plus we didn't have any money anyway. Still we never really considered leaving. Most of our friends had fled to a city or their hometown, and neither of these options appealed to us. Those of us who stayed formed even closer relationships with others in the same predicament, and somehow we all made it through.

Our housing situation got settled in the old-fashioned Farm way. Through the maze of the Change-over, Stephen and Susan found themselves living in a beautiful log cabin that had been converted to a duplex. When the other side became vacant, they could have done as others were doing, take over the whole place, but instead they offered it to us. We certainly weren't keeping score back to the room-under-the-stairs swap at Thunder Ridge, but the same spirit prevailed even after we all had our own checkbooks.

That was almost fifteen years ago. Our two children are out seeing the world on their own. Stephen and Susan's two children are now passing through The Farm's teen scene. Our home is a mix of communal living and simple, shared space that gives us a very real extended family. On cold nights we don't need a schedule to make sure someone stokes the fire in the basement furnace that heats both sides. It just happens.

We don't eat together that much, and each couple has its own circle of friends and hobbies, so we don't share every aspect of our lives like in the early Farm living arrangements. We're more like close brothers and sisters, foster aunts and uncles, godparents. All our kids have always intermingled, and we don't knock to go from our side of the house to theirs. Sometimes the four of us have to make a special effort to connect beyond kind of waving as you pass in the hallway, and every once in a while, over a Thanksgiving dinner or on a Christmas morning, or just out of the blue, we remember to thank each other for what has come from mutual respect, love, and a bond that has had many years to grow.

Doug Stevenson

"We All Knew It—Magic!"

The Farm School has had a colorful history. Originally, Lewis County was more than happy to have us educate our own children as the influx of so many new students would have severely strained their system. After the school became approved, The Farm built the largest passive solar building in Tennessee for our kids. It's a sawtooth design with very tall south-facing windows in each of the eight rooms and tons of mass in the walls and floor. This allows sunshine to fill and warm the entire school.

I became a part of The Farm School in 1988 when my two youngest sons were in the third and fourth grades. This was after the economic Change-over, and the school's enrollment had dropped dramatically. Still, the few of us who remained were able to pull off a high school, middle school, and elementary school.

In my first year, I taught the combined third and fourth grade class, and even though this wasn't planned, I stayed with this class of kids and remained their teacher for the next ten years. As they moved up a grade, I moved up a grade until they graduated in 1998. What a gift this has been. I am convinced that, if at all possible, this is the best way to teach children. Not only does the teacher get to really know the students, but the students also get to know their teacher, and a special bond forms. I believe this is a very rare situation these days.

Along with the academic subjects that are taught, our school recognizes the importance of vibes and energy. Even though they are not constant topics of discussion, we know that they exist and are part of us and affect us. It is especially great working with kids who respect vibes and energy, because not only does it help teach them morals, but it also enables them to appreciate special, magical moments.

One such moment occurred in the spring of 1989. Our class consisted of ten kids, eight boys and two girls. It was a beautiful spring afternoon, and we had the side windows, which had no screens, opened all the way. The kids were all working on different projects, and the classroom atmosphere was active and absorbed. All of a sudden, one of the kids noticed an unusual sound coming from the top of the solar window, twenty feet above our heads where the window and ceiling meet.

He looked up and yelled, "Look! A hummingbird!"

Everyone in the room turned, looked up, and began to yell commands and emotional out-bursts as we saw that the humming bird, trapped and disoriented, was repeatedly banging its fragile body into the solar windows.

"Get a net!"

"Kathie, do something!"

"He's going to die!"

"We'll never catch him!"

"The sound is awful!"

"Kathie, what are you going to do?!"

"He's hurting himself!"

"Oh, god!"

"Kathie, do something!"

"WAIT!" yelled James Moore, "I'll go call Robert and tell him to bring his ladder!"

With his eyes wild with excitement and determination, James ran down the hall to call his dad, who luckily worked on The Farm and had an extension ladder.

We all continued to watch the bird, and the emotional energy in the room continued to increase. The only thing I could think of to do was to take the curtains off the opened side windows. Hopefully this would make escape for the bird a possibility, but the side windows were ten feet below the ceiling where the bird was bumping itself senseless.

James ran back into the classroom and announced that Robert was on his way.

"OK, everyone," I yelled, "sit back down in your desks. Come on everyone, sit back down."

After a few more strong directives, the kids were all at their desks.

I said, "Everyone be quiet and take a deep breath. We are not doing the bird any good by being too excited and loud. He is already scared and we're scaring him more. Let's just sit and be quiet, and maybe he'll fly out the window."

There were no arguments, no silly remarks. This was a living being and the sound of its wings hitting the wall and ceiling sounded painful to us. Everyone was quiet and respectful.

After about a minute of quiet contemplation, it happened. The hummingbird flew down, hovered right by James's head, and then landed on the corner of his desk. No one in the room moved; we just stared at the little bird. James slowly reached out and cupped the beautiful little bird gently in his hands. He silently rose and slowly walked over to the side window with all his classmates, who also reverently got up from their desks and quietly followed him.

When they reached the window, James stretched his upper body out the opening, along with as many kids as could fit. He stretched his hands toward the sky and opened them. The hummingbird hovered for a second and then flew off to freedom.

The kids didn't clap, no high fives, just a quiet feeling, a good feeling. Something special had just happened and we all knew it. Magic!

Kathie Hanson

Psychic Cracks

David—One morning we received a check at the Bank Office for $4,000. It was quite unexpected, and we always tried to take such windfalls and do something that would positively affect the whole town. As Public Works Director and Treasurer, I knew that every summer our water towers would run dry because of how small the water line was linking them together. So my proposal was to spend the money on enough three-inch water pipe to complete this major step in the town's infrastructure.

Stephen heard about this, came to the Foundation Office, and argued at length about using this chunk of money for internal cable TV to link up the whole Farm. Of course, this idea had merit, but I thought the water line issue was more pressing. I finally gave up arguing and yelling with him, because I just didn't see any reason to hassle at length over it. Anyway, the check was deposited and proceeded to bounce, so we didn't get either project done right then. There was definitely a teaching in that whole interaction, but it didn't become apparent until later.

Maybe a year later, we did scam some cable TV equipment, coax, wire, etc. and got The Farm wired up with cable to most every house. This technology immediately was used to show movies Farmwide, then board meetings, and eventually Sunday Services.

Michael—The station call letters were NBS (No Bullshit Network). Our station logo was a sign with a bull's rear end, a red circle with a red diagonal line across the middle. There were a variety of programs generated on The Farm. They included skits about the state of the basic budget and The Farm's economy, gardening shows, cooking shows, skits from the high school (some in foreign languages), and Sunday Services when the weather was bad.

Gary—I think the first psychic fissure in The Farm, where the general perception of the community went from "full-scale commitment" to "doubts and disillusionment," happened on a rainy Sunday morning around 1981.

Stephen did services on TV that day. On this particular morning his talk was all about how The Farm had changed. There were fewer people living in the large households, and whole bedrooms were being given to teenagers so they could have their own rooms. He also said that when the housing coordinator called asking to move someone in, people were being stingy with their houses. Generally, Stephen was telling us that we, The Farm, had become more selfish.

The format of these televised services was that folks would call in questions or comments to Stephen much as we would have done sitting out in the meadow after meditation. Michael, who was a very respected man in the community—head of the farming crew (our largest work force) and husband of a midwife—called in and told Stephen that he was totally off the wall to tell us we were being selfish when all these years we'd been living in a skeleton of the dream we knew how to build, but because we'd always been taking on more projects, more trippers, getting pressured by the Gate to cram somebody else into our homes, do all this social work . . . that because of all that, we didn't even have enough money to keep our kitchens clean and our kids healthy and ourselves healthy.

So Stephen argued with him. Michael argued back, and within that week, Michael and his family left. It blew a lot of people's minds.

Edward—Having Services on cable into our houses made a large difference in how we perceived Stephen. Out in the meadow after meditating together, we were mostly quiet, blissed out and all. I mean there might be some disagreements on material plane stuff, but nothing major. In our households, though, we were all used to sitting around and making comments anytime the news or a show was on TV. So when Stephen started arguing back at Michael, we all looked at each other at home and went, wow, that's crazy him saying we've become selfish. It's something we would never have done out in the meadow.

David—That Sunday, Michael questioned a lot of basic assumptions about The Farm, specifically regarding Stephen setting the spiritual and material direction of the community.

I had rejoined the Tribal Council in 1978 to represent Town Planning and became embroiled in many controversies around water projects, sewage, and construction. The Council still made decisions, but it seemed that they could be undermined by Stephen if he felt they were not in the best interests of or in tune with the community's longstanding commitments.

Michael left soon after this public disagreement, but not before he and others had begun pointing out to many of us that the Emperor had no clothes. It opened many eyes about the direction of the community and what was really going on in this incredibly idealistic hippie town with its dwindling population. We had let Stephen and others run the community for years and never really criticized the direction until now. All this led to the formation of The Council of Elders, which did have autonomous power, but in hindsight it was probably too late.

Henry—That's right around when we left. I got sick but I just didn't think there was adequate medical or dental care. I figured it was fine for me to decide to live at this level, but since we had adopted kids, I didn't think it was fair for me to subject them to that.

Linda—I felt the same way and my kids were my own. In other words, if my children wanted to be hippies living in the backwoods some day, well, they should have all the information and tools to make that decision, rather than just my saying, Hey, this is where we live, and you'll get new shoes when the Petty Cash lady has some money, and they'll sort of fit. So I took them away so they could have more of a view of the world, see movies, go places, experience other things.

Henry—I started feeling like I was losing my choice, that I was starting to slip so low in my standard of living that I was no longer doing this by my choice.

Gary—In terms of the kids, it was like the adults were voluntary peasants, but the children had not volunteered.

Gary Rhine, Henry Goodman,
Linda Hunncutt, David Friedlander, Edward Dunn, Michael Cook

So Here I Was, Suddenly A Running-Dog Capitalist Pig

We lived in a large household which, like all Farm houses, was continually in need of upgrading. We're talking about new linoleum instead of unfinished plywood, so you could keep it clean and the kids and babies who were crawling on it wouldn't get grubby or sick. Or maybe some sheetrock to cover the insulation in the bedrooms, or gravel and a drainage ditch outside the kitchen sink so the whole area wouldn't smell sour and be a fruit fly breeding ground—that kind of thing.

Of course, there was no money available from the Bank Lady because she was pinned down by our creditors, so somehow along the line there evolved the concept of going out and working on Saturday, so you could use that cash to try and fix up the home scene a bit.

One of the men in our house was a lead carpenter on an off-The-Farm crew, so he hustled this job up in Centerville that the men of the household could do on Saturday. We'd been working all week nonstop, but still we got up at five on Saturday morning to drive an hour and a half, crowded into this van with our tools and lunches and everything. Our wives were all saying, "I never see you during the week, and now you're even gone on Saturdays." But they wanted the improvements as much as (or more than) anybody, so it was a sacrifice all the way around. But we felt good about it; we were doing something about our situation. We weren't just sitting around complaining.

As I recall the job lasted seven weeks. We replaced sills and rotten, termite-ridden beams in this eighteen-inch crawl space with rat skeletons and old poison bottles and pools of old drain water, just horrible. Ten-hour days we were putting in too. After about four weeks of this, the ladies were saying, "No, really. Just stay home, you need to juice the kids and hang out." But no, we decided we were going to finish this job and get our drainage field and buy new linoleum—vinyl goods this time, because only about a year earlier we'd put down cheap stuff. Now it was completely torn through to the plywood, so we were having to mop the place with iodine twice a day to protect the kids from giardia.

After seven weeks we had this pretty nice check that was really going to make a difference in our day-to-day lives. We turned it over to the Bank Lady to deposit into our household account. That's how all off-the-Farm crews got paid whether it was for regular weekly work or Saturday jobs. You got one big check that covered the whole crew instead of individual pay checks. The weekly crew checks went straight to the Bank Lady—who was besieged from all sides by bill collectors—so you ended up feeling great about really helping out, carrying a load. The Saturday job money, though, was to be deposited or earmarked for home improvements.

I think it was right after we finished and got paid, the very next day at Sunday Services, it came down—Stephen announced it had been decided to "collectivize" all the "Saturday Money." And it was expressed in this kind of Marxist rhetoric of—we're going to liberate the money of the capitalists. When those types of decisions came down, it generated a kind of herd mentality. Nobody felt like getting up and saying otherwise because: (a) you wouldn't get anywhere since it was perceived as a "moral force" decision and (b) you'd probably just gain yourself some grief.

So here I was, suddenly a running-dog capitalist pig for crawling in sour water for all those Saturdays so we wouldn't keep having sick kids from playing on uncleanable floors. I remember feeling totally ripped off but without much recourse. I knew the Bank needed money, but our house did too. After seeing all that we earned during the week go to the Bank Lady, it just didn't seem fair to change the agreement in midstream like that.

It wasn't so much that I resented the Bank getting the check, because there was so much need. It was the implications that because white males can go out there and make a buck, there was some kind of taint to it. There was the fear that two standards of living on The Farm would come about—the haves (those able to market certain skills out in the greater economy) and the have-nots (those unable to make a buck).

It seems like we were all working hard, but there was a hole in the bucket. We would spend tons of money on delivering babies for free or sending Stephen and the band to Europe, but we never spent very much on preventative health care, better diet, and sanitation. Not spending enough on those things ultimately lead to lost wages from illness, doctor bills, and overworked clinic folks. The same choices kept coming up again and again, but there was a sense of guilt about taking better care of ourselves, and I still can't figure that one out.

The kicker is that as soon as the Saturday work money got collectivized, guess what happened? People quit going out to work on Saturdays. This was a bitter pill for us to swallow, to see close-up how after so many years of all things-in-common and our incredible idealism, there really was something to the capitalist, free enterprise philosophy after all—that personal initiative should somehow be rewarded and people, even in a collective society, feel better having more individual choice over how the money they earn gets spent.

Henry Goodman

The Plenty Ambulance Center

We Walked into Potentially Very Dangerous
Situations With Absolutely No Back-Up

Susan—We drove up to the South Bronx in a camper with Taco (a Plenty director) and a visitor from Guatemala, so it was like we still had that bubble of energy going from the sheltering woods of Tennessee. As we crossed over the George Washington Bridge and saw bombed-out looking buildings for as far as you could see, it was exciting and sobering at the same time.

It quickly became apparent that some things were going to be better for us in the South Bronx than they had been on The Farm. We noticed immediately that there was a bottle of ketchup on the dinner table. Seriously, that was huge. There was a crew that went twice a week to the farmer's market, so we had all the vegetables known to man, all the tofu we wanted; we ate like kings and queens. It was a smaller, tighter ship than the Tennessee Farm, so there was—it sounds funny to say this, but it's true—money for food.

We lived in a four-story building. The ground floor was home to the twenty-four-hour ambulance service, with a crew and a dispatcher constantly on call. Within a one-mile radius there was an incredible concentration of people in various high-rises. In the summertime any rooms above the sixth floor (some of the buildings were more than twenty stories) would get no water because kids in the street would open up the fire hydrants to play in the water. So we got a lot of calls from the elderly on upper stories who were suffering heat stroke or dehydrated. The phone was always ringing, and the ambulances were constantly running in and out.

Basil—I had one of those on my first day there. Ben and I were test-driving the ambulance, trying to figure out an engine noise, when a call came in that our other unit couldn't take because it was already transporting somebody to Lincoln. Ben knew the city ambulance would take forever if it came at all, so off we went. I was totally lost except for Ben's directions.

We went up to the top floor of this ancient building, and there's an eighty-year-old man having a heat stroke because there was no air conditioning and no running water. It was the middle of the summer and it was HOT! We took him down to the ambulance, packed him in ice, and transported him. Ben drove because I was lost and amazed by the whole experience. And here we were, passing block after block of similar buildings, while I just kept packing ice on this man. I wondered how many more people were out there needing help, and how was I ever going to be able to find my way around this city.

Susan—Up and down the street there were a lot of people hanging out, obviously on drugs, just sitting on the steps all day. And the broken glass. You cannot believe the amounts of broken glass on the sidewalk, and not just other places but right in front of our building. My first day I went out with a broom, and I was like, yeah I'm going to spiff up this whole block. But no way. It was like throwing straw in the wind and having it come back in your face. The more you swept, the more there was.

Basil—For the most part the Plenty Ambulance Service was seen as neighborhood-friendly in that our vehicles on the street didn't get constantly ravaged, but sometimes the word didn't get around. One afternoon I came home, and there was a guy just going about his business removing the battery from one of our vans. I said, what are you doing? He said, taking your battery. I followed his eyes over my shoulder and saw two of his buddies walking towards me with tire irons in their hands. I just turned around and went inside. Another time I caught three homeless guys doing the same thing, but after I told them that the truck was part of the Plenty Ambulance service, they said, oh, sorry, we didn't know. They put the battery back in, clamped it down, shut the hood gently, and moved on to another vehicle a little further down the street.

Nancy—Looking back on how we handled emergency calls in the South Bronx—it's incredible how naive, foolish even, we were. We walked into potentially very dangerous situations with absolutely no back-up. We just sort of assumed we would be fine, so it worked out that way.

Ben and I worked the night shift, and when a call came into the dispatcher's phone, we'd answer and just head out the door. A couple of the single guys slept in the next room, so on those nights they would listen for our kids waking up or crying. Amazingly that was the only notice anyone in the Center had that we were out on a call.

I remember one time it dawned on me that we didn't even have radio contact like we had back on The Farm. We were in this dark basement of an abandoned building which was the called-in address, looking for an OD victim, unsure if it had been a high-end drug deal or a homicide or what. Just us and the jump kit, no communications. It was crazy, it happened quite often, but somehow we felt protected because it was our mission.

We also had quite a bit of contact with the Sisters of the Missionaries of Charity who had their own center a few blocks away. That was one way of gauging any area's need and poverty—if Mother Teresa's folks were there, then yes, you were working with the poorest of the poor. The individual Sisters used to come over to the Center a lot. They were fascinated by us. We were fascinated by them.

I think they were curious about what was going on in the outside world because that particular mission was into meditation. They prayed constantly when they weren't involved with service to the neighborhood, which meant they didn't have a clue as to outside events. So they'd come over, and we'd fill them in. In a way those Sisters reminded me of the Amish

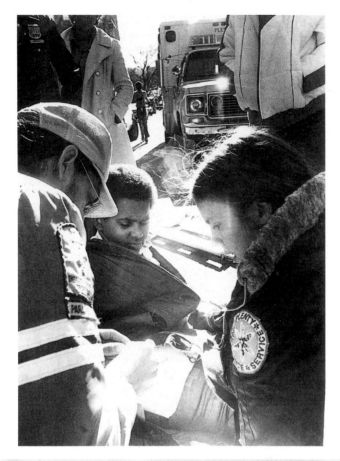

who lived close to The Farm back in Tennessee and who were curious and interested in our technology even though they, themselves, could never use it.

One afternoon I was out on the sidewalk holding my oldest son who was about two and a half at the time, and here came Mother Teresa herself along with some other Sisters. First she put her hand on Kyle's head and blessed him. Then she shook my hand and said, "Oh, The Farm and Plenty. You are the heroes of the world." She had tears in her eyes when she said that, so I started crying too. I was just so amazed. Kyle remembers that moment even though he was only a toddler. He knows he's been blessed by a saint.

Ben—When we first went to the Bronx Center, the Ambulance Service was in full swing, but we were pretty much low profile except in the immediate community. We'd get maybe a call or two a day, sometimes more, sometimes none. And it was right around that time that we decided we needed some media coverage, so Gary had a friend who had a friend on the staff of *The Wall Street Journal*, and he did a great story on the Ambulance Service that ended up on page one. The headline was: "In An Emergency, South Bronx Turns To Hippie Commune."

That story really propelled the whole thing forward. Suddenly we were hot. And of course, media attention is a two-edged sword—it was good for the exposure and opening us up to donations, grants, etc. Plus we made a bunch of contacts with agencies. But it was bad in that more and more media attention was really time-consuming, and the media tend to take stories like ours, run them through a certain lifespan, and after that, you're old news, they don't want to hear about you anymore.

The newspaper story pumped a lot of money into our project, enabling us to buy a second ambulance. Plus the article greatly increased our credibility. Our call volume went up dramatically. We began getting calls from the police and the fire department, both of whom now saw us as part of their team.

We started printing up stickers with our number on it for people to put by phones, and pretty soon all the clinics and ERs wanted more of the stickers to hand out. We stayed that way for years, a two-unit, twenty-four-hours-a-day, seven-days-a-week ambulance service with somebody always on duty ready to go.

Ambulance Calls—1980

Picked up a call off the scanner . . . EMS-911, city ambulance called, no response after thirty minutes. Plenty Ambulance Service (PAS) arrives at location at luncheonette . . . older man slouched over the counter, choked on his soup, blue in the face, unconscious and not breathing . . . administer 100% oxygen and load him for transport. En route he started breathing and fully regained consciousness by the time we reached the hospital.

PAS summoned by the NYC Fire Department . . . a man with knife wound to the chest, bleeding and unconscious with no respiration . . . firemen had begun CPR; we assist as he is loaded into the unit . . . unable to revive due to fatal heart wound . . .

Called to the scene of a traffic accident . . . drunk driving . . . car collided with the back of a parked truck . . . driver decapitated . . . two passengers injured, showing facial lacerations and fractures of the extremities. We splinted fractures, immobilized patients on spine boards, reassured one of the injured (brother of the driver), and transported them to the hospital.

Dec. 22—Solstice . . . Five emergency runs tonight including a car accident, full blown insulin shock, and severe infection . . . then from right outside our window, bam, bam, bam,

. . . well, it could be fireworks thought our paramedic, but upon peeking out the window, it looked like someone had been shot down at Sam's Uptown Bar. Within a minute we had three paramedics and an EMT on the scene. Twenty people were already there scurrying around, one guy freaking out, jumped in front of the ambulance and almost got himself run over . . . gunshot victim lying in the street, moaning. He'd been shot over one eye, in the chest, in the belly twice, and in the thigh, all by a small caliber gun . . . we got him on the gurney and loaded him into the unit, treating a couple of the wounds with bandages, and in ten minutes he was in emergency room surgery. Fifteen minutes after we left the scene, the city ambulance arrived. The victim most likely would have been dead by then. Two months later the guy showed up smiling and thanking us for saving his life. He said he really appreciated our help and left us with a $300 donation.

It Was Like We Were Out There in Orbit, But There Was No More Houston

Basil—We were in the Bronx all during the time when The Farm was going through massive changes and restructuring. We tried to keep up with the happenings and even went back to Tennessee a few times for Plenty meetings, but really we weren't in sync with the changes that were going on. It seemed that no one was as concerned with the projects as before. It was like we were out there in orbit, but there was no more Houston, no more base.

And here we were, still in the South Bronx, living together under all the old agreements, working a Plenty project, still installing windows to support the free ambulance service and the training program while back on The Farm the whole thing's changing. Which for one thing meant there weren't going to be any more replacements cycling through our crew. We were it.

I came back from a Plenty Board meeting in Tennessee; it was the one where Stephen was voted out as director of the Plenty Board. I had to break the news to everybody at the Bronx Center about what had happened and that it did not look like The Farm was going to be communal much longer. What happened was the Bronx crew got upset with me and Susan, the messengers. Everybody up there wanted things to continue on as before, and they did, to an extent, for a little while. The last of The Farm collectivity was not on The Farm.

Eventually reality set in over the course of 1983 and 1984. During the final weeks, as people began spinning off and moving out, we knew that we just did not want to abandon the building after all of the work people had put into it over the years—same for the ambulance service. We wanted to have it continue as a community-run program, but few groups were interested or had the resources to really take it over.

I remember one sunny afternoon Craig and I were up on the roof (we called it Tar Beach) trying to figure out the fate of the building. We knew once we left, it would be stripped clean immediately of everything from wiring to plumbing pipe. So while we were mulling over all that, someone came up and said, "Hey, there's a visitor downstairs. It's a nun, Sister Mary Jane." Craig and I just looked at each other and said, "What a perfect name." Things like that were always happening.

Sister Mary Jane was interested in taking over the building and starting a shelter for homeless single mothers. Fabulous. After a short meeting, we knew she was the one. We shook hands on the spot. It was like a heavy weight had been lifted off of us. And where we had been having on-going bureaucratic hassles with the city over official ownership, she marched down there, and as Susan says, she knew how to use her habit. She got the papers pushed through for ownership, sprinkler requirements waived. The city even came and worked on the building and gave her free heating oil for the winter. She turned our bedroom into a chapel because she said it already felt kind of holy. We stayed in touch with Sister Mary Jane for years afterwards.

Ben—Gradually residual fatigue began to set in; you can't run your whole life on adrenaline. The Farm was in the depths of its Change-over and replacements had stopped coming from Tennessee. One Sunday night I believe it was, we finally had to face that this was just not going to work. There's no rested, accredited crew who can staff the units tonight. We're just going to have to shut it down. So we got an answering machine, put a message on it, and hooked it up to the dispatcher's phone.

That was a very big deal—much guilt and second thoughts. It was the first time any of us, on The Farm or in the Bronx, had shut the ambulance service down. And it was kind of like a wake-up call that we were burned out and understaffed and just were not going to be able to carry on like this forever. In my mind I still haven't figured all of that out. I'm really grateful I got to do it, and I loved every minute of it, but that first awful night of shutting down the ambulance service, on a level that's what happened with all our commitments to The Farm. For years and years in the community I thought, okay, you're a small piece of a much bigger thing, and you have to set aside your own wishes and goals in order for the bigger thing to do well. And I carried that with me when I went up to the Bronx, and later on as director of the Plenty Ambulance Service. I was very adamant about that ideal.

When people first wanted to break off and use their medical training elsewhere, at hospitals or other ambulance services, I was very much hard-line against such a thing. Later though, I saw that it was natural to eventually move out, grow, and learn things away from The Farm community whether in Tennessee or the Bronx or wherever. Which undermined many of our basic assumptions. I think lots of us bumped up against that one at the same time.

Basil Campbell, Susan Campbell, Ben Housel, Nancy Housel

The Raw Footage of America Kept Showing Up

These are excerpts from the Gate logs of autumn, 1981. Even though The Farm would undergo a radical restructuring within the next few years (for example the Gate crew and other Farm services would be paid, the school would institute tuition, and the midwives would charge for births), the raw footage of America kept on showing up, remaining as varied and combustible as it ever was in the mid-1970s.

At that point there was a two-day only visitor policy. Residency Committee interviews replaced the Soakers' meeting when someone wanted to join. There was no longer a Visitors' Tent at the Head of the Roads. Visitors had to stay at a campground near the Gate or in a Farm household.

Other things remained the same—the pervasive need for greater sanitation, a single mother hitching in with two kids, a fighting couple coming "to unload their blind daughter," starry-eyed Germans, teenagers looking for sanctuary, the Gateman trying to figure it all out, make decisions, keep the agreement alive and well up at the Gatehouse while down in the woods, it was coming apart.

—T. arrived this afternoon—eighteen (according to what she put on her card)—Pretty spacey. Broke. Disappointed about two-day policy. Her aunt and uncle put her on the bus to here. She's from Florida, has been hospitalized before. Hipped her about not getting into relationships with guys here, and she acted glad about that because she has been having a rough time with guys in Florida. Didn't get any details. Right now she's the only lady in the upstairs room—possible sanctuary.

R., hitchhiked in, recently ripped off of all his stuff. Came in with G. who has traveller's checks in cashbox—drove taxi two years in Germany, read about The Farm and sold all his stuff to come here. Left Germany three days ago.

—Gate Mobile Unsafe—IMPORTANT—drivers should know that it's been jumping from park into reverse—keep foot on brake.

R. came in late last night. Two-day visit. Used to be with the Summit Lighthouse—got disillusioned.

Some of the neighbors have been feuding and bad-vibing each other for some reason. Keep an eye on this.

C. is up here about to leave. Was in mental hospital after post-partum freakout. Has been getting help from the midwives and our attorney about getting her kid back from a foster home.

H. and Z. came in afternoon. Were here in June but left and had baby in Georgia. Their main reason for being here this time is to get help or find parents on The Farm for R., their two-year-old daughter who is blind and has a negative-juice trip going with Z. They sold their land in Virginia and are here with all their stuff and three vehicles trying to figure out what to do next.

Kitchen has roaches, needs massive clean-up.

Good Morning America filmed a greeting by the Gate crew.

A tour of twenty sociology students are here for the day from Vanderbilt.

Attention clipboard folks—no joggers or berry pickers outside the Gate. Lots of guns on Drake Lane—very dumb to wander off on somebody's land picking berries.

B. came in, Swedish guy on a motorcycle, travelling around, saw The Farm on Swedish TV last year.

—H. and Z. are becoming a pain. They're here to unload their blind daughter. Very strong opinions, self-proclaimed preacher, puts the word on folks.

C. here after a year in Central America—had hepatitis in Peru, told her okay to stay till Tuesday, but keep washing those hands.

R. hitched in on H. and Z.'s bus and has been mechanicing on their bus the whole time he's been here. It would be nice to give him a tour. He's only seen the campground and the truck (from below). Decent guy, but macho.

Five guys from Germany who all speak very little English. Hard to even get their names right. Be nice to have some multilingual folks up here all the time.

D. from Twin Oaks in Virginia, full of B. F. Skinnerisms. Speed rapper.

Gatehouse mop is broken. Need new one stat.

—A nice lady, L., and two kids came in on Lawrenceburg taxi. Has one giant bag of stuff. Wants to live here. Found her a spot at Huckleberry for two nights.

All Germans okay through weekend. F. through Monday, but no promises. Try to get H. and Z. on their way. Their daughter now with family at Southern Exposure. L.—I just don't know—I leave it up to you.

—L. was in Gatehouse with her kids, two and three, but has since moved to the visitors' campground. Hangs out with bus folks there. Insists that she and kids are warm enough and dry and sleep better there than in the Gatehouse. During course of that, she let me know she is on the run from her abusive ex-husband. Decided her time was up and suggested we drive her up to the Union Mission's Women's and Children's Dorm in Nashville (check in time 4:30 p.m. for overnight—"Goldie" is house mother). L. said, no, to just drop her and kids and big bag of stuff off in the local town so they could hitch somewhere. We said no, no, gave her another day to keep trying to figure it out. Lisa made a good connection with her—L.'s pretty together, a vegetarian, digs it here, and would like to stay, but we're just too full (too many sanctuary people already). Trying to get her moving down the road before she digs in. The deal now is she wants a few more days because her period is about to start, and she doesn't want to be on the road. If she's still here Monday afternoon, residency committee will talk about her. She's freaked about the Mission deal because she thinks her name might still be in police computers from a charge in Little Rock (says she was cleared) a few weeks ago. Afraid of her ex finding her that way, afraid of having her kids taken away by the state.

V. came to The Farm in a cab from Birmingham where she lives with her mother. Saw us on Phil Donahue. Thought she might fit in. Wants to work on a crew. Newcomer to our way of doing it, but seems to be sincere in checking it out.

—H. and Z.'s. bus now fixed. Get them on their way.

Gary came in, fairly big dude, oil prospector who cut loose of his job. Saw us on Donahue.

H. and Z. story continues—now it's their starter motor. Someone from the Motor Pool is helping them out. The kicker is they say they're coming back. Be forewarned about any agreement made with them when and if they return.

L. is ready to split to Florida. She has an old social worker there to connect with. We are hooking her up with some cash and a ride to Hagerman's Truck Stop.

—W., a fifty-one-year-old dredge boat worker (now between boats) stopped by for a visit. Joined Catholic Seminary in 1941 at age of twelve and stayed until 1973.

About three in the afternoon, Samuel drives in and says one of the neighbors hit him with a big hunk of pumpkin while he was stopped on Drake Lane. He was pretty revved, wanted to prosecute the neighbor, go find him, etc. Calmed down, called Leslie.

About a half hour after that, we heard a gun shot from another neighbor's house. His wife came running out with a shotgun and trucked over to our back porch. Turns out her husband took a shot at her (boy friend?) but hit the windshield of his truck and splattered some glass. She's trying to figure out what to do with his gun.

So Close Yet So Far

Part of The Farm's original vision was to build a village for a thousand people using alternative energy systems that were economically and ecologically responsible. We believed that we could design a graceful standard of living which would be attractive to large numbers of First World people, while also being within reach of all Third World people. We hoped to build the model village, live in it, and then get funding to help build similar towns in Third World countries. We also hoped to inspire other First World groups to build similar villages for themselves.

During those years we had people living on The Farm that were at the forefront in fields such as architectural design, solar heating, and photovoltaics. We had the know-how and the man power to build the town we envisioned. But we didn't build it.

After a decade of struggling Third World-style in the woods of Tennessee, we were still living in a skeleton of our dream. Instead of building our town, we had been sending many of our most talented and energetic people to do relief work in Guatemala, Bangladesh, Haiti, the South Bronx, and on American Indian reservations. We also had a lot of our talent on The Farm tied up in dealing with social work projects such as taking care of people fresh out of jail and mental institutions, troubled teens, and hundreds of pregnant women whose babies we delivered for free.

By the early 1980s, many of the people who had been in on the original vision were tired of living in a crisis-management state of mind, with systems constantly breaking down because they weren't built right in the first place. It was frustrating because we knew how to do it right; we just didn't have the resources. So a large number of people left. I think that if at that time we had been able to build the town and been able to live within the graceful standard of living that we had envisioned as "voluntary peasants," a lot of us would not have left. We were so close yet so far.

Gary Rhine

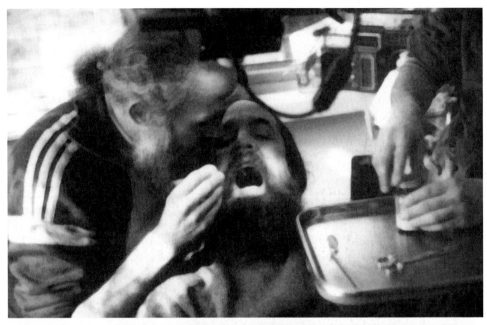

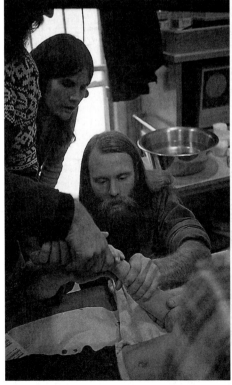

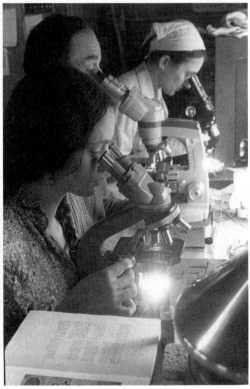

It's Far from Over

By closing the chapter on our communal economic experiment in 1983, people had to decide whether or not living with a lot of their friends in rural Tennessee was worth doing. Being communal all those years had given everything we did a certain cachet, a nobility, in that we were doing things together, for each other, as one. By giving up on communalism and making each family responsible for its own economic survival, we became, in the eyes of some members, just a glorified hippie subdivision.

There were not a lot of economic or cultural opportunities in our area of Tennessee. For people who had grown up in rural America, this was not a big deal. But for folks who had been raised in more urban settings, there was a feeling that to stick around was to become stagnant. There was a better standard of living to be had by going where the good-paying jobs were. There were better schools and more cultural activities for kids in the cities. Many people also had older parents who were starting to need more care. When everything was added up, most people felt the scales tipped in favor of leaving.

We entered a period of both grief and relief. On one hand, it was like settling an enormous divorce involving hundreds of people. Justifying the loss of your dream was a lot like justifying lost love—sometimes it involved resentment, dismissing the object of your affection as unworthy, declaring the whole thing a waste of time. At the same time, there was a world of possibilities that opened up to us when the ties of communal living were let loose. People could be entrepreneurs, developing businesses based on their interests and talents. They could go back to school to learn new skills. They could bring home foods from the supermarket that they hadn't had in years. They could even apply for government assistance to get help with medical problems, food, etc. People bought cars, installed flush toilets, washing machines, dishwashers, and microwave ovens.

Those of us who remained spent the mid-1980s reassuring ourselves that we were going to make it as a community. We had been left with hundreds of thousands of dollars of collective debt, but with some years of belt-tightening and the sale of some community assets, we were able to retire it. There were, and always will be, individuals who have a harder time than others making ends meet, but by the early 1990s most of us were modestly comfortable and carving out a new community existence for ourselves. No longer were we able to spend our energies on numerous community endeavors—at first, just keeping the bills paid and the roads repaired was an accomplishment. But we found we still loved each other. Too much water had passed under the bridge to be ignored—too much time feeding each other's families, doing each other's laundry, caring for each other when sick, nursing each other's babies. It was hard not to do something together. Here and there, groups of individuals coalesced to work on a number of projects: land preservation, ecovillage planning, a summer camp for needy urban kids, a conference center, and community beautification.

We had realized the limitations of our psychic healing abilities. We were not going to be able to mend every broken mind and spirit. Along with the rest of American society we began to learn more about the realities of mental health—the effects of alcoholism, drug abuse, spousal and parental abuse, sexual abuse, etc.—and saw that the healing promise of community had attracted many people who ended up suffering here in silence. We had formerly preached a philosophy of self-reliance, pulling yourself up by your boot straps. What we learned is that there are people who have no boot straps. Our attempts to understand mental health problems, get our friends professional help, and stand by them as they faced the long road to recovery became an important postcommunal focus.

We're reaching a point in our history where a part of The Farm diaspora may be heading home. Many people who left the community have been able to create a comfortable lifestyle for themselves, maybe a house and a career. Their children have grown up; dependent parents have passed away. Some are reaching the point of "Now what?" The Farm looks appealing to them again, and more and more are inquiring about coming back. There will be many opportunities to pick up where we left off and to continue the experiment. There's no telling where it will go next, but it's far from over.

Cynthia Holzapfel

Afterword: Blowin' in the Wind

There have been tens of thousands, perhaps hundreds of thousands, of experiments just like The Farm in American history. Estimates of those still in existence today run from five hundred (according to the *Directory of Intentional Communities* or *Encyclopedia of American Religion*) to three thousand (*America's Alternative Religions*). It has always been a part of the American fabric to experiment with alternative social matrices, a penchant that first drew deTocqueville's attention two hundred years ago.

In one of the early Sunday Morning Services in the old Horse Barn, Stephen Gaskin held up a pamphlet he had been reading and then passed it around for others to read. It told of some of the better known of these experiments—Oneida, Amana, New Harmony, Nauvoo, Bishop Hill, Pleasant Hill. In part because of its awareness of history, The Farm was able to pick its way through the moving minefield which historian Donald Pitzer has termed "developmental communalism."

The Farm avoided the power-hungry-leader-and-zombie-follower syndrome of Peoples' Temple and Heaven's Gate; the run-ins with police and government that dogged the Mormons and Community in Island Pond; the free-love marriages that complicated Oneida and Kerista; the centralized industrial complex that made Amana vulnerable; and the destructive transitions from early collectivity to cooperative association that splintered Bishop Hill and many others. Adroitly stepping past one assigned fate after another, The Farm continues to amaze both outside observers and its own members with its staying power.

There is a curious quirk of memory that seems to afflict those who leave The Farm and do not return. They assume that The Farm has remained frozen in the social structure, philosophical

debates, and whatever internal issues it had in flux at the moment they left. In actuality, The Farm never had a fixed point of reference for its religion, philosophy, economy, language, or rules that lasted for more than a year. As time passes, changes within the community continue. This explains some of its staying power, but change alone does not confer survivability.

If there is an explanation for why The Farm continues to evolve, continues to have disproportionate influence on the national culture, and continues to amaze its members and former members, it probably lies in the inner fabric of an underlying contract. Since "the agreements" were never codified, they are only discerned by an examination of The Farm's oral history.

I recall a crisp, clear morning in 1985 when the sun had come up on a fresh foot of snow and The Farm was all a-shimmer. I grabbed my camera, stuffed some rolls of slide film into my pocket and headed for the door. Up at the Horse Barn I started shooting from the interior looking out, and I noticed an abandoned wing of the Book Publishing Company across the way, its windows and doors gone, and thought that might afford some similar shots.

Walking in over the buckling floors, I had to step carefully, uncertain what holes the snow might cover, but as I picked my way to a better vantage point, something in the indoor drifts caught my eye. I reached down and picked up a glossy 8 x 10 of the Farm Flour Mill.

The memories came flooding back. This was the building where I had worked back in the mid-1970s. I remembered how we had gone out scrapping for old mill parts and once been trapped in a boarded-up water mill by the angry owner with a shotgun. I thought about how, on a Christmas Eve, I had crawled underneath and repaired the ancient bucket belt and pulley system in the two-brake feed mill that was making pastry flour. I remembered how we would fry up field corn for lunch while the grain sifted and how I got my hernia lifting a three-hundred-pound steel roller, the injury sending me to a desk job.

Photos and scraps of typescript were everywhere. Where the floor had given way had been our first office, the original aging frame house that had stood on the land when the buses rolled in. Here in the snow was a rotting cardboard box, and in it original, one-of-a-kind transcripts of interviews and lectures by Stephen in distant cities. An overturned file cabinet held original correspondence from all the twenty or more satellite farms back to home base, to ground control. I wondered how many of those letters went unanswered in the upheavals of the early 1980s.

I was standing in the ruins of what had been the Farm Book office. Here Patrick, Cornelia, Leon, and many others had transcribed from taped conversations, culled through contact sheets, and over the course of more than two years had put into rough form an epic work on the early history of The Farm. When the change came, the Book Company drastically downsized its workforce, from dozens of artists, printers, binders, editors, shippers, strippers, photographers, and databasers to two or three staffers to take and fill orders. Every work in progress was canceled. The new "Softwave" software spin-off was unspun. Scheduled reprintings were postponed. The printing presses and ten-terminal computer system were sold at scrap value. For the next few years, the Book Publishing Company would exist only by selling inventory. And here, amid the blowing snow, was the wreckage of a labor of love, a book that was carried halfway to term but yet unborn.

Gathering up the fragments and finding boxes to put them in, I took them home and dried them by the fire. The next day I visited the Book Company managers and asked for permission to continue work on the book in my spare time. My spare time has been scant since then, and so The Farm history was largely untold, but was still being amassed. A ten-year battle with the Justice Department over the national security of the United States ultimately yielded The Farm's eight-hundred-page FBI dossier. Visits to former Farm Book editors produced a smattering of pages that hadn't been entered into the defunct computer system. We found the archival digital tapes of the book, but even a very good computer lab was unable to decode them. A trip to Princeton produced a Fletcher Kneble memoir, although the one-hundred-and-fifty hours of taped interviews that the famous author recorded at The Farm in 1974 were destroyed before we found the old garage that stored them.

But none of these efforts would have produced a printed title before the end of this century had it not been for Rupert Fike.

The Book Publishing Company contacted Rupert in 1996 about doing a book of stories from Farm members. He contacted Sylvia Anderson, who published The Farm Net News, a free-form, sometimes fractious, on-going conversation of former and current Farm residents that has spanned more than fifteen years, and Sylvia helped him put out the word that a book was being planned.

Rupert pulled what he needed from the snowblown cache—ancient Gate Logs, five or six notebooks of unassailable experiences written the very day things happened, in the heat (or cold) of the moment. Mailed-in taped conversations of group remembrances began arriving from both coasts. Unexpected submissions from visitors, prisoners, and those still living on the land. Much email, file decodings, airports, rental cars, and negotiations. As the pie started

smelling good, more and more cooks started jamming the kitchen, all of them under the guidance of Rupert and Michael Cook who took these stories and made them a book.

In deciding what material to use from everything that became available to us, it became evident that it would take more than one volume to tell The Farm's story. In many ways, we have only scratched the surface here. If you enjoyed these voices, stay tuned; there should be more to come. If you are one of the voices we haven't heard from yet, speak up! There is much more that can be told. We look forward to sharing these memories with you and with those who may never have been on The Farm, but would enjoy a taste of the experience.

Albert Bates

Farm Information
For general information on The Farm, visit www.thefarmcommunity.com

The Farm Welcome Center
100 Farm Rd.
Summertown, TN 38483
931-964-3574
www.thefarmcommunity.com
vickie@thefarmcommunity.com
Information on visiting The Farm

Plenty International
P.O. Box 394
Summertown, TN 38483
931-964-4864
www.plenty.org
plenty@plenty.org
Local and international outreach and assistance, with special focus on indigenous communities and protection of the environment

Ecovillage Training Center
P.O. Box 90
Summertown, TN 38483
931-964-4474 (voice)   931-964-2200 (fax)
www.thefarm.org/etc
www.I4AT.org   www.gaia.org
ecovillage@thefarm.org
Whole systems immersion, classes, on-site and off-site consulting, access to information

The Farm School
151 Schoolhouse Rd.
Summertown, TN 38483
931-964-2325 (voice)   931-964-2362 (fax)
www.thefarmcommunity.com
farmschool@bellsouth.net
State approved alternative educational facility, elementary through high school, boarding students accepted

The Farm Midwifery Center
198 2nd Rd.
Summertown, TN 38483
931-964-2293
www.thefarmmidwives.com
For Midwifery Assistant and advanced Midwifery workshops: 931-964-2472 (mornings)
www.midwiferyworkshops.org
midwives@themacisp.net

Swan Center for Wellness
166 5th Rd. Summertown, TN 38483
931-215-7516   swancenterTN@gmail.com
Holistic sessions, classes, individualized retreats for personal growth and renewal

Book Publishing Company
P.O. Box 99
Summertown, TN 38483
931-964-3571 (voice)
931-964-3518 (fax)
888-260-8458
www.thefarm.org/businesses/bpc
bookpubl@usit.net
Vegetarian cookbooks, alternative health and Native American titles

The Mail Order Catalog
P.O. Box 180
Summertown, TN 38483
931-964-2241 (voice)
931-964-2291 (fax)
800-695-2241
www.healthy-eating.com
info@healthy-eating.com
Quick-to-cook vegetarian meat substitutes, nutritional yeast, vegetarian cookbooks, health and Native American titles - free catalog

Mushroompeople
P.O. Box 220
Summertown, TN 38483
800-692-6329 (voice)
931-964-2200 (fax)
www.mushroompeoplec.om
mushroom@thefarm.org
Mail order supply firm for specialty mushroom growers, spawn, videos, books, and supplies

Village Media Services
The Farm Catalog
P.O. Box 259
Summertown, TN 38483
931-964-2590,   800-258-9336
www.villagemedia.com; www.farmcatalog.com
douglas@villagemedia.com;phil@villagemedia.com
**Video production, web site development;
Farm books, food, crafts, Native American arts and crafts, audio CDs**

The Farm Educational Conference Center
150 Schoolhouse Rd.
Summertown, TN 38483
931-964-4927
Facilities for events and conferences, catered vegetarian meals and overnight dorm space

Look for these books from Farm authors in your
local bookstore or order from:
Book Publishing Company
P.O. Box 99 Summertown, TN 38483
Toll free: 800-695-2241
www.healthy-eating.com

Spiritual Midwifery
Ina May Gaskin
978-1-57067-104-3
$19.95

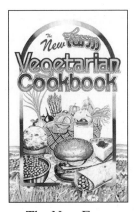

The New Farm
Vegetarian Cookbook
Louise Hagler
978-1-91399-060-5
$12.95

This Season's People
Stephen Gaskin
978-0-91399-005-6
$7.95

The Caravan
Revised Edition
Stephen Gaskin
978-1-57067-195-1
$14.95

Monday Night Class
Revised Edition
Stephen Gaskin
978-1-57067-181-4
$14.95

256

Look for these books from Farm authors in your
local bookstore or order from:
Book Publishing Company
P.O. Box 99 Summertown, TN 38483
Toll free: 800-695-2241
www.healthy-eating.com

More Fabulous Beans
Barb Bloomfield
978-1-57067-146-3
$14.95

Tofu Cookery
Louise Hagler
978-1-57067-220-0
$21.95

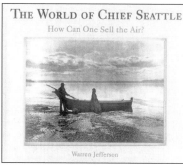

The World of Chief Seattle
Warren Jefferson
978-1-57067-095-4
$13.95

Colloidal Silver Today
Warren Jefferson
978-1-57067-154-8
$6.95

The Neti Pot for
Better Health
Warren Jefferson
978-1-57067-186-9
$9.95